Joseph Hammond

Concerning the Church

Course of Sermons

Joseph Hammond

Concerning the Church
Course of Sermons

ISBN/EAN: 9783743351929

Manufactured in Europe, USA, Canada, Australia, Japa

Cover: Foto ©Lupo / pixelio.de

Manufactured and distributed by brebook publishing software (www.brebook.com)

Joseph Hammond

Concerning the Church

PREFACE.

I AM induced to publish these Sermons in the hope that some of my brother clergy may think them not unsuited for reading in their Churches or for lending or recommending to their parishioners.

To one who believes, as I do most firmly, that the Church is GOD'S own society, His chosen instrument and organization for the regeneration of mankind through CHRIST, and the ordinary channel of His gifts of grace, few things are more distressing than the ignorance, and, I may add, indifference of so many Churchmen as to what this same Church, of which they are members, is; as to its *raison d'être*, its principles and constitution and claims on their allegiance. As far as my experience extends, not one Churchman in a thousand can give a valid reason, as distinguished from mere *preferences*, for his Churchmanship, or even say, often as he professes his faith in it, *what* he "believes" about "the Holy Catholic Church."

And this is the more to be lamented because, as a rule, our separated brethren, both Roman and Genevan, can give some reasons, and often very specious and persuasive reasons, for being what they are and believing what they do. It is the more distressing because this ignorance of what the Church is, or of what our LORD designed it to be, lies at the root of our unhappy and destructive divisions. It is only, in my humble opinion, because the teaching of Holy Scripture and of Christian antiquity on this subject has been so largely lost sight of or obscured that Dissent in its many forms has come to exist amongst us.

I am very far from suggesting, however, that Churchmen, or rather Church laymen, are entirely to blame for the present confusion and distress; at least an equal share of blame belongs to the clergy, who have, as I think it will be admitted, so seldom given definite and careful instruction on this cardinal question. I have said that not one layman in a thousand can give a consistent and intelligent account of " the Church "; the main reason is that not one clergyman in a hundred ever explains its character and design. The ninety-nine have left their congregations to form their own conclusions on the subject, and this when it was morally certain, in the great majority of cases, that they could not arrive at right conclusions. For the exercise of private judgment is a delusion and a snare when we have only a part of the evidence before us, and when that part is very liable to be misconceived. An uninstructed decision may easily be worse than none at all.

It is only fair to add, however, that the clergy have not been altogether without excuse. They may well shrink, as things are, from giving detailed instruction on the Church and its ordinances. How many of them, in the first place, **have ever received** any full and careful instruction themselves ?—I had not, for one, at the time **of** my ordination. Moreover, they remember that this is debatable ground—*quot homines,* **tot** *sententiæ*—and that controversy often breeds little but strife and ill-will. They do not care to be denounced as uncharitable bigots, as they probably will be, if they maintain, as I must do, that there is, and only can be, one Church of God, and that self-constituted ministers are not ministers of Christ **at all.** Their **own** flocks will, in some cases, resent the most guarded **and** charitable exposition **of** Church principles as an attack upon Dissenters. **Can** we wonder if they have preferred to steer clear of such vexed questions, and to confine their preaching to those primary truths as **to** which **we are** nearly all agreed ? The temptation is a powerful one, and we can hardly be surprised if some have succumbed to it. Still, the result is the same; we have left our people to frame their own theories, for some theories they must have—"individual Christians," it has been well observed,[1] "if they ever grow into the manhood of reason, must have a theology, or cease to be religious "—we have left them to shape **their** own theories when we **could** not but foresee that they would be coloured by, if not constructed after, the prevailing misbeliefs, and would therefore be largely erroneous.

And so I have tried for some time past to serve the Church of God, according to my lights, by discussing, almost "in season and out of season," a subject which,

[1] Aubrey Moore.

as Dissenters allow, cries aloud for consideration, namely,
" What is the Church ? " I honestly thought, and I
think still, that it was time something should be said on
this question, said in a popular way, and in a loving spirit.
I have only to repeat what I have said elsewhere, that
we have in this Cornish parish of 5,700 souls no less than
nineteen chapels and eleven different denominations ;
that many Christians " have lost all consciousness of the
Church as such,"[1] and that some of them think that
they are doing GOD service by disparaging and deriding
the historic Church of the land and its prayers and sacraments and usages, to show that there was a need for
plain and definite teaching, such as I have endeavoured
to give in *Church or Chapel ?* in *English Nonconformity and
CHRIST'S Christianity*, and, more recently in my little
book, *The Christian Church—What is it ?*

But, as we have recently been reminded, " three
persons out of four in this country never buy books,"
and least of all theological books. It may also be true
that three out of four never—or very seldom—" hear
sermons " ; still, the fact remains that some who do *not*
read books *do* hear sermons. It is in the hope of reaching
some of these through the ten thousand pulpits of others
that I have written these discourses. Most of them
have never been preached in their present shape : in
substance, no doubt, I have delivered them—perhaps
more than once ! Five or six have been preached on
special occasions and as many more I have circulated as
tracts. I now collect them into one volume—a volume

[1] Mr. H. Price Hughes.

which certainly embodies a systematic course of instruction "concerning the Church"—in the ardent desire of leaving no stone unturned to gain a hearing for views and teachings which are by no means popular, but which, I am firmly persuaded, are the Scriptural and Catholic views of "the Church of the living GOD, the pillar and ground of the truth."

It may be well if I add two explanations. First, the repetitions, such as they are, that will be found in this volume, are not unintentional; I have judged them to be necessary. I despair of carrying conviction to the average hearer or reader without insisting on the same truths again and again, in different forms. *Répétez sans cesse* is a rule which the teacher can never afford to neglect. Secondly, I have in one or two cases, and notably in the Sermons on Confirmation and the Holy Supper, cast the discourse into the shape which I thought would be most generally useful to the parish priest, though it may have involved some slight divergence from the continuous teaching of the other addresses. But this is a fault for which I am sure my brother clergy will readily forgive me, and the more so as I have already treated both subjects more or less systematically in my *Seal and Sacrament*. In the two Sermons on Papal Supremacy I have thought it advisable to give my authorities and to supply some further information in the shape of footnotes.

Vicarage, St. Austell,
September, 1896.

CONTENTS.

PAGE

PAGE

S. JOHN XVIII. 36.

"My kingdom is not of this world."

MALACHI III. 8, 9.

"Will a man rob GOD? yet ye rob Me. But ye say, Wherein
have we robbed Thee? In tithes and offerings. Ye are cursed
with the curse, for ye rob Me, even this whole nation."

ROM II. I.

"Thou art without excuse, O man, whosoever thou art that
judgest, for wherein thou judgest another, thou condemnest
thyself."

PSALM CXXII. 6.

"O pray for the peace of Jerusalem : they shall prosper
that love thee."

Concerning the Church.

AN APOLOGY FOR PREACHING ON THE CHURCH.

EPHESIANS V. 32.

"I speak concerning Christ and the Church."

IT is strange that, in commencing a course of Sermons on THE CHURCH, I should have to apologize for my subject, seeing that we are members of the Church, and are met in the Church, and that at every Service we profess our faith in the Church and pray for it. Nevertheless, so it is. For many Christians, yes, and some Churchmen, are extremely impatient of any addresses, of any teaching on this topic. They think—they sometimes *say*—that "we ought to preach CHRIST, and not the Church"; they are afraid that we want to put the Church in the place of CHRIST, an organization in place of the Atonement. They say that what they want from the pulpit is Christianity, and not Churchianity.

Now, we ought really to be very much obliged to these

A

earnest men; we ought to respect the feeling which
prompts this objection; it is one which every true
Christian must reverence. They are jealous for the
honour of our Redeemer. They are afraid lest we
should put Him or His work in the background. We
can only be grateful to them, therefore, for giving us
this warning. We are thankful to find that the honour
of our dear Lord is so dear to them.

But is it really the case that we do preach Christ too
little, or rather, I should say, that we preach the Church
too much? Of course, we *must* preach Christ crucified:
indeed, woe is unto us if we do not.[1] But does the
preaching of Christ leave any room for preaching about
Christ's Church?—this is the question which I have
now to consider. For if it does not, then these Sermons
of mine are a profound mistake, and I cannot ask you to
hear them.

Now, the first thing to be observed is that whilst it *is*
our sacred and bounden duty to "preach Christ," this
is by no means the *whole* of our duty. It cannot be.
We often hear people say—Mr. Spurgeon, for example,
often spoke thus—that they "want nothing but Christ"
—"Him first, Him last, Him midst, Him world without
end": "Christ and Him crucified"—that is all they
care to hear or know about. But what a strange thing
to say—a strange thing for men who have been baptized
"into the Name of the Father," and "of the Holy
Ghost," as well as of the Son! What has the Father
done, then, that He is to be left out of our preaching?

---

[1] 1 Cor. ix. 16.

Why is the HOLY GHOST, again, to be thrust on one side? Has the CHRIST alone cared for our salvation? Does He alone love us and bless us? It is obvious, therefore, that much of this talk about " preaching CHRIST and CHRIST only " is most unevangelical, most misleading. So long as we believe in a *Triune* GOD we have a triune Gospel, and we must preach it. To speak exclusively of CHRIST and His work is really to dishonour the FATHER, Who made us and all the world, and the HOLY SPIRIT, Who sanctifieth us and all the elect people of GOD.

But it may perhaps be said that the true preaching of CHRIST *includes* the proclamation of the FATHER's love and of the SPIRIT's work, because He is one with the FATHER and one with the SPIRIT. Be it so! Then our answer is obvious : The true preaching of CHRIST may also include, and, indeed, *must* include, the preaching of the Church of CHRIST, because He is one with the Church. He must be one with it if the Church is—and we are told it is—" His *body*." [1] Unless the figure which compares CHRIST and the Church to a human body, of which He is the head and His people are members, [2] unless this is altogether fanciful, then we cannot preach CHRIST fully without also preaching His Church. Do not the head and the members share the same life? do they not together make up the perfect man. [3] It is partly, then, *because* we must preach CHRIST that we are bound to speak of that Church which is so closely and indissolubly united to Him.

[1] Eph. i. 23 ; Col. i. 24.   [2] Eph. iv. 15, 16 ; v. 30 ; Col. i. 18.
[3] Eph. iv. 13.

But before we allege any further reasons for speaking and writing of " CHRIST *and* the Church "[1] may we here be allowed to ask whether the clergy—yes, and those clergy, too, who have so much to say about the Church—do not preach CHRIST ; whether they do not dwell, and that constantly, on our LORD, His life, His teaching, His example, His atonement ?   I think I may venture to say for them that if any kind friend, whether Churchman or Nonconformist, will tell us how to preach our LORD better, we shall be profoundly grateful to him.   But I should have supposed, for my part, that we preached CHRIST in the English Church in a way and to an extent that He is preached nowhere else—certainly in no Chapel in the land.   For

Consider, first, that even if the sermon has nothing to say about His life, His ministry, or His death, yet every Sunday *six* portions of Scripture—two of them from the Gospels—are read in the hearing of the people.   And what are these same Gospels about but CHRIST.   Indeed, the Gospels for the Christian Year bring before us in consecutive order the whole life of our LORD, in its main features.   They are always about His work, or word, or example !   So, very frequently are the Law, the Prophets, the Psalms, and the Epistles.   Does anyone say that this is not the same as preaching ?   No, it is not the same, because it is *so much better ;* as much better as GOD's Word is superior to man's word.   But it *is* preaching, nevertheless, and the highest form of preaching.   If Moses was " preached " of old time, " *being read* in the

<hr>

[1] Eph. v. 32.

synagogues every sabbath-day," [1] then why is it not " preaching CHRIST " when CHRIST is read of in our Churches? No sermon can ever preach the gospel as the Gospels themselves do. Six Lessons, then, six portions of that Scripture which testifies of CHRIST,[2] and which maketh wise unto salvation,[3] are read every Sunday in the Church, and I have known the Scripture read in Chapel to be limited to six verses—six verses, and then a discourse of an hour's duration! And yet some of these good people charge us with not preaching CHRIST. The very revivalists, whose preaching is almost entirely about feelings, and experiences, and ecstasies, and who have been known to *apologize* for reading a brief portion of Holy Scripture, will have it that we do not preach the pure gospel because we think that GOD'S Word preaches it better than ours.

And, then, what shall we say of the Church's *prayers?* Are *they* silent on the subject of CHRIST? Have they no message for us? On the contrary, so evangelical, so full of CHRIST's work are our Liturgical forms that no man can go away from Church without hearing the gospel of GOD. John Wesley said that if there was chaff in the pulpit, there is corn in the prayer-desk. All the main outlines of the Gospel story can be collected from the Church's forms of prayer. And the same may be said of her *hymns*. A well-known evangelist [4] has claimed for himself that he goes about "*singing the Gospel* of JESUS CHRIST.*" But if so, why may not the Church's

---

[1] Acts xv. 21.   [2] S. John xv. 26.   [3] 2 Tim. iii. 15.
[4] Mr. Sankey.

Hymns contain the Gospel as well as his? Are those always silent about the SAVIOUR of mankind? I observe that to a large extent the same hymns are sung at Church and at Chapel—that is to say, the best hymns are heard everywhere. Do they, then, preach CHRIST in the one place and not in the other? Why should they do so?

But here another question suggests itself for consideration, namely this—Must all preaching be addressed to the *ear*? Can there be no " sermons in stones "; no Gospel without the human voice? No, that can hardly be maintained. It will be readily allowed that CHRIST can be preached in a printed sermon, one *read* at the fireside as well as in that *heard* in the pew; in other words, the story of the precious life and death may be conveyed to the mind and heart through the *eye* as well as through the ear. But can it only be conveyed by print; may it not also be proclaimed by pictures? Assuredly it can, for we constantly use them to teach the story of the Cross to our children. Paintings, then, can preach as well as sermons—perhaps more eloquently than sermons. And so the Church has pressed pictures into her service, and by means of her storied windows, in which the Man of Sorrows hangs on the accursed Tree, or in which He is seen ministering to the afflicted, rising from the dead, or ascending up to where He was before, she strives to preach CHRIST from age to age to the hearts of her children.

And there is yet another way in which she silently but powerfully preaches CHRIST and Him crucified. For what is the Holy Communion which in so many Churches is celebrated every LORD's Day, and on many week-days too, what is this but a picture and memorial and re-presentation of the precious death ? No doubt it is *more* than this, for it is a feast, a supper, a sacrament, but it *is* this. As oft as we eat this bread, and drink this cup, we "proclaim," both to GOD and man, "the LORD's death until He come."[1] These holy mysteries are "for a continual remembrance of His death." And yet, though we of the Church show the LORD's death perhaps ten or twenty times as often as it is showed in the Chapel—and show it, too, in GOD's own appointed way—yet we are told that we do not preach CHRIST ; we are bidden to hold our tongues about the Church, and to learn how to preach the Gospel.

Our answer, therefore, to those who accuse us is this, that *we do preach Christ;* very imperfectly, we know, very inadequately, yet still to the best of our powers and in every way at our command—by prayers, by hymns, by lessons, by symbols, by painted windows, by the sign of the Cross, by the sacraments—in every way that we can think of we do preach CHRIST. And we further say that if any of our Christian brethren will tell us how we can preach our Adorable LORD more, or more effectively, we shall be grateful to them. If we have not preached Him, it has not been for want of the will so to do, but the power ; it has been because of our incapacity, and not always by our fault. But the real question now before us is not about the preaching of CHRIST, so much as about the preaching of the *Church*. The question is, whether the

1 1 Cor. xi. 26.

full and faithful preaching of the Gospel *excludes* or *includes* the preaching of the Church of CHRIST.

Well, we have already seen that the Church is repre-sented in Holy Scripture as " the body of CHRIST," as a part, that is to say, of Himself. He is the Vine, we are the branches ; He is the Head, we are the members ; He is the Corner-stone, we are the building. But if so, how *can* men preach CHRIST fully, so long as they ignore or pass over the Church which He has thus espoused and united to Himself—which, in fact, is one with Him ? A man's body is not the whole of a man but it is a very essential part. That is no picture of the Vine, again, which takes no account of the branches.

But let us now take up fresh ground. The Church is mentioned in one way or another more than *one hundred times* in the New Testament. And it is repeatedly implied where there is no express reference to it. For example, something like one half of this same volume consists of *Epistles*. But what are these ? They are letters either to the Church generally or to particular churches or to the officers of churches. In other words, a large slice of the Sacred Volume exists because of the Church—it was called forth by the circumstances of the Church, in one place or another. And the other half of the book is principally composed of the four *Gospels*. But the Gospels are nothing else than memoirs of the Church's Head designed for the Church's use.[1] The Acts of the Apostles, again—it is a brief history of the early Church. In fact, it is no exaggeration to say that the whole body

[1] S. Luke i. 1-3.

of Scripture implies the **Church** and was written **for the Church. And yet many** Nonconformists and some Churchmen **will not have us tell what** this same Church **is, or** what it exists for. Though the Scriptures of GOD **are by** no means silent about **it, yet the** ministers **of GOD must** not say much on this subject. But can we be justified in virtually blotting out these hundred texts from the Bible? If this institution occupies **so much space in** Scripture, **why must** it occupy **so little in our** sermons? What right have **we to leave out what** *God* has put in? Are we, then, wiser than He? Are we going to re-write the lively oracles to suit our ideas? No; so **long as the** Bible **speaks of the Church, so long** as it is the Book **of the Church,** and everywhere implies the Church, and **only exists because the Church exists, so** long must we " speak concerning CHRIST *and the Church.*"

Especially when we consider the **terms in which the** Scripture speaks of this institution. " MY Church " our LORD calls it.[1] **S. Paul** describes it as " the Church *of God,* which He purchased with **His own blood."** [2] **Else-** where he tells **us** that " CHRIST loved the Church and gave Himself up for it " [3]; and in the **same** passage he compares its relation to our LORD with **that of the wife** and **her** husband. He says that **as a** man " nourisheth and cherisheth " **his own** flesh, so does CHRIST **the** Church.[4] **In the** Apocalypse, **again,** the Church is des- cribed as " the bride, the LAMB'S wife," [5] so dear is the Church to **her** LORD. **But if** this **is** so, how can it

---

[1] S. Matt. xvi. 18.   [2] Acts xx. 28.   [3] Eph. v. 25.
[4] Eph. v. 29.   [5] Rev. xxi. 2, 9; *cf.* xxii. 17.

dishonour CHRIST to speak of what He has so signally
honoured ?   If this is so, how can we disparage the
Church without dishonouring Him ?

But it is not only from the page of Scripture that we
learn how dear the Church is to CHRIST, and how large
a part it formed in His plan; we can cite testimony of
another kind.   Let me now remind you that this Church
was all that our Blessed LORD left behind Him as the
fruit of His three years' ministry.   He did not leave any
writings—neither Creeds, nor Gospels, nor Epistles—
but He left a little Society, a band of men and women
whom He had carefully taught and trained, a Society
with its officers, principles, prayers, institutions, and
traditions.   This was His legacy to the world—a brotherhood, and not a book.   The book came later on.   The
Church was His organ for carrying on the work, and it
did carry it on, and for years, without any writings at all.

But yet another reason may be alleged why we must
preach about the Church, why we must perhaps treat of
it more fully and more frequently than the Apostles did
in their writings.   It is because the subject is now so
much misunderstood.   It must be remembered that,
when the Apostles wrote, they were then under the
guidance of the HOLY SPIRIT, and fortified by the
commandments of CHRIST,[1] fashioning, ordering, and
governing the Church.   There was no need for them to
write much about it, when in place after place they had
themselves constituted it, had appointed its officers,[2] and
had instructed them by word of mouth[3]; when, in one

[1] Acts i. 2.   [2] Acts vi. 3; xiv. 23.   [3] Acts xx. 17.

word, they were still making it. There was then no misunderstanding as to its nature and design. Men did not
then use the word in contradictory senses, as they do
now. *We* are compelled to speak about the Church
because so many Christians are hopelessly confused and
perplexed about it; because they are asked to profess
their belief in " the Holy Catholic Church," and to pray
for it,[1] and they do not know *what* to believe about it,
or what they are praying for. A leading Nonconformist
minister[2] gives it as a reason for not discussing this
question that men are so divided upon it. " I would
never," he says, "dare to discuss the Church in this
congregation. We should be at sixes and sevens
directly. . . . If I were to ask you for your definition
of ' the Church,' we should have as many definitions as
there are people here." But this appears to me to be an
imperative reason why we must face the question. For
obviously these people, with their differing definitions,
cannot all be right ; the bulk of them must, in the nature
of things, be wrong. Are we, then, to leave them to be
wrong, just because they now differ : are we to abandon
them to misbeliefs—for something they *must* believe
about it—and to misbeliefs, too, which will colour all
their ideas of religion ? Why, they only cherish these
misbeliefs because they have been left without instruction ; the first Christians had no delusions on the subject,
as their writings show. No ; we are only justified in

---

[1] In the Collects, in the Prayer for all sorts and conditions of men, and
especially in the Prayer for the Church Militant.

[2] Mr. H. Price Hughes.

shelving the question if we are persuaded that Almighty
GOD expressly designed to leave the Church in ignorance
as to its own nature and constitution ; if we are sure that
the truth can never be discovered about that very institution which the Bible calls "the pillar and ground of
the truth."[1]   And how can we be sure of this until we
have examined the question ?   On every ground, therefore, we are bound to speak " concerning CHRIST *and*
the Church," because it is one with CHRIST—His body
and His bride—and we cannot preach Him unless we
preach it ; because He loved it and gave Himself for it,
and we cannot love it if we do not know what it is ;
because both He and His Apostles spoke of it constantly,
and we cannot understand their words about it without
understanding it ; because we must believe *something* on
the subject, and it can never be GOD's will that we should
believe what is untrue ; because we have duties towards
it, and we cannot discharge them until we have recognized
it and know where to find it ; because there are blessings
to be had in it and through it, and we must be in it in
order to enjoy them.   And this is my apology and my
justification for these Sermons on the Church which I
hope to begin on Sunday next.

[1] 1 Tim. iii. 15.

"THE BODY OF CHRIST'S CHURCH."

S. MATTHEW XVI. 16.

" I will build My Church."

HERE is one part of our Blessed LORD's work, one portion of New Testament teaching as to His ministry, which to many Christians is almost a dead letter.

The life He lived amongst men, the example He set them, the teaching He gave, the sufferings He endured, the death He died—each of these receives more or less of recognition. And no wonder, for not only is each of these conspicuous in the Gospels, but it is kept before our gaze by the Church's Services, by the cycle of the Christian Year. But the part of CHRIST's work which— too frequently—is not recognized, or not understood, is of a different order. It is not conspicuous in the four Evangelists ; that is to say, it does not stand out sharply and prominently, as do the rest, but it comes before us, so to speak, incidentally—a trace of it here and a trace there, and it is not specially commemorated in our Services. It is something like the foundations of a building which are largely underground ; they are almost lost to view, and therefore are made of little account. And yet on those same forgotten foundations the whole superstructure rests.

And what *is* this part of Christ's work which is so often unobserved by Christians, this foundation which lies almost hidden beneath the surface? I refer to the steady and constant and careful provision He made for the continuance of His work among men; I am thinking of that part of His ministry which did not aim at *immediate* results, which was concerned with the future rather than the present. For our Lord not only "went about doing good"; not only preached in synagogue and by the sea-shore; not only healed the sick and blessed the children—all of which things had an immediate use—but at the same time He was silently founding a society; He was ordaining a ministry for the future; He was ensuring the continuation of His gracious work in after centuries, down to "the consummation of the age." Just as He *prayed* for those who in later days should believe on Him, so He *provided* for their believing; He made arrangements for their conversion and instruction and protection.

And perhaps nothing shows more clearly than this silent and inconspicuous work of our Master His divine patience and prescience. I say His patience. You will understand this better if you consider how very different His way of working was from ours. *We* want immediate results : we are disappointed if we do not achieve them. But *His* labours had very little immediate result. To outward appearance His work was a failure ; it resulted—

in His crucifixion! And how little there was to show, at the time of His death, for that marvellous ministry and those words such as never man spake before! Not even His brethren believed on Him. His own country-men said He was a Samaritan and had a devil, and they went about to kill Him. Many of His disciples, again, went back and walked no more with Him, whilst one of His Apostles betrayed Him to death. At the time of the Ascension He had but one hundred and twenty followers in all Jerusalem. Was that work, then, a failure? We know that it was not; the Christendom of to-day shows that it was not. And it was not a failure because, though HE had accomplished but little, yet He had provided an organization for taking up the work where He left it. His teaching should be heard from other lips; the works that He had done others should do also. The foundations were laid, though as yet the building made but little show. Yes, His was a Divine patience—"GOD is patient, because He is eternal." And this same preparation-work shows His prescience. He has a calm assurance of ultimate success. Though the end of *His* labours must be the Cross, yet He never swerved, never hesitated. For He remembered—what He has impressed upon *us*—that "one man soweth and another reapeth"; remembered, too, that "except a corn of wheat fall into the ground and die, it abideth alone, but if it die, it bringeth forth much fruit." And so, though He saw Himself "lifted up," suspended on the Cross of shame, yet He also saw Himself drawing all men unto Him. What if His life were taken away from the earth? still, He would leave

behind Him a machinery, an organization which, taught
and animated by His SPIRIT, should do the work and win
the triumphs which He Himself had failed to achieve.

But does someone still ask, " What was this organization, this instrument which He had prepared for the
regeneration of the world ? "   *It was His Church ;* it was
the band of disciples which He had gathered round Him,
with the officers He had appointed over them and the
ordinances He had given them.   The disciples welded
into an organized community—this was His machinery ;
these were the foundations which He had silently laid ;
through their agency He would go forth conquering and
to conquer.   I say that one main part of our LORD's
work was to found and organize and instruct a Church
or community of men to carry on the crusade which He
had begun.   It was to this He trusted to echo His words
and assert His claims and dispense His gifts and manifest
His compassion to the ends of the earth and to the end
of all time.

And that this is so you will see if you carefully observe
what our LORD left behind Him at His departure.   Not
a book, not a system of philosophy, not even an outline
of doctrines or a code of laws ; no, but a *society*, a *body*,
a *brotherhood*, the members of which had been, for the
most part, eye-witnesses of His works and hearers of
His words and sharers of His sorrows ; a society which
had no documents and very few gifts or endowments ;
which, in fact, had little more than the memories and
precepts of a mysterious Person Who was full of grace
and truth and fairer than the sons of men.

I say that our Sacred LORD left no documents behind
Him. It is necessary to remind you of this because it
is a common idea among Protestants that He trusted to
the New Testament as a means for carrying on His
work. It is often said that "our religion rests on the
Bible." If it is meant by this that it can and must be
proved by the Bible, well and good; the words are true
enough; but if more is meant, they are untrue. For
it is obvious that CHRIST did not and could not commit
the conservation and extension of Christianity to a book—
just because not a line of the New Testament was penned
for more than fifteen years after His Passion, whilst
the whole was not in circulation until a century
and a half later. He could not, consequently, employ
what did not exist. No, He employed *persons* to do His
work, not documents. As the FATHER had sent Him, a
living Person, to begin the work, so did He send living
persons to continue it.[1] Human agency, and the agency
of men combined in a society—this has been GOD's plan
all the way through; this is the meaning of the Old
Testament economy. There is no trace in the Bible
itself of the exaggerated importance which we attach to
its pages, as a means of evangelization and instruction.
It never encourages us to think that Christianity will
make its way in the world if we only circulate a sufficient
number of copies of the Scriptures. The Scriptures are
indispensable as standards, as warrants, as assurances,
but there must be the living agent, there must be the
community. "The Church to teach, the Bible to

[1] S. John xx. 21.

B

prove "—this is CHRIST's plan. Our LORD did not
trust to documents. It is significant that He never, so
far as we know, put pen to paper. He did write on one
occasion, but it was on the ground, in the sand—His
words were presently obliterated. So far as we know,
He did not leave one scrap of writing behind Him. Nor
did He leave a creed, or a body of doctrines, or a system
of theology—indeed, His teachings were anything but
systematic; they could not be so, seeing that His audiences
were for ever changing, and that His addresses were
suggested by the circumstances of the time and place.
There are inferences, there are doctrinal conclusions to be
drawn from His discourses; the articles of a creed may
be based on them, but these inferences He left it for His
Church to draw, these creeds it was for His Church to
frame. He did not even draw up a directory of public
worship; He said nothing, so far as we have any record,
to bind the assemblies of His people to any sort of liturgy
except the LORD's Prayer and the Holy Supper; He left
it to the Christian society to adapt the Services of synagogue or temple to Christian use, or to devise new ones.
He even left it to the Church to frame its own rules and
byelaws, which rules and byelaws He promised to ratify.
Whatsoever its officers should bind on earth should be
bound in Heaven, and what they loosed on earth should
be loosed in Heaven.[1] Nothing can be more certain than
that a living society, not a system or a book, was CHRIST's
plan, or than that much of His work was merely preparatory: He did not complete it Himself because He

[1] S. Matt. xviii. 18.

preferred to commit it, under the guidance of the HOLY
GHOST, to the community which He would and did leave
behind.

And here it may be well to observe that in founding a
society for the propagation of His Gospel and the spread
of its blessings, our LORD did nothing new or unusual.
Why, He was Himself by Divine appointment, a member
of a religious society, of the commonwealth of Israel,
and He joined a religious society—that of John—at His
Baptism. Moreover, He only did what men always do,
by a sort of instinct, if they have any cause to advance,
any wrongs to redress, any ideas to diffuse. Given the
cause, the society follows as a matter of course. And
for obvious reasons—because " union is strength ";
because a hundred men can do a hundred times as much
work as one man ; because a hundred men, working with
combined effort, can accomplish more than a thousand
working in isolation and independently. You have only
to remember the prodigious number of societies which
exist in this and every progressive country, and for all
sorts of purposes, to understand that the experience
of mankind has found in societies the most effective
machinery for attaining its objects. Any reformer, indeed, who trusted to his own personality, and his own
unaided efforts, would be doomed to disappointment. It
has often been pointed out that the work of the Wesleys
was lasting whilst that of Whitefield was evanescent,
just because the former did and the latter did not found
a society. So that our LORD only did what any sensible
man would do in committing His revelation to the

guardianship of an association. Indeed, had He not done so, it is difficult to see how, without a perpetual miracle, Christianity could have been maintained in the world. As Bishop Butler has said, " Had CHRIST and the Apostles only taught, and by miracles proved religion to their contemporaries . . . . Christianity must have been in a great degree sunk and forgot in a few ages." Without a visible Church to keep them alive in the minds of men, His precepts, and even His Passion, would soon have sunk into oblivion.

Yet this part of CHRIST's work, essential as it was, is but imperfectly recognized and understood. Many of us read our Bibles without realizing that He was any-thing more than an Example, and a Teacher, and a Redeemer. But He was also an Organizer; He was the Founder of a religious community, the Head of a corporate body. Perhaps we do not realize it because it was done so quietly. It was His way to do things silently—" He shall not strive nor cry, neither shall any man hear His voice in the streets "—what wonder if His " Kingdom cometh not with observation," or if we fail to mark its beginnings. And yet it was among His chief concerns. It has been said, indeed, that " the Church was His *one idea*"; it was certainly a prominent idea in His mind, and I now proceed to trace its rise, to mark its gradual growth during our LORD's brief but blessed ministry.

I begin by observing that our SAVIOUR's disciples, the converts which He made, were baptized. It may be that He did not baptize one with His own hands ; still,

His disciples baptized in His Name and with His approval and authority. S. John tells us that "JESUS made and baptized more disciples than John." Now what was the meaning of the Baptism which He or they administered? It was the outward and visible form by which men were admitted into CHRIST'S body or community. I do not say that that Baptism served no other purposes, but it certainly served this, and, had we lived in those days, we should have recognized it at once as the ordinance of initiation into the Christian Society, just as Circumcision was into the Jewish. For remember, our LORD was not the first to baptize; His forerunner was a "Baptist," John the Baptizer, and the Rabbis had apparently baptized before John did, and they all employed Baptism as the form and rite for admitting converts. It was consequently the recognized ritual in that day for initiating men into a new religious communion, and had we lived then we should have understood this at once. Nay, we should understand it perfectly had we worked at the present day in the Mission Field. There, by Pagans and Christians alike, Baptism is well understood to be the dividing line, the Rubicon, between the one religion and the other. A man may attend the instructions of the missionaries for years, but no one accuses him of joining the Christians until he is baptized; it is that rite, and that alone, which admits him to their communion and which severs him from his own people. We see, then, in the very Baptism administered to CHRIST'S converts, the first beginning of the Church. It was not enough that His followers should hear His words and

copy His life; they must be enrolled into His brotherhood, enlisted into His army, formally admitted into
His school.   There must be membership in His Society,
because that Society is His chosen instrument for carrying on His work in the world.

But a society, every society which is not to be an
anarchy, must have officers as well as members, and
especially one which, like the Church, is to be a school,
an army and a sanctuary.   For a school consists of
teachers as well as scholars; an army has its captains
as well as its privates; a sanctuary has its priests as
well as its worshippers.   And so we find our SAVIOUR,
at the beginning of His course, summoning the Apostles
to be the office-bearers of the new association.   And they
were not only called, they were commissioned; He "gave
them authority"; He employed them to teach, to heal
the sick and to cast out devils.   Just as the disciples
were formally admitted, so the Apostles were formally
appointed.

And so the framework of the new society of GOD is
already constructed; the membership and the ministry
are alike provided for.   And now we observe a third
point—that both members and officers, both disciples
and Apostles, are trained for their respective duties by
our LORD.   It often escapes observation, though the
Gospels are explicit on the subject, that He gave separate
and special instruction to them, apart from and additional
to that which He gave to the multitudes.   Some of His
discourses were addressed to the Apostles only—as, for
example, that in the tenth chapter of S. Matthew;

others—the Sermon on the Mount is an instance—were addressed to the disciples. In other words, He gave private and esoteric instruction both to the scholars and the teachers. The parables were spoken to the multitudes; the *explanation* was often reserved for the disciples—" When they were alone He expounded all things to His disciples." It was given to *them*, He said, " to know the mysteries of the Kingdom of GOD," as it was not given to the crowd ; hence it was that from time to time He took them apart privately. So that He was not content with starting an organization ; an organization is of no value unless it is trained and equipped for the work it has to do. After constituting the new community, He teaches both the members and the ministers ; the three years were largely spent in giving them instruction. And so much of His official life was devoted to this purpose that as a thoughtful writer [1] has justly remarked, if we called the four Gospels " the institution of a Christian ministry, we might not go very far wrong."

But He made yet other provision for His infant Church. We have seen that He did not give them a creed, or leave behind any writings. But one thing He *did* give them—a form of prayer for their use: one weapon they must learn to wield, and He put it into their hands. It would seem to have been usual for Rabbis and teachers to provide their followers with a special collect for their private use. Such a collect John had provided for his disciples ; such a collect—the LORD'S Prayer—our SAVIOUR gives to His little flock. And it

[1] F. D. Maurice.

was for their use *alone ;* it was not supposed that others
would care to use it ; it was to be a mark and badge of
His divine brotherhood. His followers must not only
be taught what to believe and what to do ; they must
also be taught how to pray, and they must all pray the
same prayer.

And so the society is now provided with four con-
stituents—its membership, its ministry, its precepts,
its prayer ; to these our LORD presently added a fifth.
Just before the end came, He bestowed on it another
boon.   Three years before He had adopted Baptism as
the sacrament of admission ; He now gives them the
sacrament of the Eucharist, as a sign and seal of union,
as a badge of brotherhood and a means of communion.
And He gives it for their exclusive use ; it was an institution peculiar to the community, just as Baptism was ;
it was another distinguishing mark of the members of
His body.   And with this last provision the outline, the
framework of the Church was complete.   That outline
will be filled up later on, but it will not be varied.
The Church will always consist of members—members
admitted by Baptism, and in no other way ; of officers
appointed, even if indirectly, by CHRIST Himself; of
members and officers enrolled in order to be taught of
CHRIST ; of officers commissioned to teach others, to
heal the spiritually sick, and to cast out the devils of
ignorance and lust ; of men who have a gospel to
believe and to preach, a gospel which they have received, and which they are to transmit; of men who
meet for and are distinguished from other men by the

breaking of the bread. Such a community, with such objects and such sacraments, our CHRIST has constituted. And its organization is no sooner completed than the same night He surrenders Himself to death. The cause will not suffer, because the Society, strengthened with supernatural power, will take it up.

But we must now observe the place which this same society takes after the Resurrection. It is hardly too much to say that everything else disappears ; the society, with its ministry, its message, its sacraments, and its prayers, alone remains. He reveals Himself to the Apostles or disciples, and reveals Himself to *repeat* or revive what He has said and done before. He renews the commission He had given to the twelve, He charges them again to carry on the work.[1] They are to preach the Gospel which He had preached and they had learned[2] ; they are to " make disciples " as before ; they are to use the rite already in use.[3] The converts they make are to be joined to the society, and joined in the same way. He gives them still further instruction. All through the forty days He was " speaking of the things pertaining to the Kingdom of GOD " and " giving commandments to the Apostles whom He had chosen."[4] He is still building His Church, and building on the old foundations—the same sort of membership, the same ministry, the same work for them to do. His care for the community, His reliance on its work, is even more conspicuous after His Resurrection than before.

[1] S. John xx. 21.   [2] S. Mark xvi. 15.   [3] S. Matt. xxviii. 19.
[4] Acts i. 3.

And so in the rest of the New Testament it is of the society and its operations, its growth and development, its finances and its faults, its sufferings and triumphs, that we read. In the Acts we have the history of its early days. The Epistles are letters written by its officers to other officers or to members. We now see the society at work; it is carrying on CHRIST's work, and there is nothing else in the world to do it.

And this Society, need I say, in conclusion, exists still, and it exists to do the same work. It is CHRIST's organization for the purpose. It has been sorely tried and grievously divided, but it is CHRIST's still, and only by it can His work be done—" GOD's work must be done in GOD's way." And into it *we* have been brought; we were put into it at our Baptism, and put into it that we may carry on to its glorious completion the work which our Holy LORD came to do.

THE STRENGTH OF THE CHURCH.

" Tell me, I pray thee, wherein thy great strength lieth."

EVERY thoughtful Churchman, or rather every Churchman who has given any thought to the subject, knows well that our Blessed LORD did not leave behind Him at His Ascension a book, a creed, a system of theology, or anything of the kind. What He *did* leave was a *Society*, the community of His believing and baptized followers, with its gospel, its morality, its prayer, and its sacraments. That was all—all that visibly remained of His mission. If, therefore, His work was to be continued, if the world was to be won for Him, there was nothing but the Society, the body of disciples with its band of Apostles, to do it. Only this agency, this organization, stood between Him and oblivion.

But if any Christian supposes, because our LORD founded a community, organized it, and trusted to it for the maintenance of His religion among men, that He therefore trusted to that organization *alone*, that He looked to its unassisted efforts to effect the conversion

of the world, he makes a great mistake; he thinks very
meanly of Him in Whom are "hid all the treasures of
wisdom and knowledge." And that just because the
Society was altogether unequal to such a task; it *could
not*, of itself, accomplish it.

Consider for a moment, I pray you, what that work
was. They were not only to "make disciples of all
the nations," not only to "preach the Gospel to every
creature," but the Apostles were to make men new
creatures, to "open their eyes,"[1] to bring them to
repentance, to "turn them from darkness to light, and
from the power of Satan unto GOD"; they were to
"cast down strongholds, and to bring every thought
into captivity to the obedience of CHRIST."[2] In one
word, they were to make the whole world Christian—
thoroughly Christian in heart and life.

Now we know, or some of us do, how much it takes
to make a true Christian; we know how difficult it is to
win one man for CHRIST. For His religion, beautiful
and beneficent as it is, is not acceptable to flesh and
blood; it does not accord with our likings; nay, it runs
counter to our very nature and constitution. A religion
of discipline, of self-denial, with its "strait gate," and
"narrow way," and daily cross, will never be popular. If
it succeeds, it must be in the teeth of world and flesh
and devil; the man who embraces it must be prepared
to "hate father and mother and wife and children . . . .
yea, and his own life also."[3] It is the religion of the
Cross, and few they are that find and follow it.

[1] Acts xxvi. 18.   [2] 2 Cor. x. 5.   [3] S. Luke xiv. 26.

But not only was it an unattractive creed for which they had to win converts, but it had in their day its special difficulties to surmount. For one thing, its Prophet and High Priest had just been crucified: He had died a felon's death. That fact was not calculated, by itself, to commend it to a hostile world, and the world, wherever they turned, was bitterly hostile. The Jews cordially hated our LORD, and not without good reason— He had reproved their evil deeds, had denounced their greed and formalism and hypocrisy. To them again, He was "accursed,"—they esteemed Him "stricken, smitten of GOD, and afflicted," for He had "hung upon a tree."[1] The Greeks, on the other hand, despised Him. They were nothing if not philosophic; they wanted a wisdom of this world and of such CHRIST had none to give[2]; to them the Apostles were "babblers."[3] The Romans, proud masters of the world, would have none of Him. He had neither power nor pleasure to offer them, and He thwarted and contradicted them at every turn. They were hard, sensuous, gluttonous; give them the bath, the circus, and the supper, and they wanted nothing more. Remember, too, that both the Judaism of the Jew, and the Paganism of the Gentile were interwoven with all the habits and customs of their daily lives, and the latter at least offered its votaries the attraction of "pleasant vices"—of idol banquets and of fornication: in Corinth, the unchaste priestesses of Aphrodite were over a thousand in number. Why, the world

---

[1] Gal. iii. 13. The Rabbis often speak of Him as "the hanged."
[2] 1 Cor. i., ii., *passim.*   [3] Acts xvii. 18.

was then at its worst, at its most bestial and brutal age—it is always darkest just before the dawn. And this was the citadel which the Christians had to storm : these were the strongholds which had to be cast down !

But we must not only consider the magnitude of the work to be done and the " many adversaries," we must also remember the feebleness of the workers. For pray what qualifications, what aptitudes had the Apostles for this herculean task ? With one exception—that of S. Paul—they had none. They were no match either for the Rabbis or the Romans. They were rude peasants and fishermen—"unlearned and ignorant men." They were not chosen because of their wisdom ; they were rather chosen because of their weakness.[1] Even after the three years training their ideas were still low and mundane ; they were " of the earth earthy."[2] A vivid writer[3] tells us that the first disciples at Rome were "a longshore population, clad in malodorous stable slops, sleeping on straw and smelling of garlick." Of some such stuff the early Church was made, and more unlikely men to effect a great moral and spiritual reformation it would have been difficult to find.

And yet these peasants, these fishermen, have somehow accomplished the work they were appointed to do. Explain it as we may, they have succeeded ; they have been " more than conquerors." At the very first sermon they preach, three thousand converts are made[4]; within a few days, the society embraces five thousand *men*[5];

---

[1] 1 Cor. i. 27, 28.   [2] Acts i. 6.   [3] M. Renan.
[4] Acts ii. 41.   [5] Acts iv. 4.

a little later "believers are added to the LORD, *multitudes* both of men and women,"[1] and again a little later, "the disciples are multiplied exceedingly," and "a great company of the priests are obedient unto the faith."[2] And they are equally successful outside Jerusalem. The Samaritans, the hereditary enemies of the Jews, believe a gospel preached by Jews and are baptized.[3] They are equally successful outside Palestine. Soon we hear of a "great number" of Greeks turning to CHRIST at Antioch[4]; then of "a great multitude both of Jews and also of Greeks" who believe at Iconium.[5] Everywhere the work proceeds by leaps and bounds. Ignorant and unlearned though the preachers were, their preaching was with power. Before fourteen years have passed the Apostles are establishing churches and ordaining elders in all the principal cities of Asia Minor[6]; at the end of twenty years they are spoken of in Europe as "the men who have turned the world upside down."[7] Even in Cæsar's household, in Nero's profligate palace, converts are made[8]; even in Corinth, the "eye of Greece" a church is planted, and even in Pergamum, where Satan's seat was.[9] Nor was the success of the Church confined to that age; it has been winning its way ever since. Century after century it has been overthrowing the idols and purifying the tribunals and freeing the slaves and cherishing the sick and comforting the sorrowful, and now four

[1] Acts v. 14; *cf.* iv. 32.   [2] Acts vi. 7.   [3] Acts viii. 12.
[4] Acts xi. 21.   [5] Acts xiv. 1.   [6] Acts xiv. 23.   [7] Acts xvii. 6.
[8] Phil. iv. 22.   [9] Rev. ii. 13.

hundred millions of men—about one third of the population of the world and three fourths of its civilization—
are professedly Christian. True, its work is not yet
completed ; we see not yet all things put under CHRIST's
feet ; even the Christian nations have much to learn of
Him still. All the same, the march of our religion has
been marvellous. It may perhaps be said that its con-
quests have not been so much greater than those of
Mohammedanism, but even if that is so, there is no
comparison between the two religions ; Christianity has
not been propagated at the point of the sword, nor has it
any voluptuous delights to promise its votaries. For
such a creed as ours to have commended itself to so
many nations, and those precisely the foremost nations
in the world, is in itself a testimony to its superhuman
origin ; hence a great thinker[1] has said that *Christendom*
is one of the evidences for Christianity. And by the
confession of its adversaries the triumphs of the Church
have been prodigious. If it has, as they allege, "destroyed
two civilizations,"[2] that fact at any rate proves its power.
Yes, and I may remind you here that it is not only the
most civilized and influential races that are Christian,
but some of the greatest minds amongst them have been
CHRIST's most ardent disciples. It was said recently by
Mr. Gladstone, himself a pillar and ornament of the
Church, that of all the leading statesmen with whom he
had been associated in the course of his long political
life, there were only five who were not convinced
Christians. So that as we look back to-day on the

[1] S. T. Coleridge.   [2] Prof. W. K. Clifford.

history and progress of the Church through nearly nineteen centuries, and as we think of the place which the gospel and precepts of the Crucified occupy in the world at this moment, we are impelled to cry with Julian the Apostate, "Thou hast conquered, O Galilean." In spite of all obstacles Christianity has won its way; it has triumphed over opposition and persecution, and the instrument by which the work has been done—it is the Church, it is the community whose officers were at the first, as they have sometimes been since, "unlearned and ignorant men."

But if this is so—and that it *is* so you will not deny— then we find ourselves confronted with the question, "What is it, what influence has been at work to accomplish the change?" If the successes of the Church have been so splendid, whilst the Church itself has been so feeble, then how has it come to pass that a third part of the world has been Christianized? How has the "great mountain" of European Paganism become a "plain"; how has Judaism been discredited and displaced; how have the Greek philosophy and the Roman power alike been brought into captivity to CHRIST? The mere Society, as we have seen, could not do it. Then what has wrought this revolution? "Tell me, I pray thee, wherein thy great strength lieth?"

To this inquiry only one answer is possible. There is "one SPIRIT" as well as "one body." The Church has been but the organ, the instrument, the handmaid of GOD the HOLY GHOST. He, "the LORD and Giver of life" has been the life and strength of the Society. The

c

Church has had and has still a supernatural power
working in it and for it. Such "help from on high,"
our Sacred LORD promised it. " Ye shall receive power,"
He said to the Apostles, "after that the HOLY GHOST
is come upon you."[1]   In this power they were to witness
for Him to the uttermost part of the earth.   Did I say
that He "promised" the HOLY GHOST? He *conveyed*
it—in part at least. "Receive ye the HOLY GHOST "
were His words on the day of His Resurrection, and as
He spake He breathed the HOLY SPIRIT into them.   He
sends forth His breath that they may be created, and
that He may renew the face of the earth.[2] And all
through the forty days it was through the HOLY GHOST
that He gave them His commandments.[3] He did not
start them on their work until He had first[4] "strengthened
them with might by His SPIRIT in the inner man."[5] No,
the work has not been accomplished by a mere organization, it could not be ; the organization has been but
the medium, the vehicle of the Almighty SPIRIT.   " Not
by might nor by power, but by My SPIRIT, saith the
LORD of hosts."   " Not with enticing words of man's
wisdom, but in demonstration of the SPIRIT "[6]—it is here
its strength has lain.   The Church is no more than the
armoury, the machinery of the SPIRIT of GOD ; it is but the
earthen vessel which holds the heavenly treasure ; but the
golden spout through which the golden oil is emptied
on to the whole earth.[7] This is the secret of its success :
" HE dwelleth with you, and shall be in you."[8]

---

[1] Acts i. 8.   [2] Psalm civ. 30.   [3] Acts i. 2.   [4] S. Luke xxiv. 49.
[5] Eph. iii. 16.   [6] 1 Cor. ii. 14.   [7] Zech. iv. 12.   [8] S. John xiv. 17.

And we can easily trace, at least in outline, the operation of the SPIRIT, LORD and life-giver, in the early
Church. But a few days after the Ascension it was
poured out in its fulness upon the disciples. And it
brought with it, in the first place, the *power to speak ;*
they received the gift of tongues. Whether they were
enabled to speak languages which they had never learned
may perhaps be doubted, but there can be no doubt as
to the "wisdom and the spirit by which they spake."[1]
Already are CHRIST's words fulfilled, "It is not ye that
speak, but the SPIRIT of your FATHER which speaketh
in you."[2] His words in their mouth are as fire, and
the people are as wood.[3] "With great power" the
Apostles gave their witness of the resurrection of the
LORD,[4] because the SPIRIT of truth bore witness through
them, and testified of CHRIST.[5] Out of their belly flowed
rivers of living water because of the SPIRIT which they
had received.[6] They were CHRIST's witnesses, and so
was also the HOLY GHOST.[7]

But scarcely less remarkable than this gift of "thoughts
that breathe and words that burn" is the change which
has come over the Apostles themselves. In them was
fulfilled the word of Samuel respecting Saul ; not only
did they "prophesy" when the SPIRIT of the LORD came
mightily upon them, but they were turned into other
men. Here is S. Peter, for example, who but lately
quailed before a maidservant, and denied his LORD with
curses : he now charges the Jews, and to their face, with

[1] Acts vi. 10.   [2] S. Matt. x. 20.   [3] Jer. v. 14.   [4] Acts iv. 33.
[5] S. John xv. 26.   [6] S. John vii. 38.   [7] Acts v. 32.

killing the Prince of Life. He has manifestly been
" baptized with fire."[1] Do you observe how the "*boldness* of Peter and John " astonished the Council? it would
almost seem to have astonished themselves; the prayer
they offer for "*all* boldness " betrays a consciousness of
the new courage which they had acquired. No, it is
not their *words* alone that are changed; the men themselves are transformed; the fear of man is gone; they
hold not their lives dear unto them. Now they *are*
ready to go with CHRIST to prison and to death.

And the change in their *hearers* is no less wonderful
than that in the Apostles. As they hear, they are
" pricked to the heart " by the power of the SPIRIT. Our
LORD had told them that the HOLY GHOST should
" convict the world of sin." Already, on the occasion of
the first sermon, we can trace His work in the soul. It
was by no eloquence or arguments of the Apostles that
the three thousand were brought to self-knowledge and
compunction; it was by a supernatural power, by the
sword of the SPIRIT. The LORD *gave* them repentance,[2]
He " opened their hearts," as later on that of Lydia.[3]
The gospel came to them "in power," because it came
" in the HOLY GHOST."[4] What our LORD could not
do—for His discourses often fell on heedless ears, or
provoked vehement opposition—the SPIRIT has done.
CHRIST never made three thousand converts in a day;
the HOLY GHOST was not then given.[5]

And let us now observe the work of the SPIRIT in

---

1 Acts iii. 14, 15; iv. 13.   2 Acts v. 31.   8 Acts xvi. 14.
              4 1 Thess. i. 5.   5 S. John vii. 39.

adding these new converts to the Church. It is in and by Him that they are "builded together for a habitation of God."[1] It is very noticeable that the first thing to be done, even on the day of Pentecost, after Simon Peter's sermon, is to admit these converts into the Society. The SPIRIT has not dispensed with the organization: that is still the instrument by which GOD's work is to be done. And it is the SPIRIT that brings them into the organization: " by one SPIRIT were they all baptized into one body."[2] The Society is GOD's, and only the SPIRIT of GOD can admit men into it. The baptism which brought the three thousand into the Church was a new birth "of water and *of the Spirit*"; it owed all its efficacy to the operation of the HOLY GHOST.

And the next thing we notice is that the members, regenerated by the SPIRIT,[3] admitted by the SPIRIT into the one body, are *strengthened* and *confirmed* by the same SPIRIT. In Acts viii. we first hear of the laying on of hands—except for the purpose of ordination[4]—in the Christian Society, and we find that in and through that laying on of hands the HOLY GHOST was given. Nor was it given exclusively to the Samaritans; in the nineteenth chapter we find it imparted to the Ephesians, and we cannot doubt, from the way in which the rite is mentioned, that it was administered in many other cases which are not recorded. The book of the Acts is not a register of all that was done in the early Church; all that it attempts to do is to preserve for us certain salient features of the Church's history. It does not

[1] Eph. ii. 22.　　[2] 1 Cor. xii. 13.　　[3] Titus iii. 5.　　[4] Acts vi. 6.

tell, therefore, of all who were confirmed, any more than it tells of all who were baptized. But it does convey to us that through the laying on of hands, wherever administered, the HOLY GHOST was given, and it was "given to every man to profit withal." This part of the Church's machinery was made effectual by the SPIRIT. They were "sealed by the HOLY SPIRIT of promise." "It is the SPIRIT that quickeneth"; mere ceremonial profiteth nothing.

And here it may be well to say a word about the supernatural *gifts* which, as well as the SPIRIT's *grace*, were conveyed by the laying on of hands, for these were two separate endowments. It has been rashly concluded from the fact that powers and portents accompanied the imposition of hands that it was for this purpose that it was administered, but this was not so. And that it was not so—that Confirmation was not ministered merely for the sake of these miraculous signs—is obvious when we remember that such signs in that age always followed in the SPIRIT's footsteps. It was necessary that it should be so ; men must know by many infallible proofs that a new Power was at work in the world. A spirit is invisible; only by such miraculous manifestations could they be certified of a real though spiritual Presence. Anyhow, it is indisputable that with the SPIRIT went the sign. Thus, at our LORD's baptism, the SPIRIT of GOD descended as a dove[1] ; so, at Pentecost, the sound of a mighty rushing wind was heard, and cloven tongues as of fire were seen ; and so, when the HOLY GHOST

---

[1] S. Matt. iii. 16.

THE STRENGTH OF THE CHURCH.   39

fell on the Gentiles, " they heard them speak with tongues
and magnify GOD."[1]   Even in the preachings and prayers
of the infant Church there were supernatural manifestations.[2] So that, not in Confirmation only, but wherever
the SPIRIT was ministered, the signs followed.   But none
of these ordinances were for the sake of the sign ; the
sign was for the sake of unbelievers.[3] Miracles and
prophecy are the recognized signs of GOD's presence.
In fact, as a great German has said,[4] " The purpose of
GOD in working miracles is to manifest Himself . . . .
There, where miracles and prophecy are, is the evident
manifestation of GOD, and GOD *cannot* reveal Himself in
any other manner."   And thus, the signs which proved
the presence of the SPIRIT served also as the credentials
of the Apostles.   The word was " confirmed " by the
signs which followed.[5]   Hence we read that the multitudes " gave heed unto Philip when they heard and saw
the signs which he did."[6] But these signs were not the
HOLY GHOST, nor were they the chief object for which
the HOLY GHOST was given. Charity, we are told, is
greater than tongues and miracles and prophecy,[7] and
so the signs were but proofs of the awful Presence, but
the skirts of His luminous robe ; they were demon-
strations to an unbelieving and hostile world that GOD
was among the disciples indeed.[8]

But it was not only in Baptism and Confirmation, not
only in tongues and interpretations, that the HOLY GHOST
wrought in the days of the Apostles ; His presence and

---

[1] Acts x. 46.   [2] 1 Cor. xiv.   [3] 1 Cor. xiv. 22.   [4] R. Rothe.
[5] S. Mark xvi. 20.   [6] Acts viii. 6.   [7] 1 Cor. xiii.   [8] 1 Cor. xiv. 25.

power pervaded and quickened the most ordinary and perpetual ministrations, " the doctrine and the fellowship, the breaking of bread and the prayers."[1] The HOLY GHOST shaped their teaching—He it was Who guided them into all truth. The HOLY SPIRIT inspired the fellowship, for that had its root and nourishment in " the fellowship of the HOLY GHOST."[2] And the same SPIRIT that brooded over the font,[3] and moved on the face of the waters,[4] converted the bread and wine into the Blessed Body and Blood. " The communion of the Body of CHRIST[5] depended on the communion of the HOLY GHOST." Even in the prayers the SPIRIT made intercession for the saints,[6] and inspired them ; they themselves " prayed in the HOLY GHOST."[7] The whole body of the Church was thus illuminated, the whole life of the Church was maintained by the HOLY GHOST the Comforter. The love which marked these first Christians was " the fruit of the SPIRIT "[8]—so was the goodness, and righteousness, and truth[9] ; so was the faith, and hope, and joy.[10] They were being sanctified by the HOLY GHOST.[11]

And the power which wrought thus effectually in the members, also provided the Church's ministers ; the SPIRIT which made men members made some of the members ministers. It was the HOLY GHOST that had Barnabas and Paul separated to their work ; it was the HOLY GHOST that sent them forth.[12] So S. Paul reminds

[1] Acts ii. 42. [2] 2 Cor. xiii. 14. [3] Titus iii. 5. [4] Gen. i. 2. [5] 1 Cor. x. 16.
[6] Rom. viii. 26.   [7] S. Jude 20.   [8] Gal. v. 22.   [9] Eph. v. 9.
[10] 2 Cor. iv. 13 ; Rom. xv. 13 : xiv. 17, etc.   [11] Rom. xv. 16.
[12] Acts xiii. 2, 4.

the elders of Ephesus that it was the HOLY GHOST that had made them bishops in the Church of GOD,[1] and reminds Timothy that the same SPIRIT *dwelt* in them.[2] So when we read of the Apostles, prophets and teachers set in the Church of GOD,[3] it is mentioned as one of the works of that "one and the selfsame SPIRIT" Who divideth to every man severally as He will.[4] The Church owed its officers to the action of the Eternal SPIRIT. And the officers were indebted to that SPIRIT for guidance—it was the HOLY GHOST that charged Paul and Silas "to preach the word in Asia"[5]; it was "the SPIRIT of JESUS" that suffered them not to go into Bithynia[6]—for guidance and wisdom and for every helpful gift.[7]

And this supernatural Power—it abides in the Church still. When the Comforter was first promised, it was promised that He should "abide with us for ever."[8] It is still the Church's Life and Light; still are men "endued with power from on high." But for this we should abandon all hope of regenerating humanity. For the work which lies before us now is no less arduous and difficult than that which confronted the Apostles. Many things have changed since those days, but the devil has not changed—save, perhaps, that he is cleverer and more experienced. Many things have changed, but the human heart has not; it is still "deceitful above all things, and desperately wicked."[9] The forms of evil may vary, but the battle rages as fiercely as ever:

---

[1] Acts xx. 28.   [2] 2 Tim. i. 14.   [3] 1 Cor. xii. 28.   [4] 1 Cor. xii. 11.
[5] 1 Cor. xvi. 6.   [6] 1 Cor. xvi. 7.   [7] 1 Cor. xii. 3-11.
[8] S. John xiv. 16.   [9] Jer. xvii. 9.

> " No wider is the gate,
>   No broader is the way,
> No smoother is the ancient path
>   That leads to light and day ;
> No feebler is the foe,
>   No slacker grows the fight,
> No less the need of armour tried
>   Of shield and helmet bright."

No, it cannot be pretended that the Church needs the supernatural power of the SPIRIT less than it did of old time. It was quite unequal to the conversion of the world then : it is just as unequal to the task now. And so that power is still promised, is still conveyed. But for this we should utterly despair. But we cannot despair whilst GOD is on our side. You may remember John Wesley's dying words—" The best of all is, GOD is with us." Let us therefore go forth, as our fathers did, in the power of the SPIRIT, for CHRIST is with us " always, even to the end of the world," [1] and the SPIRIT of GOD and His CHRIST abides with us for ever.

[1] S. Matt. xxviii. 20.

THE LIFE OF THE CHURCH.[1]

S. JAMES II. 26.

"The body without the spirit is dead."

HERE is, I imagine, no branch of the Holy Catholic Church, nor is there any religious communion in universal Christendom, so rich in all material resources as is our dear mother, the Church of England. By the generosity of her children in the past, as well as at the present time, she has been—I will not say *amply* or *sufficiently*, but still *liberally*, provided with the machinery for discharging her mission, with the means for carrying on the work which our sacred LORD founded the Society of His Church to do. She has, as we are specially reminded to-day, her stately and storied and venerable cathedrals—one such has recently risen up in our midst, and we are now keeping its eighth birthday—it has its cathedrals, and they are cherished and cared for and maintained as in no other Christian country ; it has its noble and beautiful parish churches, some of them cathedrals in miniature, and nearly all of them have been lovingly and even lavishly

[1] Preached in the Cathedral Church of Truro on the eighth anniversary of its consecration.

restored; they have not only been restored, but they have been equipped with all possible aids and accessories to worship. Of cathedral and of parish church alike it might sometimes be said that its " foundations are sapphires, its windows of agates, its gates of carbuncles, and its borders of pleasant stones."[1] At the cost of untold millions the men of this generation have " made the places of His feet glorious." She can boast again, this august and stately mother, of considerable endowments, so far happily preserved from confiscation, endowments provided by the piety of English Churchmen of a past age; she can point to the still larger sums freely contributed by her living children. And she is rich, not only in materials, but in men. It is often, and I believe truly, affirmed that no other Church has had so thoughtful and learned and dignified a clergy; it is freely allowed that this body of clergy—with rare exceptions—is now conspicuous for its earnestness and devotion and high sense of duty. Certain it is that our Bishops and Priests and Deacons of late years have manifested a zeal and a fervour which would have amazed our forefathers, and which have provoked the admiration of our contemporaries. And did ever Church number more illustrious names amongst its lay members? Among " the sons that she hath brought forth,"[2] it is the most eminent who have rendered her the most eminent services. Can any other country or any other Church tell of four Lord High Chancellors in succession who have spent a part of their Sundays in teaching the children

[1] Isaiah liv. 12.   [2] Isaiah li. 18.

of the poor ?   Do I say that she is rich in *men ?* she is still richer in her brave and patient women ; in that " exceeding great army " of unpaid workers who, as district visitors and deaconesses and Sunday School teachers, spend their leisure, if not their lives, in her service.   Yes, she is rich, this ancient Church of England, surpassing rich in all the things which make for a Church's efficiency.

And if you should have any doubt on the subject, you have only to compare our position and our resources with those of the churches and communions of other lands.   Do you know that many of the French clergy are so miserably poor that they are only with difficulty saved from starvation—they eke out their attenuated stipends by saying masses ordered from South America ; that there are bishoprics in Italy of less value than three hundred pounds a year ; that some of the German pastors, and those men of erudition, are " passing rich on forty pounds a year," whilst the edifices in which they worship are bald and unlovely to a degree, and their parsonages are mere cottages compared with our ample and substantial vicarages ?   If you have any doubt as to the exceptional advantages which we enjoy from a *temporal* point of view, a brief visit to other Christian countries would speedily remove it.   You would realize then, as perhaps you have never done yet, the great possessions and the lofty position of the English Church.

But I do not know that there is any need to go abroad to learn this lesson ; you have only to study the Dissenting communities at home.   It is true that some few

of the ministers are infinitely better paid than the great
bulk of the clergy, especially during the present distress ;
it is also true that some are provided by their congregations with all the necessaries for their work ; still, it
is obvious at a glance that they have nothing like the
endowments and resources which we enjoy.   Their
chapels—as they would be the first to admit—will not
compare " for glory and for beauty "[1] for interest and
attractiveness, with our Churches; their ministers, able
and eloquent as many of them are, have not the learning
or the culture—they have never had a chance of acquiring
the learning—which the clergy have had every opportunity of obtaining.   Their congregations again, earnest
and generous as they are, seldom have either the influence
or the opulence of ours.   I repeat that we have only to
glance at the position and the means of the various
denominations in order to understand what a splendid
coign of vantage is that occupied by the ancient Church
of the land, and what singular opportunities she has for
doing good.

And now I invite you, the sons and daughters of the
Church, on this Church anniversary, calmly and dispassionately to consider whether the work we *have*
done or *are* doing is at all commensurate with the extent
and excellence of our machinery.   It is of no use to say
that it is infinitely more so than it was in a past age ; *that*
we may thankfully and yet sorrowfully admit.   It has
been said—said by Mr. Gladstone—that the services of
our Church—parish churches and cathedrals alike—

---

[1] Exodus xxviii. 2.

even half a century ago, were a positive scandal to Christendom. I am not here to reproach the dead, but it does belong to my subject to point out that we certainly have not used our great resources—at any rate, till quite recent times—as we ought to have done, either for the glory of GOD or for the highest good of the community. No one can pretend that the history of our Church since the Restoration and the Act of Uniformity has been an illustrious one. There are chapters not a few in that record which we can only read with shame and pity. How unworthy has she been of the position of the Bride of CHRIST; how seldom has she known the things that made for her peace! It would almost seem as if "blindness in part had happened" unto her. Some of you may remember the pathetic words in which John Henry Newman lamented her perversity. " O mother of saints!" he cried, " O school of the wise ! O nurse of the heroic ! of whom went forth, in whom have dwelt, memorable names of old to spread the truth abroad, or to cherish and illustrate it at home ! O thou from whom surrounding nations lit their lamps! O virgin of Israel ! wherefore dost thou now sit on the ground, and keep silence . . . O my mother, whence is this to thee, that thou hast good things poured upon thee, and canst not keep them, and bearest children, yet darest not own them ? Why hast thou not the skill to use their services, nor the heart to rejoice in their love ? How is it that whatever is generous in purpose and tender or deep in devotion, thy flower and thy promise, falls from thy bosom, and finds no home within thine arms? Who hath put this note upon thee, to have a miscarrying womb and dry breasts, to be strange to thine own flesh, and thine eye cruel to thy little ones?" Yes, and we cannot say that such language is undeserved when we remember that *somehow* our spiritual mother has lost her hold on *one half* of her children at home, and a much larger number abroad; when so many have deserted her temples to seek their souls' bread in the prosaic chapels of the sects, there must have been grave faults some-where. She has had pre-eminent advantages and prodigious resources, but she has not known how to use them.

And though the last half century has wrought a wondrous change, a change which, it has been said by a Dissenting writer, is without a parallel in the annals of Christendom, we may still ask whether the work we now turn out is at all proportionate to the resources we enjoy. The Church exists to make men good; to preach the gospel; to overthrow the strongholds of sin; to make life purer, kinder, happier. This is the end—the glory of GOD in the service of man; our cathedrals and churches, our sapphires and agates, our organs and anthems, even our holy sacraments are but *means* to that end. Well, is that work being done? Are we doing more for it out of our abundance than foreign churches, or the denominations at home, out of their poverty? Are our people as a rule better men or better-instructed Christians than the chapel people? Are they more CHRIST-like? Do they win more souls for CHRIST? Do we teach more children, shelter more penitents, reclaim more drunkards than they? Do we give as much—as much in proportion to our possessions—for the evangelization of the world? Are our offerings for Foreign or Home Missions greatly in excess of theirs? They *ought* to be *much* greater; it is reasonable to expect that where more has been received, more will be given. But is it so? I am half afraid that it is not so. I am not sure but that some of the half-starved churches of the Continent have more to show—more *in proportion*—than we. I do not know what is the case now, but a few years ago, the much oppressed and flouted Church of France sent more missionaries into the field than all the rest of Roman Catholic Europe. And certainly she has taught her children as we have never taught ours. "Perhaps there is no part of the Church," says Canon Gore, "which has sinned, as the English Church has sinned, in the neglect of definite religious teaching." The French clergy, again, though they are often *hated*, as we, thank GOD, are not, are also *loved* as we are not. A recent writer remarks on the tender and touching relations which exist between them and their flocks—you may see it illustrated in that recent book, *Un Curé de Campagne.* And when we pass to the denominations at home, we still find much food for reflection. If, as has been said, "the religion of the Son of Man is the religion of *enthusiasm*"—I do not know that it is altogether true—in that case we should have to admit that there is more religion in the Chapel, or rather in the crudest forms of Dissent than in the Church. I say "the crudest forms of Dissent," for I greatly fear that the more respectable

D

and cultured forms are less fervent and spiritual than
we are—Mr. Spurgeon certainly held that they were.
Consider this one statistic—that the Salvation Army
raises eight hundred thousand pounds a year out of the
pennies of the poor ; remember, too, that it has its weeks
of self-denial as we have not—weeks of self-denial too
for men who are *always* denying themselves ! Such facts
as these make us wonder sometimes whether *some* forms
of Dissent—utterly unjustifiable as we may consider
them to be—are not doing *more*—not of course by virtue
of their Dissent, but by virtue of their Christianity—for
the regeneration of men and the leavening of our land
with Christian ideas than our venerable and dignified
and cultured and endowed Church.

But, if this is *not* so; if you stoutly deny that the
Church of England suffers by comparison, either with
foreign Churches or with certain Christian bodies at
home—and I freely allow that in *some* respects she does
not suffer—still, the question remains, whether either
she or they are doing anything like the work they ought
to do. Yes, the question still remains whether the work
the Church accomplishes is at all proportionate to the
means with which GOD has entrusted her for doing it.

And if it is not—and I for one must affirm that it is
not; it certainly is not in my own parish—then *why* is
it ? Our Church, we are persuaded, is a *true* branch of
CHRIST's Holy Catholic Church; she has retained the
Apostolic order ; she preaches " the faith once delivered";
she has an admirable Liturgy ; she is the envy of the
reformed Communions—the Presbyterians of the Synod

of Dort only " wished they could establish themselves on this model"; it was of her John Wesley wrote that " with all her blemishes, she is nearer the Scriptural plan than any other in Europe "; it was of her that Adam Clarke spoke as " the purest national Church in the world"; of her it was said by the Presbyterian Penny, " Many daughters have done virtuously, but thou excellest them all." Yes, she *has* many virtues, many excellencies. Whence, then, this " miscarrying womb " and these dry breasts? Whence this lack of holy enthusiasm—I may say this dread of *all* enthusiasm ? Why is it that, being so gifted, she so often lacks the grace to use those gifts aright ? I believe the main reason to be this—that we do not sufficiently recognize and remember that the Life, the *only* Life of the Church, the Power, the *only* power which can inform the Church is the HOLY SPIRIT of GOD. We forget, I fear—not in theory, perhaps, but in our practice, what others not so favoured as we are forced to remember—that *the body* of the Church may be ever so perfect, its machinery ever so complete, its officers ever so learned and eloquent, but yet that, " as the body without the spirit is dead," so the body of the Church without the SPIRIT in the Church is dead also. I believe that our danger has been this— that we have been tempted to *trust* in those material resources which have been so generously given to us— to trust in an arm of flesh, in our own wisdom and power and holiness. Those who are strong are tempted to rely on their strength ; those who are weak are con- strained to " look to the strong for strength." Yes, I

incline to think that our weakness has lain here—in the
fact that we have been, humanly speaking, so strong;
we have forgotten that our " power " is " from on high,"
that the Church can only " receive power "—power to
bear her witness and to do her work—" after that the
HOLY GHOST is come upon her "; forgotten that " when
we are *weak* then are we strong," and that, if we are to
fulfil our mission, it cannot be by human might, nor yet
by earthly power; it can only be by the SPIRIT of the
LORD.

I do not mean for one moment that the English
Church, in her standards and services, forgets or dis-
honours the Presence and Governance of GOD the HOLY
GHOST : if I were to say anything of the kind, her formularies would at once contradict me.   But she does not.
On the contrary, I question if there be any branch of
the Church which recognizes this more in theory.   There
is never a day but our congregations are urged in the
Absolution to pray for the HOLY SPIRIT ; never a day
but the prayer, " Take not Thy HOLY SPIRIT from us,"
is put into their lips, whilst not a few of the Collects are
petitions for this gift.   Why, we are sometimes reproached
for our belief in the HOLY GHOST, which we profess
every Sunday of our lives; we are reproached, for
example, because our bishops bid our ordinands
receive the " HOLY GHOST," for which we and they have
prayed ; reproached because we maintain that the HOLY
SPIRIT is given in Confirmation now, no less than in
Apostolic times ; we are even reproached because we
believe in a Baptism " of water *and of the* SPIRIT."   No,

I do not know that we could reverence the ever Blessed Comforter *in our Confessions* much more than we do; it is in our conduct, our practice, that we fall so short. Some of us have no idea of anything like " unction," nor would you say that the clergy as a class exhibited or desired it. Some of us do not seem to know that we are " priests," and I should hardly dare to say that spirituality was one of our characteristics, any more than, I fear, of Congregationalists or Baptists; you would hardly say that it was the mark of our synods and conferences and sermons: we have possibly heard of unspiritual Confirmations and mechanical Ordinations. Someone has even said that our Cathedral Service is " a job." It *is* a job, if there is no " praying in the HOLY GHOST "; in fact, singing and praying and preaching are all jobs if we are not inspired; if " the thoughts of our hearts " are not " cleansed by the inspiration of GOD's HOLY SPIRIT." And this fair cathedral—I know of none fairer, because of its virginal purity—this cathedral has been, will be, an imposture, a whited sepulchre, if it is not builded for " a habitation of GOD through the SPIRIT "; if it is not consecrated by the fire from Heaven; if its work and its worship are not begun, continued, and ended in the power and under the guidance of GOD the HOLY GHOST.

Brothers, we hear much of Church Reform. And I do not say that it is not needed. It *is* needed; it would be strange if it were not. The Church of the living GOD, being composed of fallible men, must always need reforming. But, believe me, there is no reform so much needed as that in ourselves. "The soul of every improvement is the improvement of the soul." The way to reform the Church is to reform Churchmen. And the one reform that Churchmen need, the reform that involves all others, is that we should, each in his vocation and ministry, surrender himself to the heavenly guidance of GOD the HOLY GHOST. This, by itself, would reform and transform the Church. How it would change our *characters* ; if the wind of GOD should "blow upon our garden," then would the "spices thereof flow out."[1] How it would transform our *sermons.* Then we could never "preach ourselves"; then we should get rid of that so-called "eloquence" which is the bane of some pulpits, and especially of Dissenting pulpits; of those

> "swelling epithets thick laid
> As varnish on the harlot's cheek ; the rest,
> Thin sown with aught of profit or delight."

"Self-emptying," says a Nonconformist theologian, "is an essential condition of witness-bearing ; no man can bear witness to CHRIST and to himself at the same time. *Esprit* is fatal to unction . . . . the power of the HOLY SPIRIT is only felt when the witness is unconscious of self and when others remain unconscious of him. No man is being blessed by the HOLY GHOST, when his hearers say, ' What an able sermon that was to-day.'"[2] How it would reform our *labours !* How different the results would be if every District Visitor and Sunday School teacher ever cried, " Behold the handmaid of the

---

[1] Cant. iv. 16.   [2] Denny, *Studies in Theology.*

LORD ; be it unto me even as Thou wilt " ; ever remembered that he and she could do no good of themselves : that when they were weakest, then were they strongest : that they were of no avail in the battle against sin and ignorance, except as the organs and vehicles of the SPIRIT ! How it would reform our *worship* if our congregations aimed at " praying in the HOLY GHOST "; if our singing men and singing women realized that they were " temples of the HOLY GHOST " ! Then would their tongues be tongues of fire, and their voices voices of comfort. How it would bring about, not reform only, but reunion ! We could not pursue our different ways any longer ; we could not perpetuate these odious and mischievous divisions, if we were all led by " one and the self-same SPIRIT." Where the Spirit of the LORD is, there is not only *liberty* but *unity.* How it would make our religion a power and a praise in the earth, if its professors were " filled with the SPIRIT " ! Then would the world acknowledge that " GOD was in us of a truth "; then would the Church go forth " conquering and to conquer." Brethren, let us walk in the SPIRIT ; let us live in the SPIRIT. For " the body without the spirit is dead."

THE CHURCH—ONE BODY.[1]

1 COR. XII. 13.

" By one SPIRIT were we all baptized into one body."

THERE are many earnest Christians, and there are some Churchmen—possibly you who now hear me are of the number—who are firmly persuaded that CHRIST our LORD has any number of visible churches, a " Baptist Church," and a " Methodist Church," a " Methodist Episcopal Church," and a " United Methodist Free Church," and so forth. They do not perhaps think that " one church is just as good as another," but they do believe that each is just as much a " church " as the others. They call it arrogance or impertinence to claim the name of CHURCH for any one body however ancient—in England or elsewhere— to the exclusion of the rest : they contend that each and all of our two hundred and fifty differing and competing denominations has an equal right to the title. In fact, they no longer believe, as all Christians did for fifteen centuries, in " ONE Catholic and Apostolic Church," but in a vast variety and a great multiplicity of " churches."

[1] This Sermon is published, in substance, in Tract shape, under the title *Polychurchism at the Bar of the Bible.* London : C. Taylor.

You have only to take up a religious, or even a secular newspaper to see how widespread and deeply-rooted is the idea that men can found churches at their own will and pleasure ; that they have only to meet in Christian fellowship, to choose some of their number to act as ministers, and that, forthwith, they form a true and lawful and fully-constituted Church. And this is the belief to which the name of *Polychurchism* has of late been given. That word means no more than this—that there are or may be *many* visible and separated Churches of CHRIST in one city or in one country.

I have said that very possibly *you* are of this way of thinking ; if you are, it is only what many of your neighbours are. But, if such is the case, may I beg you to consider, patiently and honestly, whether this view is scriptural ; whether it is really the idea of GOD's Church which is given us in GOD's Word. I shall hope in this address to prove to you that it is not : that, however popular or however liberal is this opinion, it is in direct opposition to all Bible teaching. I say nothing about the *ancient belief*, to which the creeds bear witness— that there is one visible Church and no more—because some modern Christians care very little for the ideas of the early Christians, but I appeal exclusively to Holy Scripture. I undertake to show—and in a way which you cannot dispute—that the Bible (to which we all appeal) knows of one Church, one *visible* Church only. I shall say nothing in this sermon again about the " invisible Church," if there is such a thing : no such expression (it is admitted) is ever found in Holy Writ.

No, I am speaking of the visible Church, or visible churches—whichever it is—and I engage to prove that by GOD's appointment this Church is one and not many; that this name belongs, and must be restricted, if the Bible is to be our guide, to the one Society, or to branches of the one Society founded by CHRIST Himself, the Society endowed with His SPIRIT on the day of Pentecost, the Society once ruled and ordered by His Apostles and since officered and instructed by their successors, the same Society which has descended in an unbroken history from their days to our own. I affirm— and I shall give you ample Scripture proof for what I say—that this is *the* Church of GOD, and that the various " denominations," however earnest their members may be, and however able their ministers, and however great their apparent success, are not Bible " Churches " at all, but are " private Christian clubs," private asso- ciations of Christian men, and no more. I begin by observing that

1. Though the Bible often speaks of " the churches "— in the plural—*it never once uses the word as the Polychurchists*— those who take the view which I am combating—*use it.* For they use the word " churches " of the different *sects* or *denominations* of Christians, which, they say, are so many " separate and independent churches " of CHRIST, and the Bible uses it of the congregations of the same body or community in different places. They employ it, you will observe, to designate *separate*, if not rival, *communities* in the same city or country, whilst the sacred writers only apply the word to branches of one

and the same community, in different regions. The Bible tells us of the "churches of Galatia,[1] of Asia,[2] of Macedonia,"[3] and so forth, and it does *not* tell of Baptist or Methodist or Unitarian churches : it is only in pulpits and platforms and newspapers, *never* in GOD'S Word, that the word is used in the latter sense. We are, therefore, true to Scripture when we speak of the (Parish) "churches of England," and we are false to Scripture—we are using the word in an unscriptural way—if we speak of the differing denominations as Churches. This is beyond all dispute. It cannot be, and I do not know that it is, denied by any careful and honest student of Scripture. But this is a point of such importance that I must put it before you in a different way. I observe

2. That "the churches" of the Bible are nothing else than *the societies or congregations of Christians in various places*, composed of *all* the Christians in those places ; it knows nothing of different *kinds* of Christians, nothing of denominations, or of separated or Dissenting communities. The churches of the New Testament are always described by their geographical position, never by any particular doctrines which they held, or any discipline which they preferred. We read of the Church of *Corinth*, of *Thyatira*, of *Ephesus*, of *Antioch*,—never of the *Congregationalist* Church of Corinth, or the *Methodist* Church of Ephesus, or the *Episcopal* Churches of Asia, or of anything at all like this. In other words, there were no sectarian Churches, no, not one : all the

---

[1] 1 Cor xvi. 1 ; Gal. i. 2.   [2] Rev. i. 4, 11 ; 1 Cor. xvi. 19, etc.
[3] 2 Cor. viii. 1.

Christians, even when they assembled in houses[1] belonged to one and the same community. I do not think
you will question this, but if you do, then you will surely
be able to produce *one* instance—I ask for no more—one
instance where the name of " Church " is applied to a
new or Dissenting body. But you cannot do it ; you
will not be well-advised if you try to do it ; a second
or separatist Church is unknown to Holy Scripture.
Moreover,

3. The Churches of the New Testament are *always
represented as* GOD's *Churches or* CHRIST's *Churches ;*
never as this man's or that party's ; never as constituted by man. Not only are all the congregations of
that age, all the parts and branches, that is to say, of
the Church, described collectively as " the churches of
GOD," [2] or of CHRIST,[3] but each separate congregation is
said to be His. Even the Church at Corinth, corrupt
as it was, is still called " the church of GOD, which is
at Corinth."[4] Similarly, the congregation at Thessa-
lonica is called " the church of the Thessalonians which
is in GOD the FATHER and the LORD JESUS CHRIST," [5]
and so with the rest. The Church is always represented
as GOD's building, GOD's husbandry, GOD's property ;
never as founded by man or a body of men. Yet the
" Methodist Church " speaks of Wesley as its " venerable founder " ; the " Congregationalist Churches " trace
their origin to Robert Browne ; the " Bible Christians "

[1] Rom. xvi. 5 ; Col. iv. 15 ; Philemon 2.
[2] 1 Cor. xi. 16 ; Thess. ii. 14.   [3] Rom. xvi. 16 ; Gal. i. 22.
[4] 1 Cor. i. 2 ; 2 Cor. i. 1.   [5] 1 Thess. i. 1 ; 2 Thess. i. 1.

owe their beginning to William O'Bryan, and so forth.
You see what this means. It means that we are true to the
Bible if we give the name of " churches " to branches of
the ancient Society founded by CHRIST, and false to Scripture if we give the name to societies begun and constituted
by man. It means that branches of CHRIST'S Society are
"churches," although they may have become corrupt, as
corrupt, indeed, as the Society at Corinth, or as "dead"
as that at Sardis, and that sects are not "churches,"
however pious and earnest they may be. It means that
CHRIST has appointed a certain Society to do His work,
and that it is not for man to start another because he
thinks that this will do the work better. Again,

4. Those who say there are many Churches—" separate
and independent churches "—*contradict our* LORD *and His
Apostles,* who speak expressly of the Church as one.
They contradict our LORD, Who said, " On this rock I
will build *My church* "[1]—not, " My churches." They
contradict S. Paul, who charged the elders of Ephesus
to "feed the church of GOD "—not "the separate
churches,"[2] and who writes that " GOD hath set in the
church "—not " churches "—Apostles, Prophets, etc.,[3]
and who affirms that " the church "—the *visible* church,
because Timothy was to learn how to behave himself
therein—is " the house of GOD, the pillar and ground of
the truth." [4] But they contradict him in another way.
He says distinctly that the Church is "the BODY of
CHRIST,"[5] and as distinctly that it is " ONE body,"[6] and,

---

[1] S. Matt. xvi. 16.   [2] Acts xx. 28.   [3] 1 Cor. xii. 28.
[4] 1 Tim. iii. 15.   [5] Eph. i. 22; Col. i. 24.   [6] Eph. iv. 4.

therefore, not two or two hundred " bodies "—as it must
be if the " Methodist body," and the " Baptist body,"
and all the other " bodies " are churches. And that
he means by " body " what *we* mean when we use the
word, a visible society, a body corporate, is clear from
the one consideration that it is of the essence of a body
to be visible and tangible : an " invisible body " is a
contradiction in terms. It is also clear from the fact
that this " body " is placed in contrast with " Spirit "—
the tangible with the intangible. Polychurchists, consequently, say there are many churches; our LORD
spoke of *one*, and no more. Polychurchism tells of over
two hundred church " bodies ": S. Paul recognizes *one*
such body, and no more. They cannot both be right ;
on which side will you take your stand ?

5. And that there is *one* church revealed to us in the
Bible, and that no provision is made for a second is
clear, not only from the considerations just alleged, but
also from the fact that GOD has appointed *the way of
admission into the Church*—He admits men to membership
Himself by the sacrament of Baptism—and no other
way of initiation can be devised. All who are baptized,
however unworthy they may prove themselves to be,
are admitted into the Christian Church : their unworthiness no more proves that they are not members than did
the idolatries and immoralities of the Jews prove that
they were not members of the Jewish Church. GOD, I
repeat, has ordained the form of admission into *the*
Church, into *His* Society; all that man can therefore
do, by the use of any other form or rite, is to admit

into a private society, a society other than God's. The
Wesleyans, for example, admit to their body by giving
a ticket of membership. This ticket does not and cannot make men members of a "Methodist *Church*"—a
ticket is not God's way of admitting to the Church : it
is a mere contrivance of man : it can only admit into a
society of man. I may be told that the Wesleyans
baptize much as the Church does. Yes, but that
baptism does not make men Wesleyans, but Christians.
It may admit into *the* Church, but admit into another
church it cannot. Similarly, God has appointed the
ministry, the Eucharist, and other institutions of His
Church. The ministers appointed in His way are
thereby made ministers of the Church : ministers not
of *the* Church are ministers of *no* church, but are officers
of a private society. I say, therefore, that the very
form by which God has constituted the Church, and the
very institutions which He has given it, exclude the
idea of a second church : they show that there is but *one*.

6. But a final reason, fatal to this idea of Polychurchism, is this—that *it means division among Christians*—open
and avowed division—and that Christ's religion is *dead
against all division.* He came to *unite* men—to "gather
together into one the children of God,"[1] to give "peace
and goodwill," and Polychurchism means disunion,
estrangement, separation, strife. It cannot exist without them. It is only because we are so accustomed to
rival "Churches" that we do not see that they contradict
the first principles of Christianity. They also contradict

[1] S. John xi. 52.

the prayer of CHRIST—that His disciples might be visibly
one;[1] they contradict His precept—that His disciples
should obey, in all things lawful, the teachings of the
wicked scribes,[2] because of their official position ; they
contradict the Apostles, who denounce all divisions,
even those *within* the Church as carnal;[3] how much more,
therefore, separations *from it*, and who proclaim that the
Church is " one body "—one visible community, for the
word " body," as we saw, cannot mean anything else :
the word must mean *in* the Bible what it means elsewhere—ONE body, not a " Wesleyan body " and a " Bible
Christian " body, and so forth.   With S. Paul the " one
body " is a fundamental principle—as fundamental as
the " one SPIRIT," the " one LORD," or the " one GOD
and FATHER of all "[4]; he mentions all these in the same
breath—the oneness of the Church is to him as certain
and as essential as the oneness of the GODHEAD.   Polychurchism, therefore, the belief in churches many, is as
directly opposed to all New Testament teaching as is
the belief in Gods many.   You may as well maintain
that the Church has two hundred heads (as well as
CHRIST), as that CHRIST, its Head, has two hundred
bodies.

And that this is so is now practically admitted by
some thoughtful and earnest Dissenters.   They allow—
they cannot do otherwise—that they cannot produce
a single text from the Book of GOD which favours the
idea of separate and competitive " Churches."   If you

---

[1] S. John xvii. 21.   [2] S. Matt. xxiii. 1-3.   [3] 1 Cor. iii. 3, 4.
[4] Eph. iv. 5, 6.

think they can, you have only to say what that text is : tell us where to find it, and we shall be grateful to you. But you cannot, and they cannot. No, it is allowed that CHRIST's Church was meant to be one, and in those early days *was* one. But that does not—in their opinion—settle the question. They still think that they have good reasons for setting up new and independent churches apart from the one Church, the one visible Society established by our Blessed LORD. Let us now see, therefore, what these reasons are.

1. And the first is that the *New Testament was written eighteen hundred years ago, and that everything has changed since then.* Well, we all allow that many centuries have passed since these records were penned, and that those centuries have witnessed many and great changes, but we say, first, that though "written aforetime," the Scriptures were "written *for our learning*,"[1] and that every part and parcel is for our learning. We must not pick and choose among the Scriptures of GOD. We must not accept the doctrine of the GODHEAD and reject the doctrine of the Church, or accept the doctrine of justification and refuse that of the sacraments. That is to "handle the Word of GOD deceitfully"; that is to want to have the Bible on our side instead of wanting to be on the side of the Bible. We do not pretend that the Church must now be in every minute particular just what it was then : it cannot be ; we have no prophe-syings, for example, or gifts of healing, or community of goods,[2] or unction of the sick.[3] But we do say that

---

[1] Rom. xv. 4.   [2] Acts iv. 32.   [3] S. James v. 14.

E

in all its *essentials*, and especially in the matter of its
unity, the Church should be now what it was then—and
you can give us no reason, no approach to a reason, why
it should be otherwise.   But we also say, secondly, that,
whatever changes have taken place since the first century,
they are changes in the things with which the Church
has little or nothing to do: *the things with which the
Church is concerned are unchanged.*   These changes are of
speech, customs, usages, social and political institutions,
and the like—things which in no wise affect the Church's
constitution; she does not profess to deal with such
matters; she has to do with GOD, with the soul, with
sin, with salvation, and these are *just what they were* and
stand just where they did.   It is no argument, therefore,
for many churches to tell us that there have been many
changes, for none of these changes affect the question of
Church unity.   If they did, it would be an argument
against the Bible.

   2. But a second reason alleged for setting aside the
plain teaching of the New Testament is that *its writers
did not foresee the corruptions of doctrine and the abuses that
would arise*—corruptions and abuses which (it is argued)
justify us in having many churches instead of one.   But
the answer to this is, first, that the sacred writers *did*
foresee the corruptions and errors of later days: they
did foresee them, because they expressly refer to them—
S. Paul, S. Peter, S. John, S. Jude, all speak, and in no
uncertain language, about them.   You have only to
turn to Acts xx. 29, 30, to 2 Thess. ii. 3-12, to 1 Tim.
iv. 1-3, 2 Tim. iii. 1-5, 2 Peter ii. 1-3: iii. 3, 1 John ii. 18,

and Jude 18, and you will see for yourself that this is so.
Yes, they foresaw these " grievous wolves ": these
" doctrines of daemons ": these "false teachers " : these
" destructive heresies "—they foresaw them all, and yet
they said not one word about separation, not one syllable
about a second Church. But a second answer is that,
even if they did not foresee the errors of *our* times, they
certainly perceived the flagrant errors and abuses of
their own times, for they speak of them and denounce
them. S. Paul denounces the Corinthians as carnal[1];
he says there was fornication among them,[2] and
that some among them denied the resurrection of the
dead[3]; he speaks of their " uncleanness and fornication
and lasciviousness,"[4] and yet never says one word about
coming out of *the* Church and founding a new one.
Nor does our risen and ascended LORD. He describes
the Church of Sardis as " dead,"[5] the Church of Thyatira
as seduced to "commit fornication " and to participate
in idolatries,[6] the Church of Laodicea as " lukewarm," as
" wretched and miserable and blind and naked,"[7] and
so forth, yet He never suggests in any way that it was
then, or could become later on, the duty of Christians to
come out of these corrupt communities—and He must
have suggested it if duty ever required it. We reply,
therefore, that it is no argument for starting new churches
that the old church has become corrupt, for, first, the
Jewish Church was shamefully corrupt in our LORD's
day, yet He never separated from it—if you say He

[1] 1 Cor. iii. 1.　　[2] 1 Cor. v. 1.　　[3] 1 Cor. xv. 12.　　[4] 2 Cor. xii. 21.
[5] Rev. iii. 1.　　[6] Rev. ii. 20.　　[7] Rev. iii. 17.

did, then will you tell us *when and how?* Why, His last hours were spent in keeping its Passover.[1] And, secondly, the Christian Church in the Apostles' days was stained with impurities, yet no one left it, or, so far as we can see, dreamed of leaving it, to set up a purer one ; and, lastly, though we are expressly warned that deadly errors will arise in the Church, yet it is never hinted that those errors will or can justify us in deserting it.

3. But it is said that the "*necessities of the work of* GOD" *required the formation of new Churches.* It is said, for example, that the Methodists were justified in founding a " Methodist Church " because of the great work which they have done. We do not deny that great work—far from it. What we do say is that it might all have been accomplished without a separation. Whatever good has been done might have been done *inside* the Church as well as *outside.* And here is the proof of it. The Methodists have never prospered or multiplied as they did during Wesley's lifetime. Between the years 1780 and 1790 their numbers rose from 52,334 to 134,549, a rate of increase which has never been approached at a later period. Yet those are the very years in which the society was kept in strict union with the Church ; the very years in which Wesley was most resolute against a separation. No, it is not necessary to leave GOD's Church in order to do GOD's work : it would be strange indeed if it were.

I hope, therefore, especially in view of what has been

[1] S. Luke xxii. 5.

alleged from Holy Scripture as to the *oneness* of the Church, that you will never again speak of any denomination of Christians, however amiable and Christlike their members may be, as a "Church." The members may be and are Churchmen—unconscious Churchmen—by virtue of their baptism (when they have been baptized, which is not always the case), but that does not make their denomination a Church. "Other foundation can no man lay than that is laid, which is JESUS CHRIST." GOD's visible Church is not built on Calvin or Wesley, but "on the Apostles and prophets, JESUS CHRIST Himself being the chief corner stone."

Nor must you think for a moment that this is not a practical question. There is none more so. If GOD has founded a Society, if it is part of His plan that there should be "one body" (and S. Paul mentions the one body in the same breath with the "one LORD," and "one faith," and "one SPIRIT," and "one GOD and FATHER of us all "), it cannot be right for us to divide it, or to set up a rival "body." However depraved His body may be, we must remain in it—just because it is His, and because there can be no Church but His.

THE GATE OF THE CHURCH.

"This is the gate of the LORD: the righteous shall enter into it."

IF the Church is, as I have said, the Society, and the only society, established by our Blessed LORD, and established to conserve and carry on the work which He began, the work of saving and blessing mankind, and if it is also the society, and the only society, to which He has expressly covenanted the gift and power of the HOLY GHOST, then it is quite clear that we must belong to it. All His followers must be Church-members, if only because He collected all His followers into a Church, and designed that Church to be the home and school and sanctuary of their souls. But they must also be members of the body because He is the Head, and they must be joined to the Head; because He is "the Saviour of the body," and they want to be saved. If, therefore, we *may* join, we *must* do so. There cannot be such a thing as a Christian who is not also a Churchman, in the proper sense of that word.

I observe that some who profess and call themselves Christians have of late conceived that all churches may be dispensed with. They say they want to follow CHRIST and to be guided by His precepts, but they see no need for a society; in fact, they are disgusted with the insincerities and imperfections of all Christian bodies. But they *cannot* follow CHRIST, or obey His commands, and hold aloof from His Church. His is a social, not a solitary religion. The Church is part of His plan. He founded it, and founded it that His followers should belong to it. His way of saving and blessing men is to bring them into His fold and family.

But how are we to join the Church? If we do not belong to it already, how can we become members? If we do belong to it, how did we become members? These are questions which cry aloud for an answer, for these are points on which, unhappily, Christians are very much divided.

You would be told, for example, if you desired to join a Baptist or Independent community, that you must first be converted; you must be prepared to relate your religious experiences; you must " narrate the history of your awakening to religious consciousness "[1]; you must be able to say that you have " passed from death unto life." When this is done, then they will give you the right hand of fellowship, and acknowledge you as a church-member. Similarly, if you joined the Methodists, you must profess a desire to " flee from the wrath to come," and attend a class; then they will hand you a ticket of membership, and so make you a member of their modern " church" or " body." But is this the

[1] Dr. R. W. Dale.

way in which we are to join CHRIST's Church? Is it thus that we are made members of *His* body? And if not, what is the way?

Now, before we go to the New Testament for an answer; before we ask, that is to say, how men were admitted into the Church in its first days, the days of our LORD and His Apostles, there are one or two axioms, one or two obvious truths, to be mentioned here. And the first is this—

1. That men can only be admitted into the visible Church by a visible rite. Remember, it is the *visible* Church that we are talking about; indeed, there is no other Church recognized in Holy Scripture; an "invisible Church," that is to say, an invisible *congregation*, an unassociated *association*, is a contradiction in terms. Anyhow, even if there is or can be an "invisible Church," even if that company of pious souls within the Church, whose members are known to GOD only, constitutes a "Church," we are now speaking of the *visible* society of CHRIST, and this, it is obvious, can only be entered through some visible gate. A form, a rite, a ceremony of some kind there must be to mark the members, to make them visible. Without this form or badge you could never know who belonged to the Church and who did not; there would be no test, no criterion. So that, if *we* are to be admitted members of CHRIST's Church, it cannot be by any emotions or experiences, any faith or repentance of our own; it can only be by the use of some outward observance. I do not say that either repentance or faith is unimportant—very far from it;

indeed, these are the qualifications for Church membership. But qualifications are one thing and admission is
another. Bravery and loyalty are necessary qualifications
in a soldier, but they do not of themselves admit men to
the ranks. Learning and piety are necessary for divines,
but not all learned and pious people are divines, but only
those who have been appointed such. Precisely so, those
only are Churchmen who have been formally admitted
into the Church. This is the first point. The second is

2. That if the Church is a divine society—and it is
always called GOD's Church: even the corrupt Church
at Corinth is described as "the Church of GOD which
is in Corinth "[1]—if it is a society founded and governed
by CHRIST, then CHRIST will Himself have prescribed
the visible rite or form of admission. He could not
have founded or commenced it,[2] if He had not done so:
until that rite is observed, no one is admitted ; there are
no members; the Church does not exist. If the Church
is a human institution, then, no doubt, man can appoint
the way to enter it : if it is a divine institution, with a
Divine Founder, then GOD, not man, must fix the mode
of admission. Here is a *third* point—

3. If "the body without the spirit is dead," if the
Church, that is to say, is really informed and governed
by the HOLY GHOST, then this outward and visible rite
will be used and made effective by the HOLY SPIRIT. It
will not be a *mere* form—there can be no empty forms
appointed by the SON of GOD, nor can there be any

---

[1] 1 Cor. i. 1.
[2] In its present shape GOD's Church began with Abraham.

such ordained for the community which is pervaded by the SPIRIT of GOD. Whatever the rite of admission may be, it will be but an instrument of the SPIRIT: in other words, it will be " an outward and visible sign of an inward and spiritual grace given unto us." It also follows, lastly,

4. That if men are admitted into the Church, directly or indirectly, by GOD, then only GOD can have the power to exclude them from the Church. Of course, GOD might delegate that power : He might instruct men to exercise it in His name, as He has permitted men to excommunicate—to put out of benefits—in His name, but man can have no power of himself to exclude from, or even to take himself out of the society of GOD. What GOD hath joined it is not for man to put asunder. Once in the Church, therefore, always in the Church.

I have said that these are axioms. Perhaps this may be disputed. But it will not at any rate be disputed that it was on these principles that the Old Testament Church, the Church before CHRIST, was constituted. That was a visible community—it consisted practically of the Hebrew race : it had its visible rite of admission, namely, circumcision : that rite was ordained and approved by GOD Himself, and its mark was indelible—once a Jew, always a Jew. It may perhaps be said that circum- cision was not the instrument of GOD the HOLY GHOST, but even if so, that is because the HOLY GHOST was not yet given.

And some such rite as this—an outward and visible form, appointed by GOD Himself, an outward and visible

sign of an inward and spiritual grace, we should expect
to find as the portal, the way of entry into the Christian
Church. We should expect it, not only from the *a priori*
reasons just given, but from the analogy of the Jewish
Church. For what GOD was then, He is still, and
what man was then, *he* is still, and therefore GOD's way
of dealing with men, of saving and blessing men, will
be the same still. We should expect, I say, beforehand, to enter the Church through the use of a form,
a form of GOD's appointment, which is nevertheless
not a mere form, but a channel of spiritual grace and
power.

And it is thus, and only thus, if the New Testament
is to be our guide—not to speak of ancient authors—
it is thus that we *do* enter the Church of GOD. The
New Testament proclaims that baptism, CHRIST's own
ordinance of baptism, is the way into the Church, and
that there is no other means of entering it. Those who
are baptized are Church-members—Church-members,
however bad they may afterwards become. Those who
are not baptized are not Church-members, however good
they may be. This is the institution of our LORD
CHRIST.

But I do not ask you to take my word for this: on
the contrary, I shall assume that you will not do so.
I assume that you want proof, Scripture proof. Such
proof, ample and convincing as it appears to me to be,
I now proceed to give you.

I begin by reminding you that Baptism is older than
Christianity. I do not insist on the fact, stated by

S. Paul, that the Jews were " baptized unto Moses "—
into the religion of Moses, into the Church in the wilderness [1]—" in the cloud and in the sea " [2]; no, but I refer
to the circumstance that the Jews of our LORD's day
admitted proselytes into their communion by a baptismal
rite.   If females, they were baptized; if males, they were
circumcised and baptized, and the children of proselytes
were baptized along with their parents.[8]   So that, at our
SAVIOUR's coming, Baptism was already in use amongst
the people to whom He came, and was used for the
purpose of admitting converts to their Church and
commonwealth.   It was the door through which all
must pass.

But this baptism of proselytes was not the only
baptism which preceded that instituted by our LORD.
The New Testament practically begins with the story
of a Baptizer—certainly S. Mark's Gospel does.   It is
significant that the Forerunner, the man sent by GOD
to prepare the way of the LORD and to make His paths
straight, was and is known as the Baptist.   And his
baptism was administered for the purpose—among
others—of admitting men to his new brotherhood.
" John," says a learned Dissenter,[4] " made his baptism
represent a social fact—entrance into a society. . . . It
was but in accordance," he adds, " with Oriental ideas
that entrance into the society was signified by a symbol.
Hence the command to repent was supplemented by the

---

[1] Acts. vii. 38.   [2] 1 Cor. x. 2.
[8] See Lightfoot, *Horæ Hebraicæ*, on S. Matt. iii. 6.
[4] Dr. Fairbairn, *Studies in the Life of Christ.*

command to be baptized." The disciples of John were made disciples by baptism, and, as far as appears, in no other way. Baptism was the one gate into his community. Those whom he baptized were members; others were not members.

And then CHRIST came, and He too came with a rite of baptism. He did what the Rabbis and what John had done already. Not only was He baptized Himself, in spite of the protest of John, but He administered baptism, administered it whilst John was still by baptism enrolling disciples.[1] If He did not baptize with His own hands, His disciples baptized in His name and with His authority.[2] Through their ministrations He baptized more disciples than John had done, though *he* had baptized "Jerusalem and all Judea, and all the region round about Jordan."[3] As to all this, the New Testament is explicit.

But why was it that the disciples of our LORD baptized in His name and at His bidding? Well, if we had no information on that point, we should still be clear as to one purpose at least which CHRIST had in view. His baptism cannot have meant less than John's did, and John's baptism was, among other things, for the purpose of admitting members into his society. No doubt His baptism meant more than John's, but it cannot have signified less, nor can it have meant something quite different. Everyone would understand it to be for this purpose, just because both the Rabbis and John used baptism for that purpose. If in their hands it was the

[1] S. John iii. 22, 23, 26.   [2] S. John iv. 1, 2.   [3] S. Matt. iii. 5, 6.

recognized form for admitting converts, such it must have been also in His. This much we should know, if we knew nothing else about it.

But we are not reduced to inferences. Our LORD has left us in no doubt as to its import. He has told us that it is by "water and the SPIRIT" that a man must "enter into the Kingdom of GOD."[1] You will be told, I dare say, by some that these words do not refer to baptism, but you will find, on reflection, that that view is simply incredible. I will not insist on the fact that, until recent days, no one dreamed of denying that it was of baptism that our LORD spoke to Nicodemus—for many centuries the meaning of these words was never questioned ; nor will I do more than remind you of the light which our LORD's own baptism throws upon His words—it was but a short time since "the water and the SPIRIT" were found combined in deed, as they are here associated in words, namely, at the river Jordan : I will only ask you to consider whether it is possible that our SAVIOUR would have said "water" when all the time He meant something which was not water. I affirm that it is impossible. It is impossible, if only for this reason, that He knew, as He spoke, that all Christian men—all save a handful—would understand Him, as, in fact, they have done, to be speaking of baptism. And now, you tell me that He was not speaking of baptism, and yet that He said no word to put them on their guard, to prevent this prodigious mistake. No, our Master can only speak of baptism

[1] S. John iii. 5.

here, and His baptism, He tells us, is the gate into the Church or Kingdom of God.[1]

But if any uncertainty attaches to these words, none can exist in candid minds with respect to another occasion, when baptism was expressly mentioned—I refer to our LORD's last commission to His Apostles. "Go ye," He said, "and make disciples of all the nations, baptizing them into the Name of the FATHER and of the SON and of the HOLY GHOST."[2] This shows how men were to be made His disciples, the scholars in His school. It was by baptizing them, and in no other way.

And accordingly we find, as a matter of fact, that it was always thus that men were added to His Church, to the band of His followers. I do not pretend that the baptism of every convert is recorded—it could not be— but our earliest Church History, the Acts of the Apostles, distinctly reveals that it was through this gate that men entered the early Church ; it records for our guidance the baptism of every new *class* of converts. First we hear of the baptism of Jews and Jewish proselytes on the day of Pentecost. The three thousand who were then baptized were (we are told) "*added* unto them"; added to the infant society, to the existing community,[3] and added by baptism. Next we read of the baptism of Samaritans[4]; then of the Ethiopian eunuch[5]; then of S. Paul,[6] and this though he had been miraculously converted ; then of

---

[1] I do not pause to prove that the Church is the Kingdom of God. I may refer to *The Christian Church—What is it ?* Chap. x.

[2] S. Matt. xxviii. 19. [3] Acts ii. 41. [4] Acts viii. 12, 16.

[5] Acts viii. 38. [6] Acts ix. 18.

the Gentiles in the house of Cornelius [1]; then of a woman, Lydia [2]; then of those who had been already baptized unto John [3]; then of Europeans, the Corinthians. [4] Nothing can be more certain than that all the early Christians were baptized, and that no man was regarded as a member of the Church, the community of Christians, who had not entered it through this gate.

It is quite true that the Epistles do not often speak of baptism as the portal of the Church, or the rite of initiation—they are for the most part concerned with other aspects of this sacrament. They do occasionally refer to it as the road into the Church, as, for example, in 1 Cor. xii. 13, " By one SPIRIT were we all baptized into one body," and in Col. ii. 11, 12, indirectly, where baptism is compared to circumcision, is called, indeed, "the circumcision of Christ," but I do not pretend that such references are numerous. But there is an excellent reason why they should not be so. It is because the Church existed before the Epistles were penned, and men were admitted into it years before a line of them was written, and the men who had been admitted by baptism did not need to be told that baptism was the rite of admission. " The Epistles deal generally with truths which were in danger," [5] they deal with disputed or neglected matters, and this never was disputed or neglected. It is necessary *now* to insist on baptism ; when a Nonconformist minister can make it a boast that he has never been baptized, [6] and when other Dissenters

---

[1] Acts x. 48.   [2] Acts xvi. 15.   [3] Acts xix. 5.   [4] Acts xviii. 8.
[5] Dr. R. W. Dale.
[6] Mr. J. C. Carlile, Member of the London School Board.

insist that baptism "is in no way binding upon us,"
what else can we do? But there was no such necessity
then, and this is why the Epistles, though they do incidentally pronounce on this question, do not refer to it
more frequently.

But what if anyone should say that he is still uncon-
vinced; what if he says that these Scriptures may be
interpreted otherwise? Then I reply that his interpretation or mine may easily be mistaken, for we are fallible.
If their meaning is disputed—though it never was till
recent times—then let us defer to the interpretation, to
the consent of Christians in all ages and all lands. We
are more likely to be in error than the universal Church,
or than the Church in its earliest days. And there is no
doubt but that Church has ever regarded baptism as
"the gate of the LORD," the one and only way into the
city and Church of GOD. You will not expect me to
prove this now; you know that it would be too long a
process; you will, I dare say, take my word for it that
it can be proved. In all ages of our religion, and in all
parts of Christendom, it has been held, as it is held by
some nine-tenths of Christians still, that baptism is the
one and only gate of admission into the visible Church
of CHRIST,[1] just as it was the gate by which our LORD
Himself entered upon His earthly ministry.

And this being so, you will readily understand why
we of the Church insist so strongly on the necessity of
baptism, why we say, indeed, that it is "generally
necessary to salvation," necessary, that is to say, "where

---

[1] "Entered we are not into the visible Church before our admittance by
the door of baptism."—Hooker III., i. 6.

it may be had." It is not only because baptism is the
instrument in GOD's hands of our regeneration or new
birth[1]—*it* does not regenerate, but GOD regenerates
through it[2]; not only because it is a channel through which
He conveys forgiveness to the penitent,[3] and a pledge to
assure them thereof; not only because it makes us partakers of the HOLY GHOST, the source of life and power;
it is also because it brings us into CHRIST, into His School,
His Body, His Army, " As many . . . as have been
baptized into CHRIST have put on CHRIST."[4] Without it,
whatever virtues we may possess, we are not Christians.
I do not say that we are true Christians just because we
are baptized—very far from it—but I do say that, except
we are baptized we are not Christians at all, nor have we
any right to look for the salvation which is in CHRIST.
He is " the Saviour of the *body*," and if we remain
outside the body we exclude ourselves from salvation.
It is in vain we pretend that we believe; His own
words are decisive, " He that believeth *and is baptized*
shall be saved."[5] If we are to be saved, it must be on
His terms, not ours, and one of His conditions is that
we shall enter His society, His school and His sanctuary,
and we can only enter it through the gate of Baptism.

[1] S. John iii. 5 ; Titus iii. 5.

[2] "Of sacraments, the very same is true which Solomon's Wisdom
observeth in the brazen serpent, ' He that turned towards it was not healed
by the thing that he saw, but by Thee, O Saviour of all.' "—Hooker V., lx. 4.

[3] Acts ii. 38 ; xxii. 16.   [4] Gal. iii. 27.   [5] S. Mark xvi. 16.

SERMON VII.

THE LAVER OF THE CHURCH.

TITUS III. 5.

"The washing [or laver] of regeneration and renewing of the HOLY GHOST."

ETERNAL GOD, the Giver of all good, does not bring men into His covenant or Church for nothing. It would not be like Him so to do. " The greatest Being in the world is the greatest *giver*," and one of His royal gifts awaits us at the very threshold of the Church. The font, standing near the door, is often understood to signify that Baptism is the gate, the door into the Church's fold; it may also remind us that we begin our Church and Christian life with a blessing. As we enter on it we are washed with "the washing of regeneration." He Who " loved the Church, and gave Himself for it,"[1] also "cleanses it by the washing of water with the word."[2] The rite of admission is also a rite of remission.

Yes, but there are some who do not believe in this gift of GOD. They will have it that Baptism is a mere form. They may allow that it admits into the Church, but that is all. The ancient and Catholic belief that Baptism, rightly received, brings with it the forgiveness of sins, is a doctrine which some Churchmen view with

[1] Titus iii. 5.   [2] Eph. v. 26.

grave suspicion, whilst Nonconformists as a class reject it as a relic of Popery or a " soul-destroying superstition." They cannot bring themselves to believe that GOD'S forgiveness of sins can be connected with the use of any form ; that it can in any way depend on the " dripping hand of a [possibly] thoughtless or bad man "—I quote the words of a prominent Dissenter—seems to them to be incredible.   They call this " salvation, not by faith, but by legerdemain."[1]

You see then that we of the Church are in this particular put on our defence. We must contend for the faith once delivered to the saints. It is not that we want to attack the beliefs of others ; it is that they persistently denounce our doctrines as unscriptural. And if there is one doctrine, one article of the ancient creed, more hateful to them than all the rest, it is that of the " one Baptism for the remission of sins."

And so I propose to-day to bring this doctrine to the test of Holy Scriptures.   Let us go " to the law and to the testimony " ; that shall decide for us.   Is it or is it not the case that Holy Scripture does connect Forgiveness with Baptism ; is it or is it not the case that the Font is a Laver for the washing away of sins ?

But, first, let us take care that we do not mistake or misrepresent the real question, the precise point at issue between us.   It *is* constantly misrepresented ; in fact, the fierce prejudice which is expressed against any and every idea of forgiveness in Baptism, frequently if not always, rests on pure misconception.

---

[1] Dr. Beet, *Manual of Baptism*, p. 52.

The question, then, is not whether Baptism or any rite, or all the rites of our religion put together, can remit sins, for they cannot. Remission must proceed from a *Person.* The water of Baptism can no more take away sins, of itself, than the blood of bulls and of goats could[1]; it may be a *channel* of forgiveness; it may be an *instrument* used of GOD to convey His forgiveness and to certify men thereof, but more than this it cannot be.

Nor is the question whether the man who ministers Baptism, be he bishop, priest, or pope, can remit sins—remit them in the sense of pardoning them himself—for he cannot. We have just seen that only a *person* can pardon; it is equally clear that only *the* person injured can pardon the injury. This is strict and obvious common sense. It needs no Scripture to tell us that—that none but the person wronged can forgive the wrong, whatever it may be. And the Person wronged by our sins is not man, but GOD. We may of course sin against our neighbour, but the wrong we do him is as nothing compared with the injury done to the MOST HIGH. Sins are transgressions of GOD's laws. Only GOD, therefore, can forgive sins.

Nor is the question whether GOD, Who alone can forgive, can or will, either through Baptism or any other means, extend His forgiveness to the impenitent or the unbelieving, for He cannot and will not. He cannot, because He is just and holy, and it would be both unjust and unholy to pardon men who mean to sin again; He will not, because He has declared that He will not;

[1] Heb. x. 4.

repentance is everywhere in Scripture insisted on as an indispensable condition of forgiveness when men can repent. There can be no question, therefore, as to Baptism bringing any remission to those who are un-fitted for remission, for it can bring none. It cannot do what GOD Himself cannot do.

No, the question is this, whether Holy Scripture represents the rite of Baptism as a means—no more—a means ordained of GOD for conveying His free and unmerited forgiveness to those who fulfil His con-ditions, those who sincerely repent and unfeignedly believe, and to no other persons ; whether to such persons and to such persons only it is a pledge and assurance of a pardon already granted in the counsels of GOD. This is the question which we have to submit to the arbitrament of the written Word.

And in weighing the evidence of Holy Writ upon this subject, the first thing to be observed is that Baptism symbolizes and represents a *washing*. In fact, the word means washing. " The washings of pots and cups," of which S. Mark speaks,[1] is in Greek the "*baptisms* of pots and cups." So in S. Luke, " He marvelled that he had not washed before dinner," is in Greek " that he was not *baptized* before dinner."[2] But, not to dwell on the *name*, the *thing* is a laver, a bath, a cleansing. But a cleansing of what? It can only represent, can only effect, if it effects anything, the washing away of *sin*. It can never have been designed to speak to men of the " putting away of the filth of

[1] Chap. vii. 4.   [2] Chap. xi. 38.

the flesh "[1]; it can only be an outward and visible sign of the purification of the soul.

But especially would this be its message to men of Jewish race and religion, the men amongst whom the rite of Baptism began. They could only see in it a figure, a picture of the washing away of sins. The language of the Old Testament would forbid any other interpretation. The washings of the Mosaic law, " the water of purifying,"[2] cleansed from ceremonial pollution, from an uncleanness which was not physical; thus we are told that " the water of separation " was a " purification for sin " or a sin-offering,[3] and here it is to be considered that it was out of these legal washings that the rite of Baptism in all probability arose.[4] The prophet Ezekiel, again, prefiguring, it would seem, CHRIST's Holy Baptism, has these words, " Then will I *sprinkle clean water* upon you, and ye shall be clean ; from all your filthiness and from all your idols will I cleanse you."[5] To men who were familiar with such language as this, the rite of Baptism, when it was first ministered among them, could only speak of a cleansing from sin. Whether Baptism, rightly received, carries with it any washing away of sins, may of course be doubted, but there can be no doubt that it symbolizes, and was designed to symbolize, the cleansing of the soul from defilement. The outward and visible sign of cleansing was there every time that Baptism was administered, whether

[1] 1 Peter iii. 21.   [2] Numb. viii. 7.

[3] Chap. xix. 9 (R.V.); *cf.* Heb. ix. 13; x. 22.

[4] See *Speaker's Commentary* on Ezekiel xxxvi. 25.   [5] Chap. xxxvi. 25.

any inward and spiritual grace accompanied it or not.

But I now proceed to show that an inward and spiritual grace, the grace of GOD the HOLY GHOST, sealing GOD's forgiveness on the soul, *did* accompany the Baptismal rite—when it was received with penitence and faith—in Apostolic days. Nay, I must go farther than this: I must remind you that the Baptism of John, even before the HOLY GHOST was given, brought with it the remission of sins. The gospel which John preached was not a gospel "of *repentance* unto remission of sins"; no, he "preached the *baptism* of repentance unto remission of sins." So that in this case, at least, the sign and the thing signified went together. The very rite that spoke to the multitudes of a washing away of sin, the same rite brought remission of sins to the penitent. Those who in the Jordan valley confessed their sins received in the Jordan river remission of their sins. Not *from* the rite, nor from the Baptist, but from GOD *through* the rite and through the Baptist: not by legerdemain, but by GOD's infinite mercy through the ordinance of His appointment. Anyhow it is clear from S. Mark's words[1] that, whether Baptism *with* the HOLY GHOST brings forgiveness of sins or not, the Baptism without the HOLY GHOST certainly did.

Now let us turn to the Baptism administered by our LORD's disciples during His ministry, administered, of course with His sanction and by His appointment.[2] It is true that not a word is said about its *effects;* still, we are sure that it must have brought remission to the

---

[1] Chap. i. 4, 8.   [2] S. John iii. 22 ; iv. 1, 2.

repentant. We are sure, if only for this reason—that the *Baptism* of the Son can never have been less efficacious or less blessed than the Baptism of the servant. It is quite impossible to suppose that whilst the Baptism of John *was*, that of Jesus was *not* "unto the remission of sins."

But the Baptism with which we are really concerned, which we have received, and which alone we have to defend, is that Baptism "of water and of the Spirit," of which both John[1] and our Lord[2] had spoken, and which was first ministered on the day of Pentecost. Is this for the remission of sins, or is it not? Well, if we had no explicit information on the subject, we should still have no doubt: our answer must be that Baptism "with the Holy Ghost" can never accomplish less for the faithful recipient than a mere Baptism with water. But we *have* explicit information; nothing could be plainer than S. Peter's words—and they were spoken just after the Spirit's coming, when he and his fellow-apostles were "filled with the Holy Ghost."[3] Will you hear what he says on this question? "Repent and be baptized every one of you"—there must be no exception to the rule. But why this universal obligation; why must *all* who repented be baptized? Was it for the sake of a mere form? Was it to submit to an ordinance which only *symbolized* the washing away of sins? No, it was for the sake of actual remission; it was because they would receive remission through the rite. "Repent and be baptized . . . in the name of Jesus Christ unto

---

[1] S. Mark i. 8.   [2] S. John iii. 5.   [3] Acts ii.

the remission of sins."[1]   The Baptism did not of itself
remit ; it could not : S. Peter did not himself remit ; he
could not.   But he did *bring* remission ; he conveyed and
he assured men of forgiveness, as the messenger of GOD
and the minister of Baptism.   It was GOD forgave the
three thousand penitents and forgave them as soon as
they were penitent, but His forgiveness was made over
to them, was assured to them in and through this sacrament of cleansing.

So that, if the Baptisms which are ministered now are
anything like that which was dispensed on the day of
Pentecost, there can be no doubt in any candid mind as
to their effect.   They must seal GOD's forgiveness on
the penitent soul.   But is it possible that that first
Baptism was exceptional ?   Does it, like the gift of that
day, stand alone ?   No, the remission then conveyed
was the normal gift, for we find Baptism administered
for the same purpose later on.   Why, even S. Paul,
CHRIST's "chosen vessel," S. Paul, who had been so
wondrously converted and who was so richly endowed,
must receive remission of his sins—and they were many[2]
—through the channel of Baptism.   What were the
words of Ananias to him ?   They were these—and they
prove conclusively that the Christians of that day regarded
Baptism as no empty form—they were these : "And now,
why tarriest thou ?   Arise, and be baptized, and wash
away thy sins, calling on His name."[3]   He is to use the
rite of washing for the washing away of sins.   He does
not receive remission direct from GOD, though GOD had

---

[1] Verse 38.   [2] 1 Tim. i. 15.   [3] Acts xxii. 16.

spoken to him directly in the way; he receives it in and
through Baptism. **Again** I say, If our Baptisms are
like that Baptism, then they still convey to penitent
hearts the pardon of their sins.

But perhaps someone objects that S. Paul's was a
special case. Then let us turn to his Epistles and we
shall find that the remission which he received in
Baptism, he held that others also received when they
were baptized. Consider, first, the terms in which he
speaks of this rite. He calls it the " washing " or
" laver " or " bath " of regeneration and renewing of the
HOLY GHOST.[1] And here his words only resemble our
LORD's, Who spoke to Nicodemus of men being regenerated by water and the SPIRIT.[2] But regeneration must
include remission: that would be no new birth which
left us stained and soiled with our old sins. Consider,
again, his language to the Ephesians. He says our
LORD cleanses the Church—the company of the baptized—" by the washing of water with the word."[3]
Consider, lastly, his words to the Corinthians. After
testifying that " neither drunkards, nor revilers, nor
extortioners shall inherit the Kingdom of GOD," he goes
on to say, " and such were some of you, but ye were
washed."[4] But *when* were they washed?—he refers to
some definite time. There can be but one answer to
that question—it was in their Baptism, in " the washing
of regeneration." They washed away their sins, as
S. Paul had washed away his, in the ordinance of
washing, in the sacrament of Baptism.

[1] Tit. iii. 5. [2] S. John iii. 5. [3] Eph. v. 26. [4] 1 Cor. vi. 11 (R. V.)

And if I do not cite any further texts in proof of this doctrine, you must not suppose that it is because there are no other Scriptures to cite. That is not the case. If, for example, Baptism in any sense " doth save us," as S. Peter says it does,[1] then it must *include* forgiveness ; without forgiveness there can be no salvation. No, the Scripture evidence is not exhausted, but I think that what has been already alleged will be sufficient for my purpose. It will convince any impartial mind that the Holy Scriptures do connect Forgiveness with Baptism, and that the Church's Laver is a Laver of regeneration and remission.

And so strong is this evidence that it has compelled some who once scouted the idea of forgiveness through forms to allow, in spite of their prepossessions, that Baptism does convey GOD's pardon to the believing adult. They do not quarrel now with the doctrine of "one Baptism for the remission of sins": all they now insist on is that in that remission infants can have no part. But why not, we ask, especially when they *have no sins*, properly so called, to be forgiven? For original sin, as it is termed, is not *sin* in the strict sense of the word, it implies no "transgression of the law"[2]; it is "the fault and corruption of our nature"[3]; it is nothing that we have done or left undone, but something that, by no fault of our own, we have *inherited*. If Baptism, therefore, does not bring forgiveness of sins to infants, it can only be because they have no actual sins. Birth-sin does not need forgiveness ; it needs a

---

[1] I Peter iii. 21.   [2] I John iii. 4.   [3] Article IX.

remedy, a restoration. That remedy, we say, is found, is applied, in the laver of regeneration and renewal. Unconsciousness is no bar to this blessing; they were not conscious when the taint was contracted. We remember, too, that there were some of old, who forbade the children to be brought to CHRIST. They argued, I dare say, as men do now, that little children could "do nothing"; that they were incapable of repentance and faith, and therefore incapable of blessing. But our Sacred LORD thought otherwise: He "blessed them" there and then. But if unconscious babes might be brought to Him then, surely they may be brought to Him now, and surely He will still, by His ministers and through the use of His appointed means, take them up in His arms, lay His hands on them and bless them.[1]

Moreover, this objection—that infants can "do nothing"[2]—entirely misconceives the grounds and principles of Divine forgiveness. We can none of us do anything. We are not forgiven because of anything that we have done or can do; we can never merit GOD's pardon; we are forgiven in His infinite love, when we put no *obstacle* in the way to prevent our forgiveness. In other words, we are not pardoned because our repentance or our faith procure it; we are pardoned, by GOD's free mercy, when there is no impenitence or unbelief to hinder it. Now, adults *can* put obstacles in the way; infants cannot. We have stronger reasons, therefore, for believing that the latter

---

[1] S. Mark x. 16.

[2] "The baptized [infant] does nothing whatever." Beet, p. 50.

have forgiveness through Baptism than the former, for whilst neither can do aught to earn it, adults may hinder it and infants cannot.

And so we see, I trust, that the " one Baptism for the remission of sins," in which we so often profess our faith, as our fathers did before us, is a thoroughly reasonable and Scriptural belief. More than this, no view of Baptism which excludes the idea of forgiveness is Scriptural; it cannot satisfy the plain requirements of Holy Writ. The Laver which our LORD has instituted in His Church is a " laver of regeneration and renewing of the HOLY GHOST." How strange that men should want to belittle GOD's gift, or think that they must " do some great thing," before they can enjoy it! And men, too, who are for ever protesting, and rightly so, that GOD's grace is free, " without money and without price " !

THE CONFIRMATION OF THE CHURCH.

S. MATT. VII. 21.

"Not every one that saith unto Me, LORD, LORD, shall enter into the Kingdom of Heaven, but he that doeth the will of My FATHER which is in Heaven."

"WHY do the clergy make so much of Confirmation? Why do they, year after year, approach us on this subject, or preach about it? Why all this fuss about a form?" Such questions, I cannot doubt, you have often heard—perhaps you have asked. I shall endeavour in this sermon to answer them. I shall give you one reason—one *sufficient* reason—why we are and must be anxious for your Confirmation.

But first, let me say, I hope you do not think that we want to have any one confirmed who is not *prepared* for Confirmation, and who does not earnestly *desire* it. We do not want to confirm anybody and everybody. Why should we? Neither Confirmation nor any rite can profit those who are unfitted for it. GOD never forces His grace and benediction upon us. No, we only want to have you confirmed, in the belief that you mean to do GOD's will and to lead a Christian life; and in the belief too that you desire His promised grace to enable you to

do this. If we are mistaken in thinking this of you, then
we hope that you will *not* be confirmed. We do not
want you to mock GOD or to misuse His religion.

But if you mean, really and truly *mean* to be saved ;
if you intend, that is to say, to give up sin, to put your
trust in GOD, and to keep His commandments, then
undoubtedly we do very much want you to be confirmed.
And we want it for this simple reason—because it is
GOD's *will that you should be;* because Confirmation " is
the will of GOD in CHRIST JESUS concerning you." And
this is the very point which in this sermon I am to prove.
Now, I *say* that Confirmation is GOD's will : of course I
have yet to *show* that this is so.

But before I offer you any sort of proof, it may be
well if I remind you that the Order of Confirmation, as
it now stands in our Church, the service in which *you*
are asked to share, involves two separate things ; it
involves, first, the renewal of your baptismal vows—you
cannot be confirmed without promising with your own
lips what you have promised already by your godparents
—and, secondly, it means your being confirmed, your
being renewed and strengthened by GOD the HOLY GHOST,
given in answer to prayer, through the laying on of hands.
These two things do not necessarily go together ; in fact,
it is only within the last 400 years that they have been
joined here in England. Before that time, you could
have been confirmed without making any promise at all.
But it is not so now. No one can be confirmed by the
bishop who has not first, before GOD and the bishop and
the congregation, renewed the promises made in his

name at his baptism.   Not that this however is now, or
ever can be, a part of Confirmation properly so-called:
it is merely an incident in the service, a preparatory to
Confirmation, which the Prayer Book carefully defines
as the " Laying on of hands."   Still, it stands as part of
the service.   And, therefore, if I am to prove to you that
this compound rite in which we ask you to engage is the
will of God concerning you, I must show, first, that it is
the will of God that you should vow to God a Christian
life; and, secondly, that it is His will that you should
submit, readily and thankfully submit, to the laying on
of hands, as a means of receiving His promised grace.

I take the vow first, merely because it comes first in
the Service: of course you all understand that it is
nothing like first in importance.   No, the important
thing is God's gift, not your promise.   No prelude, no
introduction to Confirmation (which is what the promise
is) can rank with the rite itself.   And I also take the
vow first, because I find that this promise, if it is sincerely made, does not provoke any comment or opposition.
People reserve their objections, and sometimes their
ridicule, for "the laying on of hands," for the rite of
God's own appointment!   Still, it may be well to show
you that this promise, though only an ordinance of man,
only the institution of the Church, is nevertheless a part
of God's will in CHRIST JESUS concerning you.

I will ask you, then, to remember that it is recorded,
and recorded for our instruction, that our LORD JESUS
CHRIST, when twelve years of age, went up to Jerusalem.
Perhaps you have not considered why it was that He

G

went. It was not only to keep the Passover, though He *did* keep that feast, and then kept it for the first time ; it was that He might be formally initiated and admitted into the observance of the Mosaic law; He then became what the Jews called *Ben Torah*, a son of the law. In fact, that visit was for Him much what Confirmation is for us : it was His public and solemn entry on His religious life. Such it was to every Hebrew boy, and such it was to the Son of Mary. He then made an open profession of His faith, if not in so many words, in deeds. Every neighbour who saw Him in Jerusalem, and certainly everybody who sat with Him at the Paschal Supper, knew that He then entered, of His own accord, on the observance of the law. And He is our example ; we are to follow in His steps. If such a profession was right in His case and pleasing to God in His case, then it must be pleasing to God that we should do the same. For the principle is the same now as then. True, He went up to the temple, and we go to the church, but He went up to make His profession and to enter upon His religious duties ; and this is just what we do. I point then to (what I may call) our LORD's Confirmation—it answered to Confirmation among the Jews—as a proof that our promises and our professions are according to the will of GOD.

But here I must say that I could not doubt this, even if there had been no such incident in the life of our REDEEMER to record. How can I possibly doubt that a heartfelt promise to do the will of GOD and live as a Christian will be acceptable to GOD ? GOD has never

condemned vows if they are sincerely made; **on the contrary, the** Bible **encourages them; we are constantly**
reading about them, from the vow **of Jacob to the vow
of S. Paul.** And it stands to reason **that if a man** really
means to serve GOD, **there can** be no harm in **his saying**
so, and saying **it with every** possible solemnity, **saying**
it in the **house of GOD and** before the people of GOD. It
stands to reason **that that vow** may of itself **strengthen**
and confirm him **in** his purpose: it may commit him to
a godly, righteous **and** sober life as nothing else will.
So that, **even if our** LORD had not set us this example, I
should still **be sure that the** Confirmation promise **was**
according to **the will of GOD. The Bible and, indeed,**
our common sense says, " Vow "; **the Church says, " Do
it now."**

Nor must you object that **it is** only the Church, **or
only the** English Church **that requires this vow before**
Confirmation. For GOD has given His Church " power
to decree rites and ceremonies " **such as this.** Whatsoever it binds or ordains on earth **shall be** bound—that is
to say it shall **be** ratified **and** confirmed—in **Heaven.**
Why, we **are to " submit to** *every* **ordinance—or creation**[1]
—of man," even **to those** of the civil power, " for the
LORD's sake." But if **I am** to obey the institutions of
the State, how much **more** those **of** the Church ! **And**
here again our LORD has set us **an example. He did**
not need the baptism **of** John : it was " the baptism of
repentance unto remission of sins,"[2] and He had no sins
to repent of, none **to be remitted.** Yet He insisted on

---

[1] 1 Peter ii. **13.** Rev. Vers. Margin.   [2] S. Mark i. 3.

being baptized. " Thus it becometh us," He said, " to
fulfil all righteousness." Similarly He kept the Feast of
Dedication[1] and other similar institutions of man,[2] and
He thereby teaches us to do the same.

But if you still have any doubt upon the subject, then
let me turn from our SAVIOUR's example to His precepts.
You will remember that He requires His disciples to
confess Him before men. He says plainly that if we
confess Him, He will confess us, and that if we deny
Him, He will deny us before the angels of GOD.[3] Now,
I do not say that Confirmation is the only way in which
we can confess CHRIST—far from it. But I do affirm that
it is *one* way of confessing Him ; yes, and of taking up
the cross and going after Him. Indeed, I fail to see
how we can more openly and effectually confess our
LORD. We promise in our Confirmation to be His
faithful servants and soldiers ; we engage to be and to do
everything that He requires. We do not promise, I
should like to say in passing, anything more than other
persons who are not confirmed have to perform, if they
mean to be saved—there is one gate, one road, one life,
one duty for all of us; still, we do promise everything
that GOD demands, and we do profess the faith of a
Christian. And some such profession as this, I repeat,
is necessary to salvation. We often forget that the open
confession of CHRIST is as necessary as heartfelt faith in
CHRIST, but the Apostles did not. " If thou shalt confess with thy mouth "—these are S. Paul's words—" the
LORD JESUS, and shalt believe in thine heart that GOD

[1] S. John x. 22, 23.   [2] S. Luke xxii. 17, 20.   [3] S. Matt. x. 33.

hath raised Him from the dead, thou shalt be saved."[1]
"With the mouth," he continues, "confession is made
unto salvation."

I venture, therefore, to hope that my first point is
proven, if it needed any proof, namely, that the solemn
"vow, promise and profession," made at the time of
Confirmation, is according to the will of GOD. You will
allow that it is the will of GOD that we should confess
Him before men. I now proceed to my main contention
—probably the only point that you or others will dispute—that it is part of GOD's will that those who have
been baptized unto CHRIST should receive the HOLY
GHOST through the laying on of hands.

And I begin by reminding you that the imposition of
hands as the outward and visible sign of blessing, the
"outward and visible sign of an inward and spiritual
grace given unto us," is one of the very oldest institutions
of religion. You might think, from the way people talk
of it, that the Church had invented it last year, whereas
it existed before the Christian Church did. It takes us
back to the times of the patriarchs. It was thus that
Jacob blessed the sons of Joseph, and we know that that
blessing was not an empty form ; what Jacob did he was
guided of GOD to do.[2] It was thus too that Moses the
man of GOD blessed Joshua, and the outward sign was
accompanied by the inward grace : we are told that
"Joshua was full of the spirit of wisdom, *for* Moses had
laid his hands upon him."[3] And this again was done
by GOD's appointment. It was "the LORD" that "said

---

[1] Rom. x. 9.   [2] Gen. xlviii. 19, 20.   [3] Deut. xxxiv. 9.

unto Moses, ' Take thee Joshua . . . and lay thine hand upon him.' " [1]   If, therefore, the laying on of hands is no part of GOD's will now, it was certainly part of His will once : the rite, that is to say, was formerly sanctioned and ordained and used of GOD, used for the conveyance of grace and heavenly benediction.

But you may be under the impression that this conveyance of blessing through the imposition of hands belongs to a past and a ceremonial dispensation; you may think that all this was done away at the coming of our LORD.   Let us turn, then, to the Gospels to see whether this is so.   Did the Divine Teacher during His ministry reject the laying on of hands as formal or superstitious ?   Was it abolished with circumcision and sacrifice and other institutions of Judaism ?   On the contrary, we find that it is more in use than ever : we find that our LORD, so far from disusing it, gives it a place and a prominence which it has never had before. He was for ever employing it ; it was His customary channel for the conveyance of healing and of blessing. I imagine that there are few Churchmen who have realized what a part this ordinance assumes in the life and ministry of our LORD.   Is a man deaf and dumb ? CHRIST lays His hand upon him [2] ; is he blind ? He does the same [3]; do they bring children to Him ? He blesses them by laying His hands upon them [4]; are His disciples to recover the sick after His departure ? it is by the same means. [5]   No, whatever changes our Lord made in the

---

[1] Numb. xxvii. 18, 22.   [2] S. Mark vii. 32, 33.   [3] Chap. viii. 25.
[4] Chap. x. 16.   [5] Chap. xvi. 18.

institutions of the old covenant, He certainly did not
scorn or disparage the laying on of hands; what He did
was to practise it more than it had ever been practised
before.

It may be said, however, that this was before the
coming of the HOLY GHOST, and you may have imagined
that when the Comforter was given to guide men into
all truth, we shall hear no more about this form, this
ceremony. Is it then the case that this rite ceased from
the day of Pentecost? On the contrary, it is thence-
forward in greater request than ever. It is now used
for a new purpose ; not merely for ordination, but for
Confirmation. In the sixth chapter of the Acts we find
" the seven," commonly called deacons, set apart by the
laying on of hands[1]; in the eighth chapter we find its
use extended to all the baptized, or all those baptized by
Philip at Samaria. It is a new and evidently a very
solemn function : it is so solemn or so sacred that Philip
may not minister it himself: it must be done by the
Apostles themselves : it is done by the very first among
the Apostles. Yes, we find S. Peter and S. John in the
year A.D. 34 doing precisely what our bishops do in this
present year of grace. They prayed for the baptized :
they supplicated for them the gift of the HOLY GHOST :
then they laid their hands upon them, and they received
the HOLY GHOST. And what SS. Peter and John do in
the eighth chapter, we find S. Paul doing in the nineteenth. He lays his hands on some twelve men at
Ephesus immediately after their baptism, and forthwith

[1] Verse 6.

the HOLY GHOST descends upon them.[1]   This is mentioned incidentally in the course of the history, as is
also the confirmation of the Samaritans—from which we
gather that these two instances are examples of many
more which are not recorded.   There is no doubt, therefore, that the laying on of hands was continued *after*
Pentecost ; it was not thrust aside as antiquated or
unspiritual ; on the contrary, it appears as a medium, a
channel through which the SPIRIT was bestowed.   We
are distinctly told that it was "*through* the laying on of
the Apostles' hands"[2] that "the HOLY GHOST was
given," and that "when S. Paul had laid his hands upon
them," then, and not before, the HOLY GHOST came on
the Ephesians.[8]   We have here, consequently, at this
early period of Church History, the laying on of hands
as a recognized institution of the Church, a rite ministered by the Apostles of our LORD, and ministered too
for the conveyance of the HOLY SPIRIT of GOD.

But I daresay you will raise the objection which is
constantly alleged against our identifying this Apostolic
rite with our present-day Confirmations.   You will say :
"The laying on of the hands of the Apostles was for one
purpose ; yours is for another.   Theirs was for the conveyance of supernatural gifts ; yours is not, because these
gifts have ceased and, therefore, the laying on of hands
should have ceased with them."   To this I reply, first :
What makes you say that the laying on of hands in the
Apostles' days was merely for the conveyance of the
miraculous gifts ? you have no warrant for any such

---

[1] Verse 6.   [2] Chap. viii. 18.   [8] Chap. xix. 6.

statement. **The Bible never says so. It says it was** for " the HOLY GHOST." For this they prayed and this they received. **It is true** that they received the **gifts** along with it, just because such gifts always accompanied the SPIRIT's footsteps in those days ; they accompanied the preachings or prophesyings,[1] and the prayers,[2] as well as the imposition of hands. But it never occurs to you to argue on that account that either preachings **or** prayers were for the sake of these gifts, or should now be abolished. Secondly, **you say that the** gifts having ceased, Confirmation ought to have ceased likewise, **and** it is on this ground that **some** Nonconformists have dropped both Ordination **and Confirmation.** Yes, but Confirmation did *not* **cease ; the** Christian Church went on with it ; it has continued it to the present day ; it is found in all parts **of Christendom, in East and** West, among Protestants as well as among Catholics. Though the early Christians perceived that the gifts no longer followed the laying on of hands, yet they continued the laying on of hands all the same. And **why ?** Obviously because it was for something else than the gifts ; it was, in fact, for what the Bible says it was—the HOLY GHOST Himself ; for His strengthening and sanctifying power, and not for any mere signs. To say that the imposition of hands should **have** ceased because **the** gifts did, is to say that you know **better than** the universal Church for sixteen centuries ; **it** is to **say that all** these Christians have been deluded, and that **you are** so much wiser and more spiritual than they.

[1] 1 Cor. xiv. 1-6 ; Acts x. 44.   [2] 1 Cor. xiv. 14, 15 ; Acts iv. 31.

And it is to say this in the teeth of a passage which mentions "the laying on of hands" as among the first principles and fundamentals of our religion. I refer to Heb. vi. 1, 2, where we have a list of the principles, the A B C of Christian teaching, the truths imparted to babes in CHRIST. They are mentioned quite incidentally —the sacred writer says we are not to lay this foundation over and over again. But what *is* the foundation? He mentions six things, and of these the laying on of hands is one. He mentions repentance and faith, and as to these we are all agreed. He mentions the resurrection and the final judgment, and as to these again we are happily agreed. He further speaks of "baptisms," as to which nearly all Christians are agreed. As to five of the foundation-stones, that is to say, there is no difference. It is only as to the sixth that we quarrel. Some virtually say that five are enough; that this is superfluous. But the sacred writer surely knew better than we do, and if he puts the laying on of hands into the list—and he does—who are we that we are to cut it out? What is this but "handling the word of GOD deceitfully"? Nor is it of any use to say that he is speaking of ordination. That cannot be so, for all the other foundation-stones concern *all* Christians; repentance does, faith does, baptism does; they would hardly be "principles" if they did not. It is, therefore, inconceivable that the next item in the list is a thing which only affects one Christian in a thousand. No, there is no escape from this text. If we want to do the will of GOD we must build on the foundation which GOD Himself has laid down, and GOD's foundation includes "the laying on of hands."

This then, dearly beloved, is the main reason why we make so much of Confirmation. It is not the only reason. We value it highly because of the opportunity it affords us of instructing our children in the principles of their religion, and of making a mark on their lives; we cherish it for other reasons. But our chief reason for clinging to it and insisting on it is that "this is the will of GOD in CHRIST JESUS concerning you." We are persuaded that it is a part, and an essential part, of CHRIST's religion. Nor are we singular in thinking it such. It is only what the Christian Church has held for many centuries; what all Christians believed until comparatively recent times; what the majority of Christians believe still. If Confirmation were peculiar to the Church of England, or to a small part of Christendom, or to a recent age of our religion, there might perhaps be some excuse for slighting it. But it is not so. We have not *invented* it; we have simply *inherited* it from the Apostles of our LORD. All that we are guilty of is this —that we have not dared to discontinue it; we have not dared to separate ourselves from our Christian brethren in other lands and our Christian forefathers in past centuries. They have regarded it, century after century, as existing by the will of GOD, and so they add their testimony to that of the Bible. We find it in the Scriptures; we find it in the Church; we know it is GOD's gift to us. And His gift for our good, for the strengthening of our souls by His own gracious presence and power.   Do you not need strength ?   Does not almost every day of your life show you your own weakness ? Are you wise, then, to reject the aid which GOD offers ? Are you wise to set up your will against His, especially when His will is to help you ; to come to you and dwell in you and guide and teach and comfort and support you ? For GOD's sake—because it is His will concerning you— and for your own sake—because it will bring you the very grace you need—I pray you to be confirmed.   You are calling CHRIST " LORD," " LORD " ; you do it in our Services, if at no other time.   But more than this is needed, if you are to " enter the kingdom of heaven." You must " do the will of our FATHER which is in heaven."[1]

---

[1] Perhaps I may be allowed to say here that the reader will find a series of instructions and appeals on this subject in *Seal and Sacrament— A Guide to Confirmation and Holy Communion*.   London : S.P.C.K. Post 8vo.

THE SUPPER OF THE CHURCH.

S. LUKE XIV. 16.

"A certain man made a great supper, and bade many."

THE Church of GOD, as I have more than once reminded you, is a school, an army, a sanctuary. But it is more than this: it is a refectory, a guest-chamber, a banquetting-hall. It is a place for eating and drinking, as well as for hearing and worshipping. The very arrangements of the building witness to this: it has its holy table, as well as its font and prayer-desk and pulpit.

And the Church of GOD has *always* had its feasts; it had them before CHRIST came, even when it was "the Church in the wilderness."[1] Long before it had any pulpit, it had its altar. The religion of Moses was full of feasting. I am not thinking merely of the three great festivals of Passover, Pentecost, and Tabernacles, but all through the year it spread a table for its sons and daughters. For the peace-offerings, the commonest form of Jewish sacrifice, involved a meal. The blood was poured, the fat was burned, the breast and shoulder was given to the priest—and given to him, remember, that

---

[1] Acts vii. 38.

he and his might feed on it—and then the rest of the
victim was returned back to the worshipper, who carried
it home and, with his family, feasted on the sacrifice.
And what is true of the " bloody offerings " of oxen and
sheep is also true of the unbloody oblations of shew-bread
and meat-offering and the like.   The shew-bread was for
Aaron and his sons : they were to " eat it in the holy
place." [1] Of the minchah, or meat offering, which accom·
panied almost every sacrifice, a portion, a " handful,"
was burned on the altar, but the rest was the perquisite
of the priests.   It is quite clear, therefore, that the earlier
form of our religion involved perpetual feasting.

And this circumstance in itself affords a strong pre·
sumption that CHRIST's religion will do the same.   We
cannot believe that the Church after CHRIST will be
unlike the Church before CHRIST, in any of its material
features, any of its *principles*.   How can it be unlike, if
the one is the shadow and the other the substance ?
Shadow and substance, in their broad outlines, must
always agree.

And there is another reason why, like Moses's Law,
the religion of our REDEEMER should have its food and
its feasts—because it enshrines a better covenant, estab·
lished upon better promises.   The Gospel dispensation
is to do more, much more for man, than the Law ever
did.   But it would do *less*, less in one particular at least,
if it had no meat and drink to offer him.   If it had no
board, no banquet, then Christianity would be, in one
particular, inferior to Judaism.

[1] Levit. vi. 16.

But it is not so. Our Most Gracious LORD, Who came "not to destroy the law or the prophets," did not destroy the sacrificial feasts; on the contrary, He ful- filled them; that is to say, He *filled up* the outline, He gave them substance and reality; He "made a great supper, and bade many." Yes, the feasts are there still, but they are transfigured and exalted. Christianity has its meat-offering and its drink-offering; the sacrifice of the SAVIOUR's death is followed by a feast upon the sacrifice. There would be no continuity between the first dispensation and the second, at least in this respect, if it were otherwise.

And so we observe that when our LORD appeared amongst us, when He manifested Himself to men, it was among other things, as the giver of food. He was not only master and teacher and healer; He was also "LORD"—in the true sense of that word. For the proper, the original meaning of "LORD" is "giver of bread": it carries us back to a time when the thanes or barons in their castles dispensed food to their retainers and dependents, just as we read in Scripture of the prodigious numbers who fed at Solomon's or Jezebel's table. CHRIST, I say, was the true "lord," the most generous giver of food. Not only did He proclaim Him- self to be "the bread of life," "the bread which came down from Heaven"[1]; not only did He promise to give His flesh for the life of the world,[2] but He illustrated His promises; He gave us object lessons, pledges and fore- tastes of His royal bounty. On two separate occasions,

---

[1] S. John vi. 48, 50.   [2] Verses 51-59.

He fed over four thousand persons with loaves and fishes; He satisfied them with bread even in the wilderness. And it is perhaps worth noticing, as we pass along, the prominence given to these miracles in the Evangelists. The feeding of the five thousand is recorded by all the four; that of the four thousand by S. Matthew and S. Mark. So that our SAVIOUR stands conspicuously forth on the sacred page as a feeder of men. This was one of the marks and features of His earthly ministry.

And this character—of true LORD, of bread giver—He still sustained, even on the night in which He was betrayed. "Take, *eat*," He said to His disciples, "*Drink* ye all of this." On that last night He instituted a feast, a supper for His followers. As they were eating, the Passover was replaced by a Christian institution. But the idea is still the same; still a feast upon a sacrifice. He had spoken in the synagogue at Capernaum of giving His flesh for the life of the world: this promise He proceeds to fulfil. "Take, eat," He cries, "this is My body." He leaves no doubt in the minds of the twelve as to whether His Church, the community which He had established, and of which they were the first officers, is to have its feasts. What He did, they are to do also. They are to do this in remembrance of Him. They are to eat this bread and to drink this cup until the day of His return.[1]

I say that our LORD left His disciples in no doubt as to the feast which He instituted on the eve of His

---

[1] 1 Cor. xi. 26.

Passion. For their conduct shows how they understood His words: it is a commentary on His command. No sooner is the Church fully constituted, no sooner is the Christian body governed and taught by the Eternal Spirit, than we find the disciples meeting for the breaking of the bread. It is possible, nay, it is almost certain, that in those early days, and for some time afterwards, the Eucharist was combined with the *Agapé* or love-feast, but it is altogether certain that the Eucharist, the feast of the Lord, was the great purpose for which they assembled; the *Agapé*, like our Matins, was but the setting of the precious jewel. Just as they were continually in the Temple, blessing and praising God, so in their private houses they were continually showing the Lord's death and eating the Lord's Supper. "They continued steadfastly . . . in the breaking of bread and the prayers."[1] If not every day, certainly every Lord's Day they met, not for teaching or fellowship or worship only, but for eating and drinking; not for psalms or sermons only, but for the communion of Christ's body and blood.[2] And the fact that they celebrated the Eucharist along with the *Agapé* shows conclusively the light in which they regarded the former; it was not a mere memorial; it was a feast. And this feast, I repeat, they were for ever celebrating—in fact, there is no record in the New Testament of any regular meetings of the early Christians except for this purpose. They never assembled, as we so often do now, to join in the prayers and hear the sermon and then go home: no, it was the

[1] Acts ii. 42, 46. [2] Acts xx. 7.

H

feast of GOD that brought them together; they partook of CHRIST's bread before they separated. The very abuses which arose in connection with the LORD's Table, and which S. Paul denounces in the First Epistle to the Corinthians, are proofs of the important position it occupied. So again is the fact that S. Paul had his account of the institution from our LORD Himself—" I received of *the Lord*," he says, " that which also I delivered unto you, how that the LORD JESUS, in the night in which He was betrayed, took bread."[1] Indeed, every mention of this rite in the Acts or the Epistles shows how much it was cherished and venerated in the early Church. It has been said that it is not referred to in the Epistles as often as it is in our sermons, and this is quite true. But then the answer is conclusive: No, because there was no necessity for constant reference to it. The Epistles are not set theological treatises—they are "occasional writings"; they only deal with things which were disputed or abused. And as to the Holy Supper, there was no dispute, and there was no neglect. We *must* refer to it, because it is undervalued or disregarded; in those days it was firmly established in every Church, and was thankfully embraced by every Christian.

And what is true of the early Church—that the Supper of the LORD held the highest and an altogether unique place in its devotions—is true, with hardly an exception, of the universal Church. All through the Christian centuries, many as have been the corruptions of doctrine, and many as are the abuses which have crept into the

---

[1] 1 Cor. xi. 23.

community, the Supper of the LORD has ever held its rightful place—or perhaps I should say, it has never occupied a subordinate place. Even in the darkest ages it was never dethroned; even in times of persecution it was never dropped. Of this sacred rite we may use those words—"*quod ubique, quod semper, quod ab omnibus*"; it has been celebrated everywhere, in every age, by every Church. Many as were the sacrifices of Judaism, the sacraments of our religion have been more numerous still. Age after age has this silent but eloquent gospel of the precious death been set forth before the eyes of Christians; in fact, there have been ages when no other gospel was preached—

> "Through the Church's long eclipse,
> When from priest or pastor's lips
> Truth Divine was never heard;
> Mid the famine of the word,
> Still these symbols witness gave
> To His love Who died to save."

And if, since the Reformation there have been some who have thought to honour our LORD by disparaging His ordinance, still they have been comparatively but few. Of the many sects and divisions of Christendom, only the Quakers have discarded it altogether, and of late many Dissenters have repudiated the low Zwinglian view of the sacrament. No, the Church as a whole, whatever its strifes and heresies, has passionately clung to its feast of charity and grace.

I have called it "the supper of *the* Church." Some of you may be disposed to resent this title; you may tell

me that it is "the supper of the LORD." Of course it
is! have I said one word to imply the contrary; nay,
have I not repeatedly called it CHRIST's feast—His
appointment, His memorial, His sacrament? All the
same, He instituted it *in* His Church and *for* His Church
and for that alone. And so it belongs to the Church,
just in the same way that the other institutions of which
I have treated belong to it. I do not call the Font "the
Laver of the Church," because the Church designed or
ordained it, for it did neither, but because CHRIST uses
it to cleanse and indeed to constitute His Church. I do
not call Confirmation "the seal of the Church," because
the Church has invented it, for it has not, but because
it is one of the endowments which GOD has given it.
Similarly, we speak of the Eucharist as the *Church's*
Supper, not because it is *of* the Church (for it is of GOD),
but because it is *for* the Church and for that society and
communion alone.

But I now come to a matter of much greater moment.
There are Christians who do not believe that this Holy
Sacrament is really and truly a feast, a banquet. They
cannot think it to be such or they would never shun it
as they do. It might be a fast or a funeral from the way
they regard it, for they turn their backs on it; they will
have none of it, or if they communicate at all, they do it
as seldom as they decently can. And so the question is
forced upon us, "Is the Supper of the LORD a 'Supper'
in any real sense of that word? Or is this name a
misnomer?"

Well, a feast means food: it involves eating and

drinking. And this sacrament involves eating and drinking. This is the very first idea connected with it. "Take, *eat*"; "*Drink* ye all of this." Whatever other objects and aspects Holy Communion may have, its primary aspect is undoubtedly that of a meal. It was instituted at the Passover : it was to replace the Paschal Supper. No one can participate in it without partaking of food. It is, therefore, a feast.

Yes, but you object perhaps that it is only a feast or supper in some shadowy and unreal and mystical way. What is this food, you ask, of which we partake? Well, a similar question was asked about the manna, which was nevertheless the only food of Israel for forty years. I grant you it is not common bread and common wine of which we partake. It *is* bread and wine, but it is infinitely more. For " the bread which we break," it is " the communion, the participation in the body of CHRIST. The cup which we bless," it is " the communion (or participation) in the blood of CHRIST " [1]— I use S. Paul's own words. This is the bread of GOD, the wine of GOD. But surely it is no less a *supper* because it is "*the* LORD'S Supper "; it is no less *food* because it is CHRIST's body and CHRIST's blood ; it is no less a feast because it preserves body and soul. The better the food, the better the feast. It comes to this—that you question whether it is a supper at all, just because, instead of oxen and fatlings, and instead of mere bread and wine, we partake of angels' food and eat bread from Heaven.

[1] 1 Cor. x. 16, R.V., Marg.

You see I assume that when CHRIST said, " This is My body," " This is My blood," we are to take Him at His word, and not to water down that word to suit our preconceived ideas. He did not say, " This is a *picture* of My body," or "This is an *emblem* of My blood," but " This *is* My body." Though He knew beforehand that millions of men would take His words literally, yet He used them, and without one syllable of warning. Similarly, when S. Paul writes, " The bread which we break, is it not the participation in the body of CHRIST ? ", I understand him to mean that communicants do partake of CHRIST's *body* and not of a mere emblem thereof, especially when I remember that He says elsewhere that the profane communicant is " guilty of the body and blood of the LORD."[1] If therefore I call the elements CHRIST's "body" and CHRIST's " blood," I only call them what our LORD and His Apostles called them ; if I say that we eat that body and drink that blood, all that you can blame me for is that I keep strictly to the very words of our Redeemer. You remember the words ascribed to Queen Elizabeth ; they are full of sound philosophy :

> " He was the Word that spake it :
> He took the bread and brake it ;
> And what that Word did make it,
> That I believe and take it."

I say therefore that the Holy Communion is a true feast, and that there is no feast like it. The more august and glorious and blessed is the food, the more right has this sacrament to be called a supper.

[1] Chap. xi. 27.

But if so, you may say, if it is a veritable banquet, a banquet of heavenly food, how is it that men shun it as they do? They do not as a rule decline all invitations to a feast. Yes, they do when their minds have been poisoned against the giver. You cannot argue that it is no supper, just because you see men excuse themselves from it; least of all, when you remember that the parable tells us of a "great supper" and a real supper, one of oxen and fatlings, from which nevertheless men were eager to be released. "With one consent they all began to make excuse." They did this, not because they thought there was no supper for them, or because they believed the food to be bad, but because some slanderer had prejudiced them against the giver. Rest assured, the servants were not the only ones who went round to see the guests; enemies of the host or his son had gone round also; it was their slanders and lies that kept men from the board. Aye, and if men shun the table of the LORD, it is because the slanderer of GOD and man—the word "devil" means slanderer—has been at work. He has prejudiced them against the feast, has persuaded them that they had better keep away. The feast is there, though "they that were bidden were not worthy."

But perhaps you raise another objection. You ask how it comes to pass, if the Holy Communion is such a royal feast as I have represented it to be—food for body and soul—that so many communicants seem to be but little better for partaking thereof? for we cannot pretend that our communicants are always distinguished from the rest by their Christian graces; we cannot claim that their characters are always higher than those of non-communicants. But does this argue anything against the Holy Supper? Is it not, on the contrary, exactly correspondent with what we see in the natural world? There are many persons whose food does not nourish them, who derive no perceptible strength from it, but it never occurs to us to blame the food; we cannot think ill of that when we observe how others thrive on it; no, we see at once that it is because of something in themselves. Food may be ever so choice and salutary, but it will not profit a sick man; he cannot assimilate it; his organs are diseased. So it is in the kingdom of grace. The bread of Heaven brings no blessing to the sick, that is to say, to the impenitent or unbelieving soul, just because of that soul-sickness. Impenitence rejects the gift of God; unbelief makes it of none effect. So the Supper is there still, "the banquet of most heavenly food," and still it is the body and blood of our CHRIST, which verily and indeed are taken and received by the faithful, although some or many eat and drink to their own condemnation.

And this suggests another remark, namely, that the Supper of God and of the Church is absolutely free: it is without money and without price; it costs the communicants nothing. We are not asked to contribute certain virtues of our own in order to make it efficacious. The common impression is that we are; that we bring with us certain recommendations, in the shape of our pious dispositions, to the board of God. No doubt we must be "religiously and devoutly disposed"; to approach the altar of CHRIST in any other mood is to profane it ; all the same, neither our penitence nor our faith are in any sense contributions to the feast. To begin with, they are GOD's gifts. If you tell me that these form " the wedding garment required by GOD in Holy Scripture," still that garment was the gift of the King : the guests did not provide their robes for themselves. We have nothing that we did not receive—our repentance, our belief, we have received from above. So that there is nothing left for us to bring but our sins and our needs. *These are our own* and these are amongst our qualifications. Our sins, because they require forgiveness ; our needs, because we want them supplied. Our fitness, in fact, consists in our emptiness, our helplessness, our hunger and thirst after righteousness.

Dearly beloved, I have reminded you of those two occasions when our Blessed LORD fed the multitudes in the wilderness. These things are an allegory : they represent to us one work of our ascended and glorified Master. Year after year are these miracles repeated in our midst. Still do our LORD's disciples sit down in companies—think how many such there have been in England, and how many more in Europe to-day! They are collected into companies—they are often small companies in our village churches. But the invisible CHRIST is present wherever two or three are assembled in His Name : He is present, and He it is Who blesses and breaks and gives to His ministers, and they give to them that are set down. And these eat at the feast of GOD and are filled.

THE SUPPER OF THE CHURCH:
HOW CAN MEN SCORN IT?[1]

S. LUKE XIV. 24.

" I say unto you, that none of those men which were bidden shall taste of my supper."

ALTHOUGH the Most Merciful GOD has spread for men a supper in His Church; although He sends forth His messengers to say, "Come, for all things are now ready," yet multitudes refuse to partake of it. As you may see for yourselves, " with one consent they begin to make excuse."

And to some such persons, I cannot doubt, I speak to-day, to Churchmen or Churchwomen who attend the services of the Church with more or less regularity; who take their part in its hymns and prayers; who are always ready to subscribe to its funds. But one thing they *never* do; they never kneel at the Holy Table, to show their REDEEMER's death; no, when the Communion begins, their worship ends. When the bread and wine are presented, Sunday after Sunday, upon the altar, so, Sunday after Sunday, do they leave the Church. The

---

[1] This Sermon is, in the main, published in tract shape, under the title, *How can you do it?* London: C. Taylor.

Supper of God is no sooner spread than they make a point of retiring.

I do not say that you are of those Churchmen—though they are not few in number—who have *never once* communicated in the course of their lives. I do not accuse you of doing what some others do, of communicating *once*, soon after confirmation, and then never again; you may, for aught I know, have been a most regular communicant in your time. But if so, you have ceased to be such. You have not communicated this year or last year; perhaps not for many years past; perhaps never.

And this seems to you, I dare say, a small thing, a trifle. You think, perhaps you *say*, that "there are many worse things than that"; you wish that you had "nothing worse to answer for"; you only "act as scores of others do." Well, you would like us, I am sure, to be perfectly candid with you; in fact, you expect the clergy, the ministers of Christ, above all things to be honest. Then I must tell you that we think it an awful thing. We think you are running a grave risk of losing your soul. Pray do not take it amiss, but I must say that we are extremely unhappy about you and all such persons; yes, we tremble for Christians who are not communicants. We ask ourselves, "How can they do this great wickedness and sin against God?"

But you must not misunderstand me. You must not suppose that we have no anxieties, no sort of misgivings about those who do communicate. On the contrary, we have many, and sometimes about our most constant communicants. We sometimes wonder whether they are *prepared* and *devout* communicants. Sometimes we are afraid, from what we see and hear, that after all their " hearts are not right before GOD."   It is not therefore for you only that we fear.   Nor must you suppose, again, that we assume that communicants are always and everywhere better men than non-communicants. We know that it is not so.   It is quite possible that you may be kinder, truer, humbler, yes, and more really devout, than some who communicate regularly. Your lives and tempers may be distinctly better than theirs. All the same, we have in your case an especial cause for concern ; we are anxious about you, as we are not about them.   They may cause us suspicions or misgivings— why, we have misgivings about ourselves—but at any rate, we and they do not regularly and persistently dis-regard CHRIST's dying charge ; we do not decline to " do this[1] or treat it as of no account."   But you do, and it is this which makes us so " unhappy " about you ; this is why we " tremble " for you.

For observe : It is not merely that you act in a way which would have filled the first Christians with utter astonishment.   They met (as we read in the Acts of the Apostles) for " the breaking of bread "—there is no record in the New Testament of any stated meetings of the early Church, except for this purpose ; the LORD's day was ever observed by showing the LORD's death.   It can never have occurred to them, they could not have believed, that a day would come when some Christians would shun the Blessed Sacrament as if it were the

[1] S. Luke xxii. 19.

plague ; when the very purpose for which they met would become the signal for others to leave. But that is not why we are concerned for you. Nor is it because we see you remain for those parts of the service which Christians have in common with Jews, those which are derived, in fact, from the Jewish synagogue, such as the Psalms, lessons, prayers and sermon, and only leave when the Christian rite—that which is distinctively and exclusively Christian—is celebrated. This does un-doubtedly strike us as most strange and inconsistent, as also does the fact that you readily and regularly join in acts of worship—I refer to these same Psalms and prayers and hymns—which, however helpful and excel-lent, are not of Divine institution, and were not appointed by CHRIST, and that the one thing you draw the line at is the one thing which CHRIST did appoint ; all this, I say, strikes us as unreasonable and extraordinary, but this is not why we are so anxious about you. Nor are we alarmed again, merely or principally, because by not partaking of the sacrament you lose the grace and strength, the life and health, which a worthy reception of the Blessed Sacrament brings—of course you do lose this, and we for our part think it a terrible and irreparable loss : how can it be otherwise if the elements are in any true sense what CHRIST called them, His " body " and His " blood," and if that body was really " given *for you* " and that blood " shed *for you* " ? Still, it is not because of this, not because we may think that He contemplated non-communicants, such as you, when He said, " Except ye eat the flesh of the SON of MAN and drink His blood,

ye have no life in you "; no, it is not merely or chiefly
because you have not taken the elements into your hands
and mouths, that we despair of your salvation; it is
because you have not the dispositions, the tempers, the
affections which GOD requires. If you had them once,
you can hardly have them any longer, the humility, the
docility, the penitence, the faith, the obedience, which
are necessary to salvation; for if you had them, you
would be communicants ; if you had them, nothing would
or could keep you from the altar of CHRIST—nothing !

I say that your disregard of the Holy Communion
shows that " you have not the dispositions and affections
necessary to salvation." For consider, I entreat you,
what you have been saying and doing all these years.
In the first place you have disobeyed your Maker. You,
who are but dust and ashes, whose breath is in your
nostrils, who are mere atoms in the universe, you have
defied the Great First Cause! It may be you did not
mean to do it, and have never realized that you are doing
it—that I can well believe; but all the same, you have
done it. You have said that you would have your way
and that He should not have His due. By your very
Church-going you have professed your faith in the
SAVIOUR Who has commanded this thing, and yet you
have said (for " actions speak louder than words ") that
you would disregard His command. And you have
disregarded it, and that not once or twice, but systematically, persistently. And you cannot plead ignorance;
you cannot say you " did it ignorantly in unbelief," or
" never gave it a thought," or " overlooked " it, for week

by week you have had the silent reminders of His will
and of His great goodness spread before your gaze, and
from time to time the clergy have spoken of this Christian
law. This, then, is what you have been doing for ten
or twenty or more years; you have been opposing,
resisting, thwarting the GOD Who made you and Who
will judge you. He has said, " Do this," and you have
practically answered, " I will not." He has said, week
after week and year after year, " Take, eat," " Drink ye
all of this," and week after week and year after year, you
have replied, " No : that is where I draw the line. I
will go to Church, I will say my prayers, I will give my
subscriptions, but I will not communicate." O how can
you do it ? Yes, I must say it : " How can you do this
great wickedness and sin against GOD ? "

Of course it cannot be pleasant for you to hear this,
any more than it is pleasant for me to have to speak
thus. But if these things are so, is it not well, is it not
true kindness that we should put them fairly before you ?
If your clergy do not perform this office for you, nobody
else will. I proceed therefore to remind you that this is
not all that you have done; it might be well if it were.
This is quite enough by itself to show where you stand,
but this is not all. You have publicly proclaimed your
ingratitude to CHRIST. If you have defied your Maker,
you have also denied your SAVIOUR. And in saying this,
I do not merely mean that you have " denied Him His
dying request," though you have done that. He Who
bare for you shame and spitting, Who bought your life
with His own blood, Who loved and suffered as never

man did before, *He* begged you to "do this," and to *Him* your answer has been, "No, not yet; I can't attend to such things now." Yes, you have refused the Crucified His last petition. But you have done more; you have virtually denied Him before men. By your conduct you have said both to the Church and to the world, "See, I hold Him and His redemption so cheap, I care so little for it, that I never do what He commanded me to do. He tells me that it is a banquet, and that GOD bids me to it; that it is a means of grace, a channel of blessing, a means of union with Himself, and so forth. You will observe how lightly I esteem His words and His work when you notice that I never communicate. And if *you* follow my example, you will not communicate either." Well, is not this a great wickedness? is it not a sin against our SAVIOUR? In your hymns and creeds you sing His praise; you call Him "Master and LORD," and yet you think so meanly of His salvation, you care so little for His dying love that you will not do the things which He says, and you indirectly teach others not to do them. O, I ask again, *how can you do it?* How can you be so ungrateful? Is it any wonder if we are led to despair of your salvation? You may be, we believe that you are, just and moral men, kind neighbours, good husbands, staunch Churchmen, and the rest, but your relations to CHRIST, the CHRIST Who will be your judge, are these, that you go on, year after year, denying Him the desire of His heart and refusing Him His last request, and this though He died for you! And yet you hope to be saved all the same—saved in direct disobedience!

And what is it, I must now entreat you to consider, *what is it* that our LORD really asks of you, and *why* does He ask it? Is it some great favour for Himself, or some difficult task, some stern self-denial. No, you cannot say, "Thou hast asked a hard thing."[1] If He had, our duty would still be clear; we must obey; we must not parley with GOD; He is stronger than we. But He has not. He has bidden us to a *feast*, a "supper"—that is all. He says, "Come, eat of My bread and drink of the wine which I have mingled." That is no hardship, and involves no sacrifice—no, indeed, the sacrifice is on *His* part, not ours. He fasted that we may feast; He suffered that we may rejoice. This is what He asks—that we will sup, will sit down to meat, with our Redeemer and King. And *why* does He ask it? Why, purely for our profit; only for our advantage. He is seeking nothing for Himself; what He desires, this Lover of souls, is to help and bless *us*. It is for our sake that He has provided these pledges and tokens; for our sake He has "made a great supper"; for our sake He charges us to partake. "Arise, eat," He says, "for the journey is too great for thee." Go "in the strength of this meat to . . . the mount of GOD."[2] Yes, *this* is why—it is all out of love for our souls. And what is your reply? Well, you *say* nothing, it is true, but as soon as ever the feast is spread, you rise up and march out of the Church. In the presence of the other guests you deliberately turn your back on GOD's board. And this, week after week, and year after

---

[1] 2 Kings ii. 10.   [2] 1 Kings xix. 8.

I

year! It would be bad enough to do it once, but you do it constantly. It counts for nothing with you, as far as we can see, that our LORD in His wondrous patience begs you again and again to remain; again and again you refuse. No, you *say* nothing, but your conduct says a great deal; it is just as if you cried aloud in the Church, " I do not believe for my part in this so-called 'supper.' I do not believe that any good is to be got there. I do not care who sees me—I do not care that CHRIST sees me, but I shall not partake. True, I have been singing hymns to CHRIST, and have offered prayers in His name, but that is nothing; it is here that I draw the line. No, I do not mind who sees me go; what I am much more afraid of is lest someone should see me stay." O brother, O sister, *how can you do it?* how can you be so inconsistent and perverse? How can you scorn your privileges and throw away your chances? how can you " count yourselves unworthy of eternal life "?

I know what you will say. You will tell me that you " are not good enough." But you cannot really suppose that this excuse deceives us, much less GOD. For, in the first place, how would you like *us* to say you were not good enough? You know that you would resent it, would feel insulted. But why so, if what you say is true? Moreover, if you are really so bad, are you striving to do better? It does not look much like it, for you give the same excuse year after year. And, lastly, where did you learn that Holy Communion is for " good " people? Was it for such that CHRIST died?

Are not His sacraments for sinners? "There is none righteous, no, not one." If you were not a sinner, you could not join in the service. That service is designed for sinners only; only such persons can use it. Surely you are not waiting till, like the Pharisee, you can tell GOD that you are "not like other men"; and this, when the prayer of the communicant must always be "GOD be merciful to me, *a sinner.*" Or is it that you are a sinner and do not want mercy? O, it is a poor lame excuse, and, honestly, I wonder how you can stoop to make it?

No, I do not say here that men will be lost, just because they never partook of the Body broken for them and the Blood shed for them. I may think so, but, if I do, it is not necessary to take this ground. It is enough for me to know that they cannot be saved if they disobey GOD; if they disregard His loving invitation; if they neglect—merely neglect—His plain command; if they dispense with what GOD has decreed; if they are afraid or ashamed to confess Him before men; if they have so little love to CHRIST as to refuse Him His request. And this is what you do. Is it not so? And so long as you do it, how can we be otherwise than unhappy about you, and despair of your salvation?

And what makes us still more anxious is that your conduct and its recompense have both been described beforehand in Holy Writ. Your case is contemplated there. For we read there[1] of men who, like you, were bidden to a supper; of men who, for one reason or

[1] S. Luke xiv. 15-24.

another, declined the invitation, as you have done; of men whose excuses were, so far as appears, not one whit more unreal than yours are; and of these men our LORD CHRIST, Who will pronounce your sentence and mine, said—" I say unto you, that *none of those men which were bidden shall taste of My supper*." O brothers, O sisters, O men and women, for whom CHRIST died, I ask again, " How can you do it ? " How can you " do this great wickedness and sin against GOD " ?

THE MINISTRY OF THE CHURCH.

2 COR. XI. 23.

" Are they ministers of CHRIST ? "

THE visible Church of CHRIST, whether it is "one body," as I have affirmed, or many "bodies," as is generally believed, must have its ministers ; it must have ministers just as much as it must have members ; it can no more be a Church without the former than without the latter. Without officials of some sort it would be a chaos and not a Church. No society, secular or religious, can exist without its managers, its leaders and rulers.

But especially must the Church have a Ministry, if it is, as we have been taught to think, a school, an army, a sanctuary. If the Church is CHRIST's *school*, then it must have teachers as well as scholars ; you can no more have a school without the one than without the other. If it is CHRIST's *army*, then you must have officers as well as privates ; an army without officers would be an undisciplined rabble ; men to give the command are just as necessary as men to obey it. If it is CHRIST's *sanctuary*, then it must have its priests as well as its votaries—men to lead the worship as well as men to follow.   Regard the Church in what aspect we will, the absolute necessity of a ministry becomes at once apparent.

And so we find, as a matter of fact, that every Christian community, including even the Quakers and the "Brethren," has its officers, its ministers of some sort or other.   There are wide differences of opinion, indeed, amongst them, as to the particular kind of ministers required, as to their place and powers and functions and appointment, but none whatever as to the necessity of a ministry.   As no body corporate *can* exist, so no Christian body attempts to exist without its office-bearers.

And these office-bearers claim for the most part to be "ministers of CHRIST"—lawfully appointed and fully accredited ministers of CHRIST.   The Baptist and the Seventh-Day Baptist, the Methodist and the Primitive Methodist minister, each claims to be CHRIST'S minister, just as much as the bishop or the archbishop—perhaps even more.   I propose in this sermon to examine this claim—ours and theirs.   I ask you to join with me in considering who are and who are not ministers of CHRIST[1] and of the new covenant.[2]

But before I embark on this examination, I must be allowed to say that there is nothing arrogant or unkind or offensive in instituting this inquiry.   Such an inquiry, I know, is constantly resented, but it ought not to be: the only persons who need resent it are "false apostles,"[3] those who say that they are ministers and are not.[4]   If there are any such persons, no doubt they will not care

---

[1] 1 Cor. iv. 1.   [2] 2 Cor. iii. 6.   [3] 2 Cor. xi. 13.   [4] Rev. ii. 2.

for their claims to be tested, but if men are satisfied as to their mission and position, then they need not fear the light ; the more of it the better. Anyhow, I for my part mean no offence, none whatsoever, by raising this question, and I further say that no person who is sure of his position has any right to be offended. The Romanists dispute our orders ; they are doing it at this present moment, but I do not know that we resent it ; *I* do not for one. For I hold that not only have they a perfect right to examine them, but that it is their bounden duty so to do ; I say that it is a duty which we owe to CHRIST and to Christianity and to our own souls to make sure who are and who are not the " ministers of CHRIST."

And it is still a duty, however much it may be resented or misunderstood, for these plain and obvious reasons— that until I know who is and who is not CHRIST's minister, I cannot know whom I am to obey, and who is to have the rule over me,[1] and whom I am to avoid ; I cannot know who is to be my teacher in CHRIST's school,[2] my leader in CHRIST's army, my representative in His sanctuary. The popular idea is that it is only courteous and charitable to recognize every man as CHRIST's minister who claims to be such ; they brand us as arrogant and bigoted, if we ask anyone to exhibit his credentials. And yet these same persons would be the first to condemn us if we acted on their principles in daily life, and more than that, they do not act on these principles themselves ; no, they act on ours. If our statesmen, for example, were to accept every man as an

[1] Heb. xiii. 17. [2] 1 Tim. iv. 11, 13; 2 Tim. ii. 2.

ambassador from a foreign power who merely *said* that
he was such, like the Ansahs who recently came to us
from Ashanti, they would have no words too severe to
condemn such folly; they would denounce them for
trifling with the affairs of State, for jeopardizing the
peace and prosperity of the country; they would say that
it was imperative to see his credentials, as the case of the
Ansahs proved. Well, ought we not to take similar
precautions about the ambassadors of CHRIST, for He
calls ministers His ambassadors.[1] Are the things of
eternity of *less* moment than the things of time ? Why
must we take every pains and precaution in the one
case, and why must exactly similar precautions in the
other case be an impertinence? So again with the
army. If our soldiers in a campaign were to follow
implicitly everyone who claimed to be their captain; if
they said they did not like to inquire too nicely as to his
commission for fear of hurting his feelings, what would
you, what would everybody say about such folly? You
would say that such an army was destined to defeat;
that it was simply courting its own destruction; such an
army has just been defeated in the Hauran.[2] It is plain,
then, that in everyday life we do and we must " try the
spirits " and test the claimants to office. But that is
not all. The very persons who so loudly denounce us
for demanding from all ministers the proofs of appointment, do precisely the same in their sect or sphere—
precisely the same; they cannot help doing it. The
Baptist or the Wesleyan does not recognize as a Baptist

[1] 2 Cor. v. 20. [2] *The Times*, Feb. 17th, 1896.

or a Wesleyan minister anybody and everybody who *claims* to be such; nothing of the kind; he only recognizes as a minister of his denomination the man who can prove that he was appointed such. He has no hesitation in asking for proofs, and if the other shows any hesitation in producing them, he suspects at once that something is wrong; he observes at once that it is only pretended ministers that have anything to fear. And if you charged him with bigotry or intolerance for so doing, he would soon reply that there was no bigotry about it, or that the intolerance was on your part; he would say that he may surely be allowed to ascertain who is his lawful minister and who is not, and how else can he ascertain except by seeing the man's credentials. Well, all that we claim is the right—which we say is also a duty—to test the credentials of *all* claimants— not only those who claim to be Baptist or Methodist ministers, but those who claim to be CHRIST's ministers. It seems to us that it is a sacred duty, one that we owe to the Church's Head, to be sure that this man or that is one of the Church's officers, one of its rulers and teachers, before we listen to him or follow him. It seems to us that it is just as wrong to recognize those whom CHRIST has *not* sent, as to defy or disobey those whom He has commissioned.

What then, you will ask, are the tests and proofs of a lawful ministry? What men shall we recognize as appointed of GOD to rule over us and to teach us? This is the question we have now to consider.

And the first remark I have to make is this—that it is

not a question of piety or ability, of character or attainments. No amount of learning or eloquence or holiness can possibly prove that this man or that has been appointed to be CHRIST's ambassador, nor can any degree of ignorance or incapacity or even of irreligion prove that he has not been so appointed. No doubt CHRIST's ministers *ought* to be able and learned and devout—as to that we are quite agreed; we are all agreed that none should be appointed to any office and administration in the Church who has not the necessary qualifications; but what we do say is that no amount of qualifications can take the place of the outward call and appointment, and that if there has been appointment without qualifications (as may sometimes happen; indeed, no minister has or can have *all* the qualifications for his sacred calling), if there has been appointment, such person is CHRIST's minister, His most unworthy minister, notwithstanding His unworthiness. It is necessary to say this, because the prevailing idea is that no *bad* man can possibly be the minister of GOD, and that His true and only ministers are those who have the appropriate gifts. But this idea, popular as it is, does not square with Holy Scripture, nor can it be made, by any amount of ingenuity, to harmonize with it. You will allow, I am sure, that Hophni and Phinehas were priests of GOD[1]—they are called such, and the ark was in their keeping—and yet their lives were so profligate that " men abhorred the offering of the LORD."[2] You will allow, again, that Judas was CHRIST's Apostle, one

[1] 1 Sam. ii. 13.   [2] 1 Sam. ii. 17.

of the twelve, yet he purloined their monies and betrayed our Lord to death, and altogether is designated as a devil."[1] You will also admit—you cannot help it—that our Lord charged His disciples to obey the Scribes and Pharisees, because they "sat in Moses' seat"—that is to say, were successors of Moses as interpreters of the law—and this although He denounced them at the same time as "hypocrites" and "blind guides" and "vipers" and "children of hell."[2] That is to say, the Word of God recognizes all these men, in their different capacities, as ministers of God and of His Church, notwithstanding their wickedness. They were ministers just because they had been *appointed* such, and other men, such as Joseph of Arimathæa[3] or Joseph surnamed Justus,[4] however high their moral character, and however great their spiritual attainments, were not ministers because they had never been appointed. In other words, the Bible regards the ministerial office as conferred by due and formal appointment, and not by mere moral or mental qualifications.

Yes, and something more must be said here. I must remind you that all the denominations do the same. Loudly as they complain because *we* do not recognize their many able and pious pastors as Christ's ministers, on the score of their gifts or successes, yet they themselves never recognize—they could not do it—any man as a minister of this or that denomination on the ground of his piety or ability. I say "they could not do it";

---

[1] S. John vi. 70.   [2] S. Matt. xxiii., *passim.*   [3] S. Mark xv. 43.
[4] Acts i. 23.

they are compelled to look at the formal appointment
just as we are ; it would plunge them into endless confusion if they were to do otherwise.   If it were a matter
of mere gifts or attainments, they never could be sure
who was and who was not their minister.   Because in
every congregation there may be members who are much
holier and much abler than the pastor, and yet they
make no claim to be pastors.   And if you ask why they
are not pastors, the only answer can be, not that they are
not qualified, but that they have never been in any public
or formal way constituted such ; there has been no outward sign or observance, not even a "recognition service"
(a recognition, that is to say, of a Divine call), to mark
them as such.   It is in vain that we urge that they have
gifts far beyond those of many pastors ; we are still told
that they are not ministers, and never were.   In other
words, Dissenters hold, just as we do, that a man is not
constituted a minister of CHRIST, nor is he marked out
as such, by any gifts or virtues whatsoever, but by
certain objective acts and ordinances.   What then, let
us now proceed to ask, are the marks of the New
Testament ministry ?

But before I answer this question directly, it may be
well that I should remind you that, if Holy Scripture is
to be our guide—I might say, " Holy Scripture and
ancient authors "—then *there is no* " *Church* "—no true
congregation or society of CHRIST—*except* THE *Church*,
the one society founded by Him, the visible society to
which men were admitted by baptism, the society over
which He set the apostles, the society which He endowed

with the gifts of the HOLY GHOST, which society, I may add, though unhappily divided and more or less confused and corrupted, has lasted to the present time. There is no trace in the New Testament of any Church but this —this or some branch thereof. *Now*, we hear of scores of " Churches," for almost every denomination claims to be a Church, however recent its origin and whatever was its beginning; in the sacred word we read of one Church and no more. This is undeniable—that such a thing as " the Church in England " or " the Church at London " is known to Scripture, whilst a " Methodist Church " or a " Lutheran Church " or a " Labour Church " is unknown to Scripture. This, then, is the first point to be borne in mind—that there are not many " churches," diverse and rival churches. GOD'S Church is but one : " one body," not one hundred " bodies."

But if this is so, then it follows

1. That there can be *no Christian ministers but the ministers of* THE *Church*, the society of which I have just spoken. Of course if there are, as we are sometimes told, " churches of the Methodist order " and " churches of the Baptist order," then no doubt there may be ministers in Methodist and Baptist orders; in fact, you may have as many sorts of ministers as you have " churches." But if on the other hand the Church is one, then the Ministry must be one also.

I have said that this follows inevitably from the oneness of the Church. But we are not left to inferences. I proceed to remind you, secondly, that just as Holy Scripture never mentions any Church other than " *the*

Church," so it never mentions any Christian ministers except the ministers of that Church. We do read of " the ministers of CHRIST,"[1] of the " elders of the church,"[2] of the " messengers " of the various local " churches,"[3] but we never hear of any " Presbyterian " or " Wesleyan " or " Bible Christian minister," nor of anything at all resembling it, and no one who knows his Bible can pretend that we do. Now I come to a second point. I ask you to observe that

2. The ministers of the Church of whom the Gospels and Epistles tell were all *appointed by the Church's Head, or by His Apostles and delegates.* They were called and commissioned of GOD, as was Aaron. We cannot find the slightest trace of a minister who had appointed himself, or of one who derived his authority from the congregation, or of one who had not received his commission from the highest order in the Church. Let us take these positions separately. I say that there is no trace in the whole Bible of any man taking the ministerial office upon himself. Why, even of the Jewish priests it is said " No man taketh this honour to himself." There were one or two who intruded themselves into the priest's office, but they died by a horrible death[4] or were smitten with a living death[5]—I refer to Korah and his company and to King Uzziah. Even CHRIST our LORD, we are told, was " called " and " sent "—" He glorified not Himself to be made a high priest,"[6] and it is very noticeable that our LORD did not begin His

---

[1] 1 Cor. iv. 1.   [2] Acts xx. 17 ; S. James v. 14.   [3] 2 Cor. viii. 23.
[4] Numb. xvi.   [5] 2 Chron. xxvi. 21.   [6] Heb. v. 4, 5.

ministry until He had been **publicly baptized and until**
a voice **from Heaven** had proclaimed **Him to be GOD's**
beloved **Son** ; even He was anointed to His ministry.[1]
So were His ambassadors ; they were never **self-**
appointed. It may be **that** the " prophets " of whom
S. Paul tells **us**[2] had no sort of ordination, but then
they were marked **out by** inspiration, and, moreover,
their **functions were** altogether exceptional and **tem-**
porary—as **temporary as were the** supernatural **gifts ;**
they **were limited to the** Church's infancy. **Presently**
they pass away, **and we hear of** them no more. **It may**
also be that the **first Christians, whether** elders or **lay-**
men, spoke **of CHRIST to all with whom they came in**
contact,[3] **but** still **we** have **no** proof whatsoever **that**
anybody and everybody ministered in the congregation—
the Pastoral Epistles teach the **contrary.** They **show**
us that even then the Christian teacher **needed** an
authorization, and received one[4] ; even those who were
to serve tables (we learn elsewhere) must **be lawfully**
called and sent.[5] **In** the pages of the New Testament,
consequently, as in the Old, there is no trace of any self-
constituted ministry. Nor, secondly, is there any trace
of ministers commissioned by their congregations. **On**
one occasion, it is true (that just referred to), the whole
body of the disciples *selected* certain officers—" the seven,"
commonly called deacons—but that selection would appear
to have been quite exceptional ; **it was because** of the
murmurings of the Grecian **Jews**[6] ; **in the** Pastoral

---

[1] Acts x. 38.   [2] 1 Cor. xiv. ; *cf.* Acts xiii. 1 ; xv. 32 ; xxi. 9, 10.
[3] Acts viii. 4 ; xi. 19. [4] 1 Tim. iii. ; 2 Tim. ii. 2. [5] Acts vi. 6. [6] Chap. vi. 1.

Epistles S. Paul instructs Timothy as to the choice of
the deacons,[1] and in any case, whoever *chose* them, the
Apostles *appointed* them. " Look *ye* out seven men . . .
whom *we* may appoint over this business." No, there is
absolutely no trace of any officer of any sort who derived
his authority from the people, and such an appointment
would have been altogether contrary to the genius of
Christianity. It is not for the sheep to appoint their
shepherds: not for those who " obey " to say who shall
" have the rule over them "[2]; not for the disciples or
scholars to authorize the men who are to teach them.
How could such men, being their nominees, " speak and
exhort and reprove with all authority "[3]? But not only
have we no trace of any appointment by the people,
but we have proof, lastly, that all appointments were
made by superior authority, by our LORD or His Apostles.
The twelve, for example, did not run without being sent ;
our LORD " gave them authority " ;—" these twelve
JESUS sent forth "[4]; He sent them as the FATHER had
sent Him.[5] Nor did the seventy ; nothing is plainer
than that they received every shred of office or power
which they possessed from Him.[6] And after His
ascension and the coming of the HOLY GHOST the same
rule holds good. Even if we suppose that the two put
forward for the place and apostleship of Judas[7] were
designated by the hundred and twenty disciples present [8]—
which is doubtful—still, the final choice was made by

[1] 1 Tim. iii. 8-10.   [2] Heb. xiii. 17.   [3] Titus ii. 15.   [4] S. Matt. x. 1, 5.
[5] S. John xx. 21.   [6] S. Luke x.   [7] Acts i. 25.
[8] Verse 15.

God Himself.[1] The seven, again, as we have already seen, were commissioned by the Apostles; the people presented them; the Apostles ordained them.[2] The elders, of whom we hear presently,[3] were appointed in every city of Asia Minor by Barnabas and Paul.[4] Both Timothy and Titus derive their authority from S. Paul, who gives them precise instructions about the appointment of others.[5] It is quite clear from these provisions that the call and commission to the ministry, if the New Testament plan is to be adhered to, must be from above, not from below; from the Apostles or their successors, not from their peers or from the people. In the latter case, he that is sent would be greater than those who sent him.[6] Now I come to the last point.

3. The ministers of the New Testament were sent—at least after the coming of the Holy Ghost—*with an outward and visible sign, with the laying on of hands.* I am not concerned to prove that the twelve or the seventy were thus commissioned, though I think it extremely probable that they were, especially when we remember that the scribe or doctor of the law was set apart for his office with the *Semichah* or laying on of hands. But what if they were not? the Lord was still with His Church, and the Holy Ghost was not then given. What I have to prove is that, after Pentecost, Christ's ministers were made such by the Holy Ghost, through prayer and the laying on of hands. And this admits of no doubt. Take the first recorded ordination—that of "the seven": there

---

[1] Verse 24.   [2] Chap. vi. 6.   [3] Chap. xi. 30.
[4] Chap. xiv. 23.   [5] 1 Tim. iii. 5; Titus i. 5-9.   [6] S. John xiii. 16,

K

the imposition of hands is expressly mentioned.[1] So it is in the case of Barnabas and Paul. They were separated for their apostolic labours, at the bidding of the HOLY GHOST, in this way and in no other. But I may be reminded here that when Paul and Barnabas in their turn proceed to "appoint elders in every church," nothing is *said* about this ceremony. No, but it was *used* all the same. We cannot doubt it, when we remember how the ordaining apostles had themselves been separated. It is inconceivable that they could have repudiated or neglected an ordinance from which they themselves had not been exempted, especially when we remember that it was used even in the case of the lower order of deacons, and still more when we find these apostles or one of them using this same form elsewhere, and mentioning it too as the mode of appointment. Need I remind you that S. Paul speaks to Timothy of a "gift" which he had received through the laying on of his hands [2]—his hands and those of the presbytery [3]? Need I tell you again that S. Paul, when giving directions to Timothy on the subject of the ministry, bids him to "lay hands hastily on no man" [4]—using the words, you observe, as synony-mous with ordination ? Is it conceivable, therefore, that the ordinance which he ministered in the one case, he did not in the other ? in other words, that though the laying on of hands was an established usage in the appointment of teachers, and one which Christianity had taken over from Judaism, still the Apostles sometimes used it and sometimes did not—and this just because it

[1] Acts vi. 6.   [2] 2 Tim. i. 6.   [3] 1 Tim. iv. 14.   [4] Chap. v. 22.

is not expressly mentioned in every case? I say that it is not conceivable, and the less so when we remember that the history of the Acts was not written to tell Christians what to do; they had learnt that already, both from the example and the precepts of the apostles; the book only gives us some few glimpses of what the early Christians did. We cannot wonder, therefore, if the laying on of hands is not mentioned in every single case; we are sure that it was used in every single case all the same.

Yes, and it was *through* this imposition of hands, and in answer to the prayer that was offered, that the HOLY GHOST was given to make men bishops or presbyters of the Church of GOD.[1] It was thus that Timothy had received his spiritual gift; indeed, this was the ordinary channel for the conveyance of the SPIRIT of GOD.[2] GOD works by means, and this is the outward and visible form of the inward and spiritual grace of ordination.

Such then, I submit to you, are in brief the marks of CHRIST's minister. He is first a minister of *the* Church, the one society founded by our LORD, the "one body" governed and sanctified by His SPIRIT. Ministers of other "bodies," however able and devout they may be— and they may be not unseldom both abler and better men than some of the clergy—and however much their labours may have been blessed—for we are nowhere told that GOD only blesses the work of ministers—such men are officers of Christian communities indeed, but not

[1] Acts xx. 28.   [2] Acts viii. 19.

officers of CHRIST or of CHRIST's Church. Secondly, he has been *sent ;* he has not taken the office upon himself; if any man has appointed himself, either because of the gifts which he has for the work, or because of an inward call, or even because of his yearning desire to " save souls," such man may be very capable and very eloquent, but CHRIST's minister he is not; he is unlike all the ministers of whom the Holy Scriptures tell. Thirdly, he has been sent by the Church's Head ; he has been set apart by the SPIRIT of GOD. The shepherd must be employed by the "chief shepherd," the teacher by the Divine teacher. But this does not mean that any man is *made* GOD's minister by a secret call, by the voice of the SPIRIT speaking to his soul. Such call there may be, perhaps there ought to be ; but it is but a call, not a commission ; it may certify a man that he ought to devote himself to the ministry, but it cannot satisfy others that he *has* been set apart and sent. That can only be accomplished by some overt act, some *ceremony* of authorization, and that ceremony can only be performed by one who is himself a minister and a superior. So the lawful minister of CHRIST has, in the fourth place, been sent by a lawful minister, by an overseer of the Church. Such a man has GOD's authority to send forth labourers into the vineyard, and other men and inferior ministers have not such authority—at least, we never find them exercising it in the Church of the first days. And, lastly, he must have been sent, publicly and openly, in the face of the Church, for he is the messenger of the Church and its representative before

GOD, with prayer and the laying on of hands. Prayer for the gift of the HOLY GHOST ; the imposition of hands for the conveyance thereof. No doubt Almighty GOD can dispense with both—with all prayers and all form-alities, but it is not *for* us to do so. The form could hardly be simpler than it is, but such as it is we must adhere to it. We must not say, for example, that " if not superstitious, it ministers to superstition," and there-fore we will have none of it. This has been said,[1] but no one who remembers that this form is older than Christianity ; that it has been ordained of GOD Himself; that it was constantly used by our SAVIOUR CHRIST; that it was the recognized form in the early Church; that it has been continued in the Church ever since, can presume to set it aside or can recognize the ministry of those who have set it aside. No, those are not true and lawful ministers of CHRIST who, whatever their gifts, have not been sent, as " the seven " were, as the Apostles Barnabas and Paul were, as Timothy was, with the laying on of hands, the laying on of hands on the part of men who have themselves been set apart in the same way, and set apart by men who trace their authority, ultimately, to the twelve Apostles of the LAMB.

And now, in conclusion, I must deal with two objec-

---

[1] By the *Nonconformist and Independent*, the organ of the Congre-gationalists, March 6th, 1884. " The practice has, so far as we know, been gradually falling into disuse, some of the leading ministers refusing to countenance by their personal participation in it, a ceremony which, if not superstitious itself, is calculated to minister to the superstition of the less intelligent."

tions. You will be told, perhaps, because we contend
for the due and orderly appointment of officers in the
Church of GOD, because we think that such canonical
appointment to be at least as important in the Church
as in any other society, you may be told that we put
formalities before gifts and rites above personal piety.
Our answer is that we do nothing of the kind : we never
compare them at all, because they have entirely different
spheres and departments. The gifts have to do with
the *discharge* of the office ; the formalities have to do
with *conferring* it.   No amount of formalities will ensure
the efficient discharge of the office, either of bishop,
priest, or deacon in the Church of GOD, just as on the
other hand no amount of gifts will convey the appointment.   The two things are entirely distinct, and each
has its own place.

But perhaps you say that the doctrine I have laid
down is that of " Apostolical Succession." Undoubtedly
it is, but is that anything against it ?   For Apostolical
Succession only means that " the same rule holds good
in the Christian Church as in every well-ordered secular
government, namely, that officers cannot appoint themselves, but must derive their commission from the
supreme central authority, or from persons empowered
thereby."   Well, is there anything unreasonable here ?
Is it not sound common sense ?   It is such eminent
common sense that it would never have been challenged
for a moment, had not the denominations lost that
succession.   Indeed, as it is, they cannot consistently
denounce it, for every denomination has a succession of

its own, and strictly adheres to it.   But if it is so necessary to the part, to the sect, why is it so absurd in the
whole, in the universal Church ?   You will find, in fact,
that no sect objects to a succession ; all they object to is
one that *goes back to the Apostles.*

THE FAITH OF THE CHURCH.[1]

S. JUDE 3 *(Revised Version).*

"Contend earnestly for the Faith once for all delivered to the saints."

THESE are familiar words, and I dare say you hear them without emotion. But if you heard them to-day for the first time and realized their meaning, I cannot but think that they would cause you some surprise and some searchings of heart. For they proclaim two truths which, I fear, but few Christians comparatively have grasped—first, that there is such a thing as "*the* faith," the true faith of a Christian ; and, secondly, that it is a Christian duty earnestly to contend for it. I say that it is not every Christian that has realized that "the faith," as revealed by GOD to man, and as delivered by apostles and prophets, exists—that it can be found, and that it is our duty to search for it. Many of them think that the precise faith we hold and profess is a matter of very little moment ; they tell you that all forms of the Christian religion are very much alike, and that doctrines

[1] Preached, in substance, in Northfield Church, Birmingham, on Sunday, January 27th, 1895.

and creeds are of little account. Their "sentence" is—

"For modes of faith let angry bigots fight;
His can't be wrong whose life is in the right,"

and they call *this* tolerance and charity. Their model clergyman is one who never meddles with (what they regard as) men's private opinions; anyone who should hold himself ready " to banish and drive away all strange doctrines contrary to God's Word "—which is just what every priest at his ordination undertook to do—they would pronounce a " pestilent fellow " or at least " a busybody in other men's matters." Still less do they realize that they themselves are bound to hold one particular form of belief and to contend for it. They perceive that this means controversy, and they have a horror of controversy in every shape. That is not to be wondered at, for it constantly happens that " where controversy begins, Christianity ends "; there are so few who can debate points of doctrine without disgracing their religion. Still, the text does imply controversy, such controversy as becometh the disciples of Christ, for I suppose it is possible to " speak the truth in love "; possible to contend for the faith without calling names or imputing motives. It must be so, or it would not be commanded. Anyhow, S. Jude summons the Christians to whom he writes to stand up boldly for this faith. Nor can anyone doubt that, in appealing to them, he also appeals to us. It cannot be pretended that the faith was in peril then, but is in no sort of danger now; no one can maintain that that faith is better understood or more firmly held in the nineteenth century than in the first. They had not then, as we have now, over two hundred denominations of Christians ; there were no villages then, as there are now, with twelve different kinds of Christianity professed by their inhabitants. No, if the true faith has ever been obscured, it is at the present day—so much so that many doubt whether it can ever be recovered ; if controversy was ever an imperative duty, it is a duty now, here in England and in America and our colonies, where, as a Dissenting writer testifies, " no people of any age or climate have ever carried the evil of religious faction and endless division to a more extraordinary height." [1]   I think I am justified, therefore, in saying that, if you can hear my text without astonishment, it is only because you have not grasped its significance ; because you have not understood that there is one true faith and only one, and that Almighty GOD has intrusted this faith to *your* keeping and protection.

But if you have any doubt as to what this exhortation means and requires, I think you will have none if you will carefully examine it, as I now propose to do.   And its meaning, I may say at the outset, is all the clearer when we take the Revised Version for our guide.   From that we learn that S. Jude had been for some time intending and desiring—in fact, he had been " giving all diligence " —to write to the saints, the professed Christians of his day, about their " common salvation " ; that is to say, he had hoped to pen an epistle about the gospel in general

[1] *Eclectic Review*, 1831, p. 192.

when it became necessary for him—he "was constrained" by circumstances—to abandon this idea, at least for the time, and to write, and write immediately, on one point. Instead of unfolding and extolling the redemption which is in CHRIST, he was compelled to exhort those to whom he wrote to hold the gospel fast, and to hold it in its length and its breadth. And this because, as he proceeds to say, ungodly men had crept into the Church, men who even "denied our only Master and LORD, JESUS CHRIST," and utterly subverted His revelation and religion. This is why he must write at once — "the King's business requireth haste"[1]—and entreat them to contend, to contend *earnestly* for the faith which had been delivered once for all. That faith, he says, was being grievously corrupted; men who bore the Christian name were perverting and overthrowing it, and it is to this fact that the Epistle owes its existence. But for this, so far as we can see, it would never have been written, and it certainly would not have been written in its present shape.

So that, at a very early age in the Church's life, within half a century of the Ascension—for the date of this Epistle is A.D. 80 or thereabouts—at this early period, whilst the supernatural gifts of the SPIRIT still lasted, whilst the apostles still lived, whilst the Church was still being sifted and purified by persecution, there were ungodly men in the new society; there were tares among the wheat; there were wolves in the fold.[2] Already has S. Paul's prophecy been fulfilled; among the Christians

---

[1] 1 Sam. xxi. 8.   [2] Acts xx. 29.

themselves have men arisen speaking perverse things.[1]
So soon after the gospel was first preached has it been
perverted, and, as constantly happens, misbelief has led
to misconduct.   A man's life and morals must be governed largely by his creed, and so we find that these
early heretics had not only denied the LORD that bought
them—and what more " destructive heresy " could they
teach ?—but they had "turned the grace of GOD into
lasciviousness"; they had given themselves up to
" wretchlessness of most unclean living,"[2] and to work
all uncleanness with greediness.[3]   And this, remember,
within fifty years of CHRIST's passion and resurrection.
We are sometimes tempted to despair of the Church
because of its abuses, because we find the evil ever
mingled with the good,[4] and sometimes usurping the
highest places.   We shall do well to remember that the
Church of the apostles' days was similarly afflicted, as
the apostolic writings abundantly prove.   It is no new
thing has happened to us.   The Church has had its
depraved members and its dangerous teachers from its
first beginning.

But I may ask you to observe here, that, grievous as
was this corruption of the gospel, and gross as was this
immorality, yet not one word is said, either by S. Jude
or any other sacred writer, about leaving the Church.
Though ungodly men have crept into it, we are never
told that godly men are to go out of it, as we should
have been told, if secession were a duty.   The modern
idea, the idea which prevails amongst Dissenters, and

---

[1] Acts xx. 30.   [2] Art. xvii.   [3] Eph. iv. 19.   [4] Art. xxvi.

which is **urged** in justification of **Dissent, is that we must** leave any and every communion which is corrupted either in doctrine or in practice. We are told that it is **at** our peril that we remain in a Church which is **tainted** with grave error; we are warned that by so doing we become partakers of its **sins.** Yet there is not a syllable in Scripture to support this contention. **The Scripture** view is this—that the Church being GOD's Church, **being** CHRIST's body, and His chosen instrument for saving the world,[1] **we must remain** in it, if only to help to reform **it**; we must remain in it, that it **may not** go from bad **to** worse. I merely mention this in passing, **but I do think** it worthy of observation that though S. Jude writes about **the errors and** afflictions of the early Church, and about little **else, the** last idea that enters his **mind is** that **the** remedy for these errors is secession. It is also noteworthy that he does speak, in verse 19, of separatists—" these **are** they who make separations "**—but it is** only to denounce them as " sensual, having not the SPIRIT."

It is abundantly clear, therefore, that S. Jude's remedy **for** false teaching and unclean living is not separation— *that* remedy is always worse than **the** disease; it is **to** extinguish all hope **of** reform by removing the reformers —his remedy **is** not Dissent. What then, it may be asked, is it? **My** text supplies the **answer.** It is to " contend earnestly for the faith "; **it is to** remain and fight for it; it is to plunge, if necessary, into controversy **—yes,** strenuous controversy—in its behalf.

---

[1] " The instrument whereby the world shall be made Christian and be born again."—Martensen, *Dogmatics*, p. 335. (Clark's Transl.)

But I must now revert to the point with which I started, namely, that there was and there is, if we can but discover it, such a thing as the true faith ; there is a fixed and authorized form of Christian belief; one which is right whilst all other forms are wrong. There *must* be such a faith, for the simple reason that, if there were not, no one could "contend" for it ; S. Jude would in that case be commanding the impossible. But there was and there is an orthodox objective faith—" the faith of GOD's elect," as it is called elsewhere [1]; " the common faith," [2] "the faith of the gospel," S. Paul also calls it ; "your holy faith," S. Jude calls it later on. Such a faith, I say, there was, else how could some " depart from " it [3] or " deny " it [4] or " err from " it [5] or " keep " it [6] or " make shipwreck concerning" it [7] or " hold " it [8]—all of which the Scriptures say can be done—such a faith there must be, a dogmatic faith, a fixed form of belief. I suppose there is nothing of which men are more impatient, and especially men who pride themselves on their liberality and catholicity, nothing of which these tolerant persons are more intolerant than of dogma. Yet nothing can be more irrational and absurd, for dogma only means a definite belief. We cannot get away from dogmas do what we will, and they are not peculiar to theologians. The man who affirms that all theological doctrines are untrue or all uncertain, or who says that there is no GOD or no future life, *he* lays down dogmas,

[1] Titus i. 1.   [2] Verse 4.   [3] 1 Tim. iv. 1.
[4] Chap. v. 8 ; Rev. ii. 13.   [5] Chap. vi. 10, 21.   [6] 2 Tim. iv. 7.
[7] 1 Tim. i. 19.   [8] Chap. iii. 9.

and very precise and positive dogmas too. " The faith once delivered," consequently, can only have been delivered in the shape of dogmas or definite statements about GOD and His will or man and his duties. I say it again : Any faith that can be contended for must be a positive and dogmatic faith, but it does not follow that we are to contend for it in a positive and dogmatic way.

Now such a faith S. Jude affirms that there is, not only because we are to *contend* for it, but because others have "*delivered*" it. We shall do well to pause at that word. It may suggest the observation that " the faith " was not given to the world, as some people fondly imagine, in the shape of a book ; it was delivered by word of mouth ; it was " preached to them that heard it," and for a time handed on by tradition. It is undeniable that the revelation of JESUS CHRIST was not communicated to the world at first, and has not, except in rare instances, been imparted since by means of documents, that is to say, through the pages of the New Testament ; it was communicated through the sermons and instructions of our LORD and His apostles. Why, the Christian verity had been " delivered," it had been preached in diverse places for some twenty years before a line of the New Testament was in existence. Our LORD died, it is generally held, in or about the year 33, and it was not until the year 54 that the First Epistle to the Thessalonians, the earliest of the New Testament Scriptures, was penned. It was not until the year 170 or thereabouts that the New Testament writings were collected into their present shape, or invested with their

present authority.   Nay, it is not until quite recent days
that Christians have had any Bibles in their hands.
They could not learn the faith, consequently, from sacred
books, either the earlier or later Christians; at first there
were none; in later days they were not generally acces-
sible.   Add to which, that the New Testament, as its
very structure shows, was not meant to *teach* " the
faith "; it is not in " systematic form "; many portions
of it—the Epistles, for example—are mere " occasional
writings"; that is to say, writings occasioned by the
circumstances of various Churches or individuals—the
Epistle we have now before us is a case in point;
it was elicited by the heresies which had sprung up
in the Church; but for these it would not have
existed.   So little indeed were either Gospels or
Epistles meant to teach the faith, that they were
addressed to people who had already learnt it; the
Epistles were all addressed to Churches or the officers of
Churches or to Christians generally; S. Luke's Gospel
was penned that Theophilus and others like him might
" know the certainty of those things wherein " they had
already " been instructed."[1]   No, the New Testament
was not meant to teach or to deliver the faith; the
Church was to teach, the Bible was to prove.   I will
beg you to remember, therefore, that the faith was from
the first delivered, it was delivered at the time S. Jude
wrote, as for the most part it is still, in nurseries, in
schools, in sanctuaries, in the Mission Field, by the
voice of man.   " The glory of GOD," says Westcott,

[1] S. Luke i. 4.

"is a living man." A man stands nearer to Him, and resembles Him more, than any book can possibly do.

But now we come to the very heart of the question. The faith thus delivered was " delivered *once for all.*" When given to the world, it was given complete and in its final form. It may be unfolded, may become better understood, but it is not to be altered, not to be enlarged or improved. Nothing is to be added to it or taken from it. Though everything else changes, this is not to change; it has the mark of finality. There is no gospel but the original gospel. If an angel from Heaven professed to bring a new and better revelation, S. Paul says we are not to listen to him ; that angel is to be anathema.[1] GOD knows no change, no variableness nor shadow of turning, and so the gospel of GOD is capable of no improvement. The faith once given was given once for all. The creed of the first days is meant to be the creed of our days and of all days.

But I have now, alas! to remind you that this faith thus given has been corrupted, has been frightfully corrupted and changed. We might have known beforehand that it *would* be so. Because, if there is a devil, and if he can injure the religion of our LORD, he will do so, and in no way can he damage it so effectually as by corrupting it at its source. " If the *foundations* are destroyed, what can the righteous do ? "[2] Hence, you will remember, the Epistles are full of warnings against false teachers, against perversions of the gospel of CHRIST. The Apostles saw beforehand what would come, what

[1] Gal. i. 8.   [2] Psalm xi. 3.

L

indeed *must* come, and so we know of our own selves that " the faith once delivered " must be depraved. But whether this is so or not, one thing is certain, that it *has* been depraved, and in a variety of ways. You have only to remember that we have now in England some fifty or a hundred different " faiths," to see how widely we must have strayed, many of us, from *the* faith. You must not pretend that these differences are of little or no moment ; they are often such that if the one faith is right, all the rest are wrong. If either Baptists or Romanists or Quakers or Unitarians are right in their peculiar tenets, then all the rest of us are wrong. If any one of these represents the old faith, then the others do not and cannot. The more or less contradictory teachings of the different denominations are proof in themselves that error is being taught somewhere. There can be no question that, in these later days, as S. Paul[1] predicted, some have fallen away from the faith.

Moreover, we can see for ourselves, as we study Church History and the history of doctrine, *how* the faith has been altered and corrupted. Some Christians have added to it ; some have taken away from it. In the earlier days of our religion the tendency was to add to it, to teach for doctrines of GOD the commandments of men, and down to the time of the Reformation new articles of belief, plants which our Heavenly FATHER hath not planted, were constantly grafted upon the ancient Creed. Those were ages of credulity, and legends were accepted for truths. But since the Reformation the tendency has

[1] 1 Tim. iv. 1.

been largely in the opposite direction—the times of ✔
credulity have been succeeded by those of criticism and
self-will—and one article after another, one part of the
deposit after another has been sacrificed by one or other
of the sects. I have only to remind you of the portentous
cultus of the Blessed Virgin and of the Sacred Heart, of
the Invocation of saints and angels, of the doctrine of
Indulgences and works of supererogation, of the iron
Supremacy claimed for the Pope, to show you that the
faith has been added to. I have only to speak of the
denial of our LORD's Divinity and of His Atonement, of
the disuse or disparagement of the Sacraments, of the
rejection of the Apostolic rite of Confirmation, of the
repudiation even of a Church and a Ministry, for you to
perceive how "the faith" has been undermined or overthrown.

And just because this is so, because GOD's revelation
has been overlaid by man's inventions, it becomes
necessary for us to contend for the ancient faith, for the
creed "once for all delivered."

But where, you will no doubt ask me, *where* is that
creed to be found ? How can we be sure, after all these
centuries, *which* is the true faith ?

> "Lutheran, Popish, Calvinistic—all these creeds and doctrines
> three,
> Extant are, but still the doubt is where Christianity may be."

You may perhaps remind me that every sect believes
that other sects have more or less gone astray, and that
it alone preserves the faith in its purity, and you wonder

whether there can be any certainty about it. Well, I
will tell you how we may discover this ancient faith ;
how to go to work to arrive at the Creed of CHRIST and
His Apostles.

It is obvious that it is not enough to appeal to " the
Bible, and the Bible only."   It is not enough, it will not
help us, for the simple reason that every sect, including,
I believe, even the Mormons, every sect appeals to the
Bible.   I do not say that they all " want to be on the
side of the Bible "; they all " want to have the Bible on
their side," and profess that it is.   No doubt much is to
be done in the way of vindicating the Bible from private
and often preposterous interpretations ; no doubt it is
often misread, and we can show that it is misread, but
still we want an interpreter of the Bible.   At present
every man finds *his* faith in its pages, but " *the* faith " is
as far off as ever.

Nor do I honestly think that we can trust the Pope to
interpret the Bible for us, and to say what is " of faith,"
as he professes to do.   It would greatly simplify matters
if we could, but we cannot.   He tells us that he is
infallible, but we have only his word for it, his and that
of some of his followers, who not so long ago denounced
the doctrine of his Infallibity as a " Protestant invention."
Besides, I can only be *certain* that the Pope is infallible
when I am sure of my own infallibility.   If I myself
may be wrong, then I may be wrong in thinking the
Pope infallible.   And I am the less disposed to trust
myself to his guidance when I observe that, under it,
the faith has been so greatly changed.   The Papal

Church teaches many things which the **primitive Church** did not.

What, then, are we to do? I will tell you. There is **only one** thing we **can do, and it** is this: **We must** *ask those* **to whom** *the faith* **was** *delivered* **Not only the** apostles and evangelists who delivered it—whose words we have in **Holy Scripture**—but those who received it. If anybody **knows, they will know.** I repeat: **The faith** once for all **delivered can be ascertained from the men** to whom it *was* delivered.

For there **are such persons. Their names are known** to us; their writings **are preserved.** Some of them, Hermas[1] and **Clement**[2] for **example, were contemporaries and companions of the Apostles; others,** like Polycarp or Ignatius, **heard the faith from the lips of the** apostles. **Now** *they* **must have known what the** **true** faith of a Christian was in **their days, and what it** was then it is still. And they will **tell us, if** we ask them.

This is what is **called "the** historical **method," and it** is the only safe course to follow; **to interpret the Bible** according to the ideas **and** interpretations **of the** early Christians. We do not **say** that **they were** infallible. But **we** do say that they are more likely to know than the Christians **of a** later age. They had this advantage at least, that **they** drank **of the stream at its source,** before it became polluted.[3] **Men have since** their **day** put many glosses on the **Word of God. The** first Fathers are older than the glosses.

---

[1] Rom. xvi. 14. [2] Phil. iv. 3.
[3] **See** *The Christian Church—What is it?* pp. **226-7.**

But perhaps you say, " That is a long and tedious process, to collect the Faith from the Fathers. It requires time and skill and patience." Well, the search for truth is never easy ; error is easy enough ; truth hides at the bottom of a well. There is no royal road to Divinity any more than there is to mathematics. If we are to " *buy* the truth and sell it not," [1] then we must be prepared to pay the price. Many of our errors are the result of our idleness or indifference—and mental indolence is even more common than physical laziness. Things are not always easy in life or in business ; why should we expect them to be so smooth in religion ?

And is it not part of God's plan, part of His training of our souls, that we should have to search for the truth ? Is it not a test of character ? Is it not formative of character ? It was said by a great thinker [2] that if he had to choose between the pursuit of truth and the possession of it, he would unhesitatingly choose the former. The God Who gave us our minds meant that we should use them.

But you say that you have not the leisure or the learning to qualify you for this inquiry. Then I answer that the investigation has been made for you by others. The English Church has made it. She makes her steadfast appeal, not only to the Scriptures but to " ancient authors," to the very men by whom and to whom the faith was delivered. She does not put them on a level with Scripture ; no, but she appeals to them to tell us what the Scripture really means ; to say which

[1] Prov. xxiii. 23.   [2] Leibnitz.

out of this Babel of interpretations is the ancient and therefore **the true** belief.

And it **is just because the English Church, and the** English **Church** alone **in** Western **Christendom, does** this; because **she, and she alone, has shaped her stan-** dards and rites **by a** reference **to the beliefs and usages** of the **first days that we can be so confident that she** holds and **teaches the faith once for all delivered. Her** position is unique. **Other communions decline this appeal** to history. **Some Romanists do ; Cardinal Manning has** denounced it as **worse than a heresy, as a treason against** the HOLY GHOST. **The Nonconformists do, with rare** exceptions; they **think the Fathers were all in the dark,** or anyhow **were dreadfully superstitious and unevan-** gelical. **Each man, as a rule, contends for the faith** delivered in his **denomination, a faith which began a few** years ago, or **he excogitates** *a* **faith for himself;** hence individual Dissenters **so often tell us what their private** " views " **and " opinions " are. They account it a posi-** tive advantage **that** their views **are derived direct from** the Bible; they sometimes **boast that they have not** been either checked or moulded **by the beliefs of others.** The Church stands alone in **this land in submitting her** interpretation of **Scripture to the** arbitrament **of the** early Christians. **This was the battle-cry** of the Reform- ation—" Back **to** Holy **Scripture and the teaching of the** primitive Church." **The Prayer Book** consequently represents the beliefs **of** the first days; it reflects "the faith " as held by those **to whom** it **was delivered.** You may tell me that **that** faith is not always preached in our

pulpits, because the clergy differ amongst themselves. I
answer, first, that these differences, such as they are,
arise from the system of private interpretation ; they
arise from putting *our* faith in the place of "*the* faith."
If the injunction of S. Jude, nay, if the mind of the
Church herself had been regarded, these discordant
voices would never be heard, for her mind is that
" preachers . . . never teach anything . . . except what
is agreeable to the doctrine of the Old and New Testament, and what the catholic fathers and ancient bishops
have collected from that same doctrine."[1]   And I also
answer, secondly, that the faith and doctrine of the
Church are to be sought in her formularies and standards,
not in the utterances of individual men, and that these
standards exhibit the faith that was "once for all
delivered."   And I say, thirdly, that these differences
are on minute or secondary points ; as to essentials the
clergy are all agreed.

And now I come to my last point. I ask you to
observe that S. Jude is not addressing the clergy. He
writes to all "them that are called." So that he
charges all Christians to contend for the faith. He
implores *you*, my brethren, to do this office for your
religion. You must not leave it to the clergy, as you
constantly do. Nor is it enough again to build churches
and to support the clergy who minister in them ; no,
the lay people, the sons and daughters of the Church,
must become, each in his sphere, each amongst his friends
and acquaintances, a missionary for the old Church and

---

[1] *Canon. Eccles. Angl.* xix., A.D. 1571.

the old creed. This is the true method of Church extension. It was thus that the Church was built up in the first days—Andrew found his own brother Simon ; man influenced man ; it is thus that the Church must be built up again.

And is it too much to ask of Churchmen that they should first know *why* they are Churchmen, and then be ready, as opportunity offers, to tell others ? If the faith is worth having, it must be worth defending and propagating. And others do this readily enough. The Roman Catholics do; it is said that there are some 40,000 of them banded together to work and pray " for the conversion of England "—its conversion from *the* faith to a new faith. Dissenters do it ; their principles are propagated not so much by their pastors as by their young men. Do Churchmen then owe less to their communion, to CHRIST's society ? Can it be that the old faith is less vital, less salutary than the new gospels ? I pray you, brothers and sisters in CHRIST, I beseech you in CHRIST's stead, devote yourselves to the sacred duty of which you have heard to-day, " contending earnestly for the faith which was once for all delivered to the saints."

> " Ancient prayer and song liturgic,
>   Creeds that change not to the end ;
> As His gift we have received them,
>   As His charge we will defend."

SERMON XIII.

THE PRAYERS OF THE CHURCH.

1 Cor. xiv. 15.

" What is it, then? I will pray with the spirit, and I will pray with the understanding also: I will sing with the spirit, and I will sing with the understanding also."

IT is not necessary, in order to worship Almighty God acceptably and profitably, in order to join in Matins or Litany or Evensong with reality and reverence, it is not at all necessary that we should understand the plan (or what is called the *rationale*) of the Service, the principles on which it is based. We can ask God to pardon our sins or to supply our needs and we can praise Him for His great goodness without understanding the Service as a whole, or the suitability and adaptation of its different parts. It would be a sorry thing for thousands, nay, millions, of our fellow-Churchmen, living and departed, many of whom, especially in past centuries, were "ignorant and unlearned men," if the worship they offered had never been acceptable and accepted, unless they understood the principles of worship. But it is not so. We can profitably use the several parts of our Morning and Evening Prayer, the Confession, the Psalms, the Creed, the Prayers, without at all comprehending why they stand where they do, or what is the particular propriety and design of each part. All the same, it is a great help to worship, it makes it more intelligent, more of "a reasonable service," if we understand the structure of the Service and the sequence and harmony of its component parts. And to explain this to you is my purpose to-day. I shall endeavour to put before you the underlying principle of that Order for Morning Prayer in which you have just taken part, and that Order for Evening Prayer in which, I trust, many of you will take part to-night.

Now, the broad principle which governs this Office, and which has made it what it is, is soon stated. Its order is ordered after the life, the religious life of every soul. It marches with the history of every true Christian in his commerce with GOD. It reflects the "progress" of every true "pilgrim" in the way of righteousness. The parts of the Service correspond with the emotions and experiences of the penitent and pardoned soul. All that the Service does, or aspires to do, is to lead *all* the souls of the congregation, unitedly, along the path which *each* must tread in its journeyings to GOD.

Now, in the history of the Christian soul—I am not speaking of GOD's gifts to us, but of our approaches to Him—there are three steps or stages, never more or less, and these stages must always preserve the same order. They are these—Penitence, Praise and Prayer, for under one or other of these heads all our communings with GOD may be classed. I say that this order must always be preserved. For when the soul first awakens

to religious consciousness, it awakens with a cry of penitence. The beginning of the spiritual life is the realization
that we " have sinned and done wickedly." Conviction
of sin—in other words, the knowledge of self—this is the
first step heavenward. Any other beginning is fraught
with danger ; we build our house on the sand if we put
praise or intercession or works or sacraments before
penitence ; we build our steeple from the top. It is not
for us to praise GOD until we are pardoned. " Unto the
wicked GOD saith, ' What hast thou to do to declare My
statutes, or that thou shouldest take My covenant in thy
mouth ? ' " [1] " First be reconciled . . . and then come
and offer thy gift." [2] The first stage in the soul's
pilgrimage is *penitence*.

And the second is *praise*. This follows naturally on
penitence, or rather on the pardon which treads on the
heels of penitence. Almost instinctively the pardoned
soul bursts into song. It cannot receive so great a gift
in silence. GOD Himself has opened its lips, and its
mouth must show forth His praise. [3] When it looks
upward, to the hills whence its help has come, its
language is, " O LORD, I will praise Thee : though Thou
wast angry with me, Thine anger is turned away, and
Thou comfortest me." [4] When it looks around on the
congregation, it is constrained to cry, " Come and hear,
all ye that fear GOD, and I will declare what He hath
done for my soul." [5] And so, you will remember, the
Psalmist, when he summons his soul to " bless the LORD,

[1] Psalm l. 16.   [2] S. Matt. v. 24.   [3] Psalm li. 15.   [4] Isa. xii. 1.
[5] Psalm lxvi. 16.

and forget not all His benefits,"[1] is moved most of all by the thought—"Who forgiveth all thine iniquities, Who healeth all thy diseases." Praise is the natural sequel to repentance and forgiveness.

But the Christian soul cannot stop here ; it has other work to do. It has not only to think of past mercies, but of present needs and future trials. It wants grace to "go and sin no more," strength to do better hereafter, and help to serve GOD truly. Moreover, GOD's great love in delivering our souls from the pit of corruption teaches us unselfishness and solicitude for others. Now that it has learned that GOD is gracious, it wants others to share in His royal bounties and benefits. And so from praise it passes on to *prayer*, to intercession. You will remember how these two are associated in Holy Scripture. As by the Psalmist : the 65th Psalm for example begins, "*Praise* waiteth for Thee, O GOD, in Zion," whilst the next verse is, "Thou that hearest *prayer*, unto Thee shall all flesh come." As by S. Paul again : through all his Epistles you can trace, ever side by side, these two golden threads, Praise and Prayer— one of his recent biographers devotes a whole chapter to tracing this combination.[2] I repeat, therefore, that just as penitence leads on to praise, so does praise in turn give place to prayer. This is the natural order.

And this is the order preserved for us in our daily offices. What we call "the prayers," that is to say, the worship of the Church, is arranged under these three heads and in this order. Matins and Evensong, yes,

[1] Psalm ciii. 2, 3.   [2] Howson, *Character of S. Paul*, Lecture IV.

and the " Divine Service " properly so called, the cele-
bration of Holy Communion, each has its three departments of Penitence, Praise, and Prayer.   I do not mean
to say that these three divisions of worship are always
sharply divided the one from the other ; that there is no
intertwining or overlapping, for there is.   But I do say
that these are the broad features and characteristics of
each part of each office—Penitence of the first, Praise of
the second, and Prayer of the third.

I proceed to remind you, in proof of what I have just
said, that our Order for Morning and for Evening Prayer
begins with a " Penitential opening "—this is indeed the
name given to that part of the Service which precedes
the Lord's Prayer ; that is to say, the Sentences, Exhortation, Confession, and Absolution, all of which were
introduced at the second revision of the Prayer Book,
made in the year 1552 ; the first book of King Edward
the Sixth—that of 1549—begins with the Lord's Prayer.
Now, I could hardly maintain that before this date penitence had its proper place in the Service, but there is no
doubt about it now.   In the Middle Ages the daily office
began with the *Sursum corda*—" Lift up your hearts."
Now, the *preparation* of the heart comes first.   You will
observe that the whole of this introduction speaks of sin,
of its confession, of its remission and the like.   No one
can hear it and be uncertain as to its meaning and
purpose.   Its one purpose is penitence—penitence and
the pardon which follows it.   For penitence, just like
the soul's pilgrimage (of which it is a part), has its steps
and stages.   It begins with the conviction of sin ; it

proceeds to the confession of sin; it culminates in the remission of sins. Just as worship consists of Penitence, Praise, and Prayer, so does Penitence consist of **Contrition,** Confession, and Absolution. Well, the Service comprehends these several exercises, and it preserves their proper order. It starts with Contrition; that is to say, it aims at it. To this end the *Sentences* are recited—to produce in the worshippers the consciousness of sin. They are all taken from " the word of God," and that word is " the sword of the Spirit." [1] Only God the Holy Ghost can " convict the world of sin." [2] But God always uses means—uses means even to reach to the deepest recesses of the heart, and the instrument wherewith He pierces " even to the dividing of soul and spirit," and to discerning the thoughts and intents of the heart, is the "living" and "active" [3] word. We see, then, how the first notes that fall upon the ear in the house of God are designed to produce in us compunction, to bring our sins to our remembrance, and to bring us to penitence for them. And similar, of course, is the design of the *Exhortation*, which is but an exposition of the Sentences, a short sermon, so to speak, on these eleven texts—we might almost call it a " Persuasive to penitence; its ruling ideas are contrition for sin and confession of sin. Then comes the second stage; words of confession are put into our lips; we are made to speak of our sins both of omission and of commission; we are taught to cry to God for mercy. And just as conviction is followed by confession, so is confession by absolution,

[1] Eph. vi. 17.   [2] S. John xvi. 18.   [3] Heb. iv. 12 (R.V.)

and thus the goal is reached, the goal of reconciliation. " I said, I will confess my sins unto the LORD, and so Thou forgavest the iniquity of my sin."[1] The cry for mercy is followed by the conveyance of mercy to those who sincerely desire it ; all who truly repent and earnestly believe, receive, then and there, from the GOD of all grace, "perfect remission and forgiveness." And so they have peace with GOD, and may now pass on to the next stage of Divine Service, which is Praise. Now they can truly say, " O GOD, my heart is ready, my heart is ready: I will *sing and give praise* with the best member that I have."[2]

But before we proceed to speak of our Church's sacrifice of Praise, I should like to remark that this penitential preparation is one of the losses which (as it seems to me) our Nonconformist brethren have sustained by leaving our communion and fellowship. They have lost the true idea and order of worship. They begin their services, with rare exceptions, with hymns, which are acts of praise ; the penitence which should precede praise is in great danger of being lost sight of altogether. Indeed, it is to my thinking a distinct defect in Nonconformist worship that it makes so little of sin ; I mean, makes so little provision for confessing and bewailing it. There is far too little of the Publican's spirit in their public devotions; in fact, they sometimes reproach us for using the Publican's cry, and calling ourselves " miserable sinners "—*they* are not " miserable sinners," they say, but saved sinners. It was observed by Richard

[1] Psalm xxxii. 5.   [2] Psalm cviii. 1.

Baxter that " the Pharisee's liturgy is often heard in the separatist meetings," nor can it be wondered at when it is remembered that they make no provision, they have no special place for words of penitence. Our very form of Service compels us to cry, " GOD be merciful to me a sinner." It is meet that we should do so. And so the Church of GOD in all ages has begun her devotions, not with Psalms, but with self-abasement before GOD.

But I have to speak to you of our offering of Praise. You will observe that the transition from Penitence to Praise is appropriately made by the LORD's Prayer. Appropriately, because this contains both a prayer for pardon—" Forgive us our trespasses "—and a doxology —" Thine is the kingdom and the power and the glory." The same idea may be traced in the *Versicles*. " O LORD, open Thou our lips " is taken from the *Miserere, the* Psalm of penitence, *par excellence*, whilst this is its response, " Our mouth shall shew forth Thy *praise*." Again, " O LORD, make speed to *save* us" still contemplates the past, still lingers on the pardon we need, whilst the response, "O LORD, make haste to *help* us," looks forward to the worship we are about to offer, and the lives we hope to live. The *Gloria* and the *Alleluia* mark a further advance ; they speak only of Praise. The transition is now complete.

And whence does the Church derive her materials for " praising and blessing GOD."[1] Mainly from the Psalter, " the Book of Praises," the Hymn Book which GOD has bound up in the middle of our Bibles. True,

---

[1] S. Luke xxiv. 53.

M

the Psalms are Jewish hymns, and they were heard in temple and in synagogue. But, seeing that we worship the same Eternal GOD, and that " there is no difference between the Jew and the Greek, the same LORD over all," being " rich unto all that call upon Him "[1]; seeing, too, that man is the same now as then, with the same nature, and the same needs, and the same sins, the hymns of the Old Testament Church lend themselves to the New Testament worship, and the more so as we make them Christian by singing the *Gloria Patri* at the end of each. Our separated brethren discard the Psalms in public worship. The Church can never do so. It is part of the treasure which she has inherited, along with the Law and the Prophets, from her Jewish predecessor, which was GOD'S Church while it lasted ; the Psalter is also, as I have already observed, the Hymn Book which has been prepared for us by the finger of GOD. Just as we go to the Bible for our *Sentences*, so do we turn to it for our songs. We begin with the *Venite*, the " Invitatory Psalm," as it is sometimes called, for it contains within itself not only a call to praise—" Let us come before His presence with *thanksgiving*, and show ourselves glad in Him with *Psalms* "—but an invitation to prayer—" Let us *kneel* before the LORD our Maker "—and to hearing GOD's Word—" To-day, if ye will *hear* His voice, harden not your hearts." Then we sing the other Psalms " in order as they are appointed." But we do not confine ourselves to these Hebrew hymns. The same GOD who spake to the fathers by the prophets has spoken unto us

[1] Rom. x. 12.

by His Son [1]—hence we sing the *Benedictus*, the *Magni-ficat*, the *Nunc Dimittis*, all of which come from the Holy Gospel, and even the *Te Deum*, and the hymns of devout Christians of later days. It may be said that they are not inspired as were the Psalms, but there are degrees of inspiration, and we believe that GOD'S SPIRIT still speaks to man by the songs of men, by the hymns of Wesley, or Lyte, or Keble, for example. I must here remind you that our Service of Praise is twice interrupted by a Lesson, which is read not merely for "instruction in righteousness," but in order to give fresh food for praise. The *Lessons* " rehearse the righteous acts of the LORD " and " His wonderful works towards the children of men." And our praises culminate in the *Creed*, for we cannot praise GOD better than by simply reciting what He is to us, and what He has done for us. We misuse the Creed if we do not make it the vehicle of praise. And here I may remind you that the *Te Deum* is really a Creed in substance, though cast in the shape of a Psalm. It has been called an expansion of the *Gloria* Patri *;* it is also an enlargement of the Apostles' Creed. In the *Bene-dicite*, again, we make mention of creation : in the *Te Deum* we dwell on the blessings of redemption ; in the Creed we do both ; it is the crown and flower of our Praise.

And then we pass to Prayer ; " Let us pray " is an express and distinct summons to intercession. This is followed by the *Lesser Litany*—" LORD, have mercy upon us," etc. Observe, we cannot enter upon prayer, any more than we did upon praise, without an act of peni-

[1] Heb. i. 1.

tence ; once more we echo the publican's cry for mercy.
And as the LORD's Prayer marked the transition from
penitence to praise, so does it now mark our entry on
our supplications. We put the pattern prayer before us
as our model. But now we leave out the doxology—
"Thine is the kingdom," etc.—we confine ourselves to
the seven petitions, because it is with petitions that we
have henceforward to do. And as the LORD's Prayer is
our model—" After this manner pray ye "—so are the
Versicles which follow it a kind of rehearsal or outline of
the prayers we are about to offer ; they strike their key-
notes. They speak first of all of mercy—mercy again,
you observe : always the publican's cry—of " mercy "
and " salvation." And of what else do the different
Collects for the day treat ; *their* theme is mercy and
salvation too. Then we pray briefly for the Queen, for
Ministers and People, for Peace, for Grace—each versicle
foreshadowing a prayer or a collect—" The Prayer for
the Queen's Majesty," " for the Clergy and people," the
" Collect for Peace " and that for " Grace to live well."
And then we proceed, after this preparatory exercise, to
pray these prayers. If we did not join heartily in the
responses, we have still another chance ; the same gifts
are now to be sought of GOD in the prayers.

And as to these prayers—two observations must suffice.
First, that we ask the *best* gifts. Very often in our private
prayers we ask for the poorest and lowest of GOD's blessings ; we are concerned about our worldly prosperity—
about what we shall eat and drink and wherewithal we
shall be clothed. But we cannot do it in the Church's

prayers if we would. We *must* "seek first the Kingdom of GOD and His righteousness." We ask for "grace, mercy, and peace," the very things S. Paul so constantly implores for men in his Epistles. This is my first remark. The second is that we pray for the Queen and the Royal Family, not because we care more or desire more for people in high estate than for the poorest, but because such persons are "set in authority over us," and as such we are specially commanded to pray for them. They need our prayers more than others, because of their greater temptations and heavier responsibilities, and still more because on their character and conduct depend the peace of the nation and the welfare of the Church. Similarly, we pray for " bishops and curates and all congregations committed to their charge," because the Church which they together compose is the organ of GOD for renewing and blessing the world. We *must* "pray for the peace of Jerusalem," because the true happiness of mankind hangs upon it— it exists for the glory of GOD and the good of man. But we do not forget others; we make supplications for all sorts and conditions of men. It is noticeable that even here our especial prayers are for the Catholic Church, for "all who profess and call themselves Christians"; still we remember those outside its pale; we pray for missions to the heathen—that " Thy ways may be known upon earth, Thy saving health unto all nations"; not only so, but we pray "for all men " as the Apostle enjoins,[1] for " all sorts and conditions of men " includes every

[1] 1 Tim. ii. 1.

child of man. Then we remember the sons and daughters
of sorrow, whether afflicted in mind, body, or estate : we
commend them to our FATHER's goodness, asking here
as always in the Sacred Name—" for JESUS CHRIST His
sake "— and thus we conclude our prayers.

And then it seems as if we took a retrograde step,
for a General *Thanksgiving* is provided for our use :
it is not enjoined indeed, but it is generally used.
That is to say, at the end of our *prayers* we hark back to
praise. Yes, because our praises may have been, nay,
must have been, defective. The Psalms and Canticles
were our praise-songs, but what if we did not improve
them; what if we wasted our opportunity ? Then another
chance is provided for us here; we may still lay our
tribute of gratitude at the feet of GOD. Not only does
the General Thanksgiving at the close of the Service
correspond with the General Confession at its commence-
ment, but it corresponds with the Prayer of S. Chrysostom.
For as that sums up and comprehends all our petitions
in a few words, so does this final Thanksgiving sum up
our praises. And then " the Grace " completes the
Service ; we invoke the blessing of FATHER, SON, and
HOLY GHOST upon us all ere we depart. That is in
itself an all-embracing prayer. What can we want for
ourselves or for others, for our souls or our bodies, that
is not included in "the grace of our LORD JESUS CHRIST,
and the love of GOD, and the communion of the HOLY
GHOST." In a northern parish, a few years ago, an old
peasant lay dying. He was " no scholar," as he confessed, and he seemed to know no prayer but this : at

least he repeated it again and **again. And some of the** neighbours sneered ; what **sort of a prayer was** that, they said, **for a** dying man ? Yet he could not have offered a more comprehensive petition ; **not** even **the** LORD's Prayer **covers a** wider field or is more complete. **I have** understood that in the Greek Church this blessed formula stands at the beginning of some of their services. **There** are few words more fit for use at any part of the liturgy ; there **are none that I know** of **so suited to its** close.

Thus have I tried to explain to **you the** *rationale* **of our daily offices. We owe it to Him Who** hath given **us an** understanding, **to use it in our prayers ; we** are little better than **" sheep or goats, That nourish a** blind life within the **brain," if we do** not. **But we** need quite as much to sing and to pray **" with** the SPIRIT." Worship demands inspiration—do **we not** pray GOD **in** the Com- munion Office to " cleanse our hearts **by** the inspiration of His HOLY SPIRIT, that we may . . . worthily magnify His holy **name "? S. Jude** speaks of " praying in the HOLY GHOST." **We pray** in the HOLY GHOST when we yield up ourselves—our **hearts and** minds **and** wills—to His governance. **The most** familiar forms acquire new meaning and impressiveness **when** the SPIRIT **of** GOD makes intercession within **us.** What is true **of the** Church is true of the Church's prayers that the " body without the spirit is dead." O what a difference it would make, to ourselves, to **our** lives and characters, to England, to the universal Church, if **we** only prayed the old prayers and sang the **old** Psalms with the spirit and with the understanding also !

WHY WE ARE CHURCHMEN.[1]

EPH. V. 30 *(Revised Version)*.

" Because we are members of His body."

HOPE I may do you some little service if to-day I ask you to consider the practical question, *Why are you Churchmen?* It is one about which we ought surely to be fully persuaded in our own minds. If we *are* Churchmen and not Chapel-goers, then we ought to have a reason, and to be able to give our reason for being such. For it is not reason enough, I need hardly say, that we happened to be *born* Churchmen—if such is the case— though this has often been alleged as a reason why those who were born Dissenters should remain Dissenters. It is not reason enough, because if it is good for the Church-man, it is equally good for the Mohammedan and the Mormon. Nor is it a sufficient reason that we *like* the services of the Church best, or that it is close to our doors, or that there is a good preacher there, or that

[1] This sermon, originally preached in All Saints' Church, Falmouth, on the fourth anniversary of its consecration, was published by request, and has since been reprinted as a tract, entitled, *One Reason why we are Churchmen.* London : C. Taylor, Warwick Lane, E.C.

someone has asked us to attend Church. I say these are no reasons, because each of them may be urged and indeed *has* been urged as a reason for going elsewhere. No, we must have some better foundation to build on, unless we are content to be Churchmen *by chance*, by *mere accident*. And if there is a better foundation, who is to blame us if we state, temperately and charitably and affectionately, what that foundation is. Indeed, we owe it to CHRIST and to what we believe to be the truth of CHRIST so to do. If we merely thought that our mode of worship was a better mode, or that our doctrines were on the whole more Scriptural, or that our Church polity was more Apostolic, then we owe it to CHRIST and to our fellow-Christians to say so. We have no right to keep back anything that is profitable. But how much more are we bounden to deliver our souls, if we should think, rightly or wrongly, that our Church represents the Church, the only true and lawful Church in England. We may be very ignorant or very bigoted—that is quite another thing—but if we do think this, then we are verily guilty before GOD if we do not say so. I trust, therefore, that no one will resent my raising this question, but if anyone does, I shall not distress myself, because anyone who is not afraid of the truth will be thankful to have this question calmly and kindly and honestly considered.

But, before I proceed to say why we—I speak not only for myself, but for thousands of others, both clergy and laity—why we are Churchmen, it may be well if I expressly disclaim and repudiate certain reasons by

which we are often supposed to be governed. Let me
say, then, first—

1. That we are not Churchmen *because we think that
the Church is perfect.* We know very well that it is
nothing of the kind. We know that it cannot even be
pure, so long as it is composed of men. The Church,
just like the Chapel and other similar institutions, has
had its errors and imperfections and abuses ; it has some
such, to our great sorrow, still. Indeed, so far are we
from thinking it perfect or even pure, that if we did
think it such, we should be compelled to leave it at
once. We *must* leave it in that case, because we ourselves are so impure—so stained by sins, so full of
imperfections, that we should have no right to remain.
We must not make a perfect Church imperfect by our
presence. The only Church in which we can keep our
place is one which "receiveth sinners and eateth with
them." Nor are we Churchmen, secondly,

2. *Because the Church is established*—whatever that word
may mean. I say "whatever it may mean," for very
few persons can tell you what it does mean. It does
not mean, I need hardly say, that the Church was *set up*
or *established* by the State, simply because it never was
so established, as every student of history knows. Nor
was it *endowed* by the State, nor is it *supported* by the
State, nor is it *managed* or *moulded* by the State. But
whatever the word "established" means—and what it
does mean I will tell you on a future occasion—that is
not the reason why we are Churchmen. It is not the
reason, simply because, if the Church were disestablished

or disendowed to-morrow, we should belong to her just the same. Our Churchmanship has nothing to do with politics. Nor are we Churchmen, thirdly,

3. *Because the Church has or is supposed to have the support of the so-called " upper classes "*—I mean the more educated and cultured classes. We cannot be sorry, if such is the case. We think it something to be thankful for that the Church commands the respect and allegiance of educated men—say of men like Mr. Gladstone—as other communions do not. We should think it a very serious thing and a very bad sign if our doctrines or our discipline were such that only the ignorant would endure them. But we should belong to her just the same. If the Church had none but the poorest and meanest for her members, *we* should be members just the same. If the classes who now go to Church went as one man to Chapel, we should never dream of following them. Our Churchmanship has nothing whatever to do with culture or refinement or riches or poverty. Nor are we Churchmen, because

4. *We think* **other** *Christians are not good men, or because they have not done a good work.* We are very well aware and are quite prepared to admit that some Dissenters are *much better men* than some Churchmen—than ourselves, for example. And we are also well aware that they have done good and spiritual work; we never dream of denying it; we frankly and thankfully acknowledge it. But that does not reconcile us to the idea of leaving the Church. Other men, Roman Catholics and Socinians, are good men and have done a good work, but Dissenters never

dream of joining them on that account, and they would be the first to reproach us, if *we* joined them. Our Churchmanship, then, has little or nothing to do with the character or piety of Churchmen or Dissenters. Lastly, we are not Churchmen

5. *Merely because we think the Church* BETTER *than other* religious communities. We do think it better, no doubt —at least in *some* respects. We may think, for example, that she gives us much more of GOD's word and much less of man's than the denominations do. We may think her stately and scriptural and reverent liturgy far preferable to extemporaneous prayers—or at least to such as it often falls to our lot to hear. We may think, again, that she puts the sacraments where CHRIST placed them, and where the denominations do not place them. We may think that she has a truer idea of worship than many other bodies have, and that she preserves the proportion of the faith, and the old faith, as they do not. And on all these grounds we may prefer her. But these are *not* our reasons for belonging to her fellowship, for if we preferred the Chapel service, or if we found Dissenters kinder or better men than Church people, or even if we profited more by the Chapel preaching, we should still belong to the Church and not to the Chapel. It is not a question of *preferences* at all—it is a question of *principles;* not of doing what we like best, but of doing what we believe to be the will of our FATHER which is in Heaven.

But enough of these reasons, which are *not* our reasons for being Churchmen. I have now to give you one reason—I shall only give you *one*—why we are Church-

men and can be nothing else. It is this, that we have
been *put into the Church*, which is GOD'S *Society*, founded
to do GOD'S *work, and endowed with* GOD'S HOLY SPIRIT,
to enable it to do that work—we have been put into it
by GOD *Himself,* and this being so, *we must not, we dare
not leave it.* I proceed to explain what I mean. I say,

1. *That our* LORD JESUS CHRIST *founded a Society; He
collected His followers into a community, to which community
He gave the name of Church.* I do not suppose that I need
stop to prove that our SACRED LORD not only preached
and wrought miracles, but that He also established a
society, a band of disciples. This can only be denied—
so even the writer of *Ecce Homo* says—by those who
deny His mission altogether. I no sooner hear of His
preaching than I read of His baptizing. Every person
thus " baptized unto CHRIST " was thereby admitted into
the Church or company of His disciples. I will ask you
to remember that Baptism was administered by John—
John the Baptist—before it was administered by JESUS,
and that by Baptism men were made members of John's
society.[1] And what is true of John's Baptism is, of
course, also true of our LORD's—for He " made and
baptized more disciples than John "—it admitted men
into His society, His brotherhood, and that is the
Church. He calls it such, Himself. " If he will not
hear thee," He said, speaking of one Christian " brother "
who had trespassed against another, " tell it to the
Church." Elsewhere He speaks of the rock on which
He will build His Church. He does not mean that at

[1] See the testimony of Dr. Fairbairn quoted above, p. 76.

that time the Church had no existence, for its foundations
were already laid in the persons of the Apostles; He
uses the future tense because He is building the Church
still.   There can be no doubt, therefore, in the mind of
any unbiassed person, either that our LORD did establish
a Church—did establish *the* Church—or that men were
admitted into its membership by the visible rite of
Baptism.

2. And this society, this band of disciples, this Church,
thus founded by the SON of GOD, was *founded to carry on
His work in the world*.   It was *the* society for the purpose ;
there was no other.   I do not suppose that there
will be any difference of opinion among us on this point,
for every Christian, I believe, admits that the Church
exists to carry on CHRIST's work, to preach, to teach,
and so to bless the world, as He had done.   The Church
is the company of men banded together by GOD to represent CHRIST before men ; it is His organ, His instrument
for regenerating our race.   And so we find that our LORD
appointed its officers, the Apostles, and that He gave it
a bond and badge of membership, the sacrament of the
LORD's Supper, and He gave it a prayer, the LORD's
Prayer, and He gave it special teaching to prepare it for
the work it had to do and the like.   CHRIST founded a
society, and founded it as the one great agency by which
His work was to be done.

3. And to this society thus shaped, this community
thus organized, our LORD promised the gift of the HOLY
GHOST.   The society of itself could accomplish nothing ;
its members and its ministers alike were altogether

inadequate to the work which it had to accomplish. It must receive "power from on high." Its apostles must be "baptized with the HOLY GHOST." And such power it did receive; on the day of Pentecost the HOLY SPIRIT of GOD descended upon it; such power it possesses still; by this its work has so far been done. And this grace and power is covenanted to the society alone. We do not say that the HOLY SPIRIT is restricted to the members of the Church, but we do say that the Church is the ordinary field of His operations. Even if it were given to the world, the world could not receive it.

4. And this society, this Church, is the one thing— apart from His precepts and His blessed example—which our SAVIOUR left behind Him at His departure. He did *not* leave any New Testament—that was not written for many years afterwards. He left the Church and nothing else. There were not many members, it is true—there were only some hundred and twenty in Jerusalem—but still, there they were, and they were all members. And so sure were they that this Church was to continue, and was to carry on His work on His lines, that the first thing they did after the Ascension, even before the HOLY SPIRIT came, was to appoint an Apostle to take the place of Judas, and so make up the number of its officers.

5. *And this community has been continued from that day to this.* I say that it has been continued to our day. There has been no break in its existence. No new Church was set up on the day of Pentecost—the three thousand who were baptized were simply "added"—so we are told— added to the Church. At Pentecost, the Church was

endowed with power, with life, but no new Church was started nor was one begun during the lifetime of the Apostles. All who became Christians became Churchmen ; that is to say, they joined the society which had been started by the LORD, and which was now governed by His Apostles. And all who entered the Church, entered it in the same way : " By one SPIRIT they were all baptized into one body." They were " made disciples " by CHRIST's sacrament of Baptism.

6. But now, I must ask you to observe that this Church, this society of Christians, *was by no means perfect*, and never had been from the first. Even during our LORD's lifetime, one of its ministers, Judas, was a " devil," and even then there were some, our LORD's brethren among them, who believed not. Nor did the coming of the HOLY GHOST make it pure. There were grave errors and abuses in the Apostolic age—as grave, to say the least, as anything that has been seen in the Church since. We often fancy that the early Christians were all exemplary Christians, but the New Testament tells a very different tale. The Church of Corinth, for example, was grossly corrupt, corrupt both in *doctrine* and in *morals*. Among the members were some who said there was " no resurrection of the dead," and there were also fornicators of the deepest dye. The Churches of Galatia again were desolated by Judaisers—men who " preached another gospel which was not another "—*i.e.*, which was no gospel at all. The Church in Sardis " had a name to live, but was dead." The Church of Laodicea was such that our LORD threatens to " spue it out of His mouth."

In short, all the Churches **of that age** were very much what the Church has been **ever since; they** had many imperfections and errors and sins.

7. And now **mark this.** From these Churches, corrupt **or** dead though they were, *no Christian* in those days *dreamed of separating.* Not **a** word was ever said, either by our LORD **or** His Apostles after Him, about the duty of Dissenting—and **if it** *had* been **a** duty, something **must** have **been** said. But impure as the society was, **it is** undeniable that **no one** except apostates separated; no one started **a** second **Church. The idea** of **any second** Church in *competition* **with** CHRIST's own Church, the society founded by Him, would have struck **the** Apostles dumb with astonishment. It never seems to have occurred **to** them that separation was a remedy for abuses. Their idea was to remain in **the** Church in order **to** reform it. **They** *must* remain, simply because **it** was GOD's Church. If He had not left **it—and** He had not ; even the unclean Church **at** Corinth is distinctly called " the **Church of GOD** which is at Corinth "—**if** *He* had not left it, how could they dare to leave it ? And **leave it** they did not. There is no trace, **not** the slightest, of any second **or** secession Church **in** the New Testament. There are now, I believe, in England over two hundred bodies calling themselves " churches "; a " Methodist Church," and a " New Jerusalem Church," and **a " Labour** Church," and a " Theistic **Church,"** and **so** forth. In **those** days *there was but one*, " **one body** " it is called, **one** community, *the* Christian Church. **Some** of these " churches " say they were compelled to separate because

N

the Church was so corrupt. Yet we have had nothing in modern times anything like they had in Corinth or in Pergamum—no ministers "teaching the servants of GOD to commit fornication,". or denying the resurrection of the dead. Yet Corinth had one Church and no more, and we must have twenty. Yes, and so little did men then think of leaving that one Church that even parties within it, the party of Paul, or Apollos, or CHRIST, are sternly condemned. How much more, then, *separations* from it! But there *were* no separations from it. To leave the Church, the community founded by the LORD, because it has become corrupt, is a purely modern idea, in direct defiance of all New Testament teaching.

8. And this corrupt Church, founded by CHRIST, founded to do His work, this society which had "a devil" amongst its Apostles and a Jezebel amongst its teachers, it held on its way and it grew and grew, but it always grew on the same lines; its members admitted in CHRIST's way; its officers ordained in CHRIST's way. And as it grew, branches of this Divine society were established in different cities and countries—first in Palestine, then in Asia Minor, then in the different countries of Europe. And after a time—*when* we do not know, but at an early date, a branch of this same society was established here in England, and it grew here, as it had grown elsewhere, and by degrees it filled the land. It was by no means a pure Church—it had its grave errors and defects; but I do not know that it was ever worse than the Church of Corinth or of Thyatira. Anyhow, it held on its way, and for centuries no one

separated **from it** ; no one dreamed **of** setting up **a purer** Church : they never dreamed of **it because** they looked **on the** Church which they had already as CHRIST'S, and **if it were** CHRIST'S how could they leave it ? **Not even** at the time of the Reformation, when the abuses had become intolerable, did either King or Bishops or Parliament talk of beginning **a new** Church—perhaps those **who** say they did will be good enough to quote their words ; good enough to refer us to some one statute **or** ordinance or act—we only ask for **one.** No, there was no thought then of beginning a new society in opposition to CHRIST'S. The object of the Reformation, as the very name implies, was to *purify the existing Church, not to start a new one.* Down **to** the year 1568, or thereabouts, there **was no** attempt **made to** set up a man's Church side by side with GOD'S Church here in England.

9. But about that time the attempt **was** made. It **was** made by the Brownists, afterwards known as **the** Independents. But the ground they took is most striking and instructive. They said the ancient Church of England had ceased to be a Church ; they also allowed that if it were a Church, they would not be at liberty **to leave** it. (Their descendants at the present day, I may remark in passing, say the exact opposite : they allow that the English Church is a Church, but they affirm that their consciences will not allow them **to** remain in it or to return to **it. Yet,** if it is a Church at all, it must be GOD'S Church. But **let this pass.**) The Brownists began *new* societies, with **new** rules and new officers : they began them in the same towns, sometimes in the

same street, where the old Church had its meetings.
This was the beginning of separation. "Separatism,"
says Dr. Mackennal, "is the old name for what we now
call Congregationalism." The Brownists were soon
followed by the Baptists, the Baptists by the Quakers,
the Quakers by the Unitarians, the Unitarians by the
Wesleyans, the Wesleyans by scores of others. And
each of these, though begun by man, and begun as a
private society, now claims to be a Church. But the
curious thing is that though they all stand aloof from
the Church; though they all say (by their actions, if not
by their words) that we are not fit for them to worship
with—if we *were* fit, why did they leave us and insist on
worshipping apart ?—the curious thing is, that they all
go on, except the Quakers, admitting men into *the*
Church, into CHRIST's Society. Whilst insisting that
they are "separate and independent Churches," they go
on baptizing men into *the* Church. For they allow
that Baptism admits into the old Church, the Christian
Church. "By Baptism," says Wesley, "we are admitted
into the Church." "In Baptism," says Dr. Paton, a
learned Congregationalist, "a child or adult is associated
with the Church of CHRIST." "By Baptism," says the
Wesleyan Dr. Beet, "the Christians at Corinth had
been admitted into the visible fellowship of the Church
of CHRIST." I say, therefore, that they go on baptizing
men into *the* Church, for Baptism, being CHRIST's
ordinance, does not and cannot admit into a sect or
denomination. We are "baptized unto *CHRIST*"—not
unto Calvin or Wesley. And yet these same earnest

and excellent men insist on belonging to societies which
have been set up—I will not say in opposition to, but in
competition with that very society of CHRIST, into which
they themselves admit men in CHRIST's way.

10. But if you have followed me thus far, you will see
clearly why we cannot follow their example—why we
dare not do it : why, if we are Christians at all, we must
be Churchmen. We must be Churchmen, because the
Church is GOD's ; because it remains GOD's, His household and His family, in spite of its corruptions ; because
GOD has not left it ; because it is still His chosen instrument for doing His work in the world, still the vehicle,
the habitation of the HOLY GHOST, and because GOD
Himself has put us into it—His SPIRIT baptized us into
the one body—and there we must remain till GOD leaves
it or takes us out of it. It is of no use to tell us it has
this or that abuse or this or that defect ; we know it ; we
deplore it : but we say that it has not ceased, because of
these defects, to be GOD's Church. No one has ever
said, so far as I know, that the ancient Church of England
is *worse* than the Church of Corinth or the Church of
Sardis was. Yet each of those Churches was a congregation of GOD and part of the great Church of GOD.
Then, if so, what has the Church of England done to
forfeit its Church character ? If you can prove that it
never *was* a Church at all, or if you can show that it was
once a Church, but now has ceased to be such, then we
will come out of it at once ; we owe it to GOD and to our
own souls so to do ; but until that is proved, we must
remain in it : it is at our peril that we leave it. We have

been made " members of His body "—*CHRIST'S* body—
how can we leave it for Wesley's body or the Baptist
body, or any similar institution of man, however devout
or amiable the members may be? In *His* body we are,
and in His body we must remain; and the more so,
because this is the community to which He has covenanted
His grace, and to which He has entrusted His work.
This is why we are Churchmen—or rather it is the main
reason why we are such—because we were baptized into
the Church, the same society which CHRIST founded,
and it is not for us to join or to found another. We are
Churchmen because the Church, however unworthy it
is, is GOD'S; and because He has put us, however
unworthy we are, into it. This is why we mean to live
in the Church and to live for the Church, and to die in
the Church, and if necessary, to die for the Church.

WHY WE DARE NOT BE DISSENTERS.[1]

1 COR. XII. 25, 27.

" There should be no schism in the body. . . . Now ye are the body of CHRIST."

 SUPPOSE that here in England there are as many Dissenters from the Church as there are Churchmen. And many of these Dissenters are devout and earnest and excellent men. All the same we think them, or I for one think them, distinctly in the wrong. We think that their separation from us was and is, whatever their motives, a great mistake ; we believe that it was against the will of GOD that they should secede. And I propose in this sermon to give you our reasons for this belief, the reasons too which prevent us from being Dissenters ourselves.

I hope I may do this much without offence. There ought not, of course, to be *any* offence in a calm and charitable statement of the reasons which constrain us to be what we are, but, unhappily, there are Christians who cannot bear to hear or to read anything which seems to run counter to their views or to condemn their actions.

[1] This sermon is published in tract form. **London : C. Taylor,** Warwick Lane, E.C.

I must therefore point out that, in taking this course, in stating why we are *not* Dissenters, I am only following the example of Dissenters themselves. For I observe that they are perpetually publishing to the world the reasons why they *are* such, or, in other words, why they are not Churchmen—probably you have seen some of their pamphlets—and they do not confine themselves to publications; they sometimes employ lecturers to state the grounds of their Dissent. Nor do I know that any fair-minded and intelligent Churchman blames them for so doing; we should be much more inclined to blame them if they did *not* do it. For if they must separate from us, then they owe it to us as well as to themselves to say plainly why they are compelled to take such a course; to say what there is in our beliefs or our practices which makes it impossible for them to worship with us any longer. It is no kindness to us to keep this back; the sooner we know our errors, the better for our peace and the better for the world's welfare. But if Nonconformists may do this, and indeed *must* do it, in self-justification as well as in charity to us, then they should be the last persons to resent our doing the same. And the more so as their very action, their having left us, quite apart from their writings or lectures, impugns our conduct and puts us on our defence. The course they take in leaving the Church challenges our wisdom or honesty in remaining in it. The world may well think, when it sees so many high-minded men leaving our communion for conscientious reasons, that we only remain because of its *prestige*, or because of its emoluments. It is therefore just as necessary for us to state our reasons, if we have any, as for them to formulate theirs. I hope, consequently, that I shall give no offence to any Christian if in this discourse I state some plain reasons why we cannot, why we dare not, be Dissenters. I may say that these are not our *only* reasons, but these are quite enough by themselves to keep us where we are.

I begin, then, by observing that the reasons alleged by those who are Dissenters *on principle*, those who have separated from the Church on conscientious or religious grounds—with those who are Dissenters by accident, without any reasons at all, we are not now concerned; you cannot argue with such people—the reasons alleged by convinced Dissenters may all be reduced to one. They have left the Church, as they will soon tell you, and as they do tell us in their publications, because of the errors and abuses which they have discovered or think they have discovered in it. They tell us they could not remain in the Church, still less could they rejoin it, " so long as it teaches the soul-destroying error of baptismal regeneration," or so long as it is connected with the State, or so long as " some of the clergy are unconverted men," or so long as there are certain expressions in the Prayer Book, and so forth. Their reason is always the same—the Church's errors or defects—though of course different persons fasten on different points : they are all Dissenters because, as they believe, *the Church is not what GOD'S Church was intended to be :* in this particular and in that—so they say—it has departed from His plan.

Now, it is no part of my purpose to discuss here whether the views which these good men entertain of the Church's doctrines and discipline are founded in truth or not. I may say to you that I do not think they are; in fact, I am firmly convinced that they are not, and I can say this the more freely, because I once held these same opinions myself. I once thought myself that the Church was very much what they say that it is. I know exactly their difficulties, and I know that many of them are the result of *pure misunderstanding*. They mislike the Church's doctrines—take the doctrine of " baptismal regeneration " as an example—because they entirely mis-conceive it. By " regeneration " they mean one thing and the Church means quite another. They fancy that we ascribe salvation to a mere ritual act, an idea which we indignantly repudiate, and one which does not find a shred of support in the Prayer Book, which is every-where the echo of the Bible. So with the Burial Service, to take another instance. They denounce it as a solemn mockery that we should commit the body of a drunkard or a felon to the ground " in sure and certain hope of a resurrection to eternal life "—so they often misquote the words—because they think that we are expressing a confident belief in *his* resurrection to life and blessedness, whereas what we have " a sure and certain hope of " is—not " his resurrection to life," but *the* resurrection, the " general resurrection in the last day." All that the service affirms is that there *is* a resurrection to eternal life : whether this man or that will have part therein is quite a different thing. And so with other teachings and usages. I do not propose, however, to defend these, or any of these, now; I must do that, if at all, at another time. I shall now assume that the views which Dissenters hold and propound on these points are strictly and literally true; that the Church says, and is, and does what they insist that she says, and is, and does. And I shall proceed to show that, even if the Church is all this, and more than this, still we are not justified in leaving her; that we *must not be Dissenters*, however bad the Church may be, so long as it is a Church at all. And our first reason is this:

1. *We dare not separate from the Church, because it is GOD'S Church.* No one who has read the Bible carefully and without prejudice will deny that the Church is a *Divine* institution. He will not deny that Almighty GOD founded, owned, and governed the Jewish Church, the Church before CHRIST. It was GOD's creation, GOD's possession, His "peculiar treasure." Everyone must admit that that communion, in spite of its many corruptions, was GOD's, and that He always claims it as His. However wicked were its priests and prophets and people, still they were His priests, and it was His people.[1] Nor can it be denied again that the SON of GOD founded a Church—"My Church" He called it— within the bosom of the Jewish Church. He formed His disciples into a society, and that society was the beginning, the nucleus, of the Christian Church. It was not pure from the very first—there were "some who believed not," and one of the Apostles was "a devil,"[2]

[1] Isaiah i. 3, 4; v. 7; Psalm l. 7; lxxxi. 11, etc.   [2] S. John vi. 60-70.

but still it was His.   The branches of this same society,
again, established soon after the ascension, at Corinth,
at Rome, in the cities of Galatia and of Asia, were full of
errors and abuses—yes, and of graver errors and of
darker abuses than the Church of England is now
charged with—yet they are always addressed as " the
churches of God," or " the churches of Christ."   In
the Church of Corinth were some who denied the
resurrection and gloried in incest,[1] yet it is called " the
church of God."[2]   In the Church of Thyatira Christians
were taught to commit fornication, yet Christ claimed
it as His.[3]   The Church of Sardis was " dead," yet He
still owned it and ruled it.[4]   Even so, the branch of the
Church established centuries ago in this country has
often been unfaithful and impure ; it has been stained by
many and various errors and sins, yet it has not ceased
on that account to be God's Church.   And it is *still*
God's Church, notwithstanding its present corruptions,
whatever they may be.   If it is as bad as Dissenters
believe it to be, still it is the Church of God which is in
England, just as the carnal community at Corinth was
" the Church of God which was at Corinth."   At least
no reason can be assigned why the Church at Corinth
was God's Church, and yet the Church of England is
not His Church.   And being His, we dare not leave it.
It is reason enough for us to remain in it, that God
remains in it.   If He has not left it, we may not leave
it ; of course we may not.   We dare not be Dissenters,

---

[1] 1 Cor. v. 1, 2 ; xv. 12.   [2] 1 Cor. i. 2 ; 2 Cor. i. 1.
[3] Rev. ii. 20.   [4] Chap. iii. 1-4.

therefore, **because we dare** not pretend *to know better* **than** GOD, *or to be* *purer or holier than He* **is.** And this we **do,** if we reject what He retains. Our second reason is:

2. *We dare not separate from the Church because our* LORD *JESUS* CHRIST *did not separate from the Jewish Church.* We have already *inferred*—and it **is an** inference which cannot be disputed—that **if** the ancient Church of this country *is* a Church of GOD, that is to say, is a "Church" at all, we must not desert it. **But** we are not left to inferences ; **we** have the **example of** our REDEEMER to guide us. No one who has read the **New** Testament humbly **and** honestly will deny **that our** Blessed LORD became a member of the Jewish Church; He was admitted **to** membership **at** His circumcision. **Nor** will he deny **that** He continued in its membership, in spite of its many and its scandalous abuses. **He was a** member at twelve years of age, for then He went up **to** Jerusalem to be initiated into the observance of its rites, and He listened **to its** accredited teachers.[1] He was a member **after He** began His ministry, for **He** attended its temple and worshipped in its synagogues [2] and kept its feasts.[3] **He** was **a** member **"the** same night in which **He** was betrayed," **for He** then ate the Passover with **His** disciples, and **with all** the ritual, all the observances which the Jewish Church had appointed.[4] **No,** He never separated from it. Frightful as were the abuses of that **age,** and freely as He denounced them, He never dreamed **of** separating Himself, any more than the prophets had

[1] S. Luke ii. 42, 46.   [2] S. Luke ix. 16; S. John xviii. 20.
[3] S. John ii. 23; v. 1 ; vii. 10, 37.   [4] S. Matt. xxvi. 20-30

done, from the communion into which those abuses had crept. A member of the corrupt Jewish Church He lived, and a member of that Church He died. *He was no Dissenter ;* not a particle of proof can be alleged in support of that idea. He separated Himself from all its errors—and they were many—but He never by word or deed separated Himself or His disciples from its communion. Had He done so, we should hardly have found those disciples "continually in the temple,"[1] should never have found them observing its hours of prayer,[2] or teaching in its synagogues,[3] or discharging its obligations.[4] We cannot shut our eyes to the fact that He Who "left us an example that we should follow His steps" never by word or deed encouraged the idea, on which all Dissent is based, that we must leave the Church as soon as it becomes impure. We cannot be Dissenters consequently without *reflecting on His wisdom or His conscientiousness,* and we dare not do the one or the other. Here is a third reason :

3. *We dare not be Dissenters, because we dare not disobey* CHRIST. For CHRIST has distinctly told us that the Church's officers, her pastors and teachers, are to be obeyed—in all things indifferent, all things not positively sinful—however corrupt these men may be. He commanded His disciples to observe and do all things whatsoever the Scribes and Pharisees enjoined, though in the next breath He denounced these same men as hypocrites and vipers and blind guides and children of

---

[1] S. Luke xxiv. 53 ; Acts ii. 46 ; v. 12.   [2] Acts iii. 1.

[3] Acts xiv. 1 ; xvii. 1, etc.   [4] Chap. xvi. 1 ; xviii. 18 ; xxi. 26.

hell.[1] And this command by itself settles the question of Dissent, which can only exist by repudiating the authority of the Church's officers. Separate we cannot, so long as we obey this injunction. To separate is to say that *He must have made a huge mistake*, and this we cannot bring ourselves to do. A fourth reason is:

4. *We dare not be Dissenters because the Apostles of* CHRIST *forbid all Dissent.* I do not say that they ever mention Dissent by name, for they do not. It never seems to have occurred to them that any Christian could or would separate himself from the society established by CHRIST, the society which was to carry on His work, and to which alone He had promised His presence and grace, and start a rival society. But all the same, the Apostles forbid Dissent, for they forbid *all* divisions amongst Christians.[2] It may be said that they were thinking of divisions *within* the Church—and this is true—but what of that? Why, that if divisions which do *not* proceed to an open breach, to refusing to worship together, are sinful, *how much more* divisions which do! If parties within the Christian body are condemned, how much more secessions from it! To separate is to say that *we will go our way*, not the Apostles' way, and we think the Apostles' way must be the best.

5. *We dare not start or join a second body of Christians, because it is* GOD'S *will that there should be* "one body" *and no more.* We say it is GOD's will because S. Paul says so. He is very explicit on that point. He says that,

---

[1] S. Matt. xxiii. 1-3, 13-17, 24-33.
[2] 1 Cor. i. 10-13; iii. 3, etc.

just as there is " one LORD " and " one faith " and " one
SPIRIT " and "one GOD and FATHER of all," so there is
" one body." [1]   He classes the principle of one body,
that is to say, along with the belief in one GOD and one
SAVIOUR.   He knows as little of a second body, a " Baptist body " or " Methodist body," as of a Baptist GOD or
Methodist GOD.   The only body he recognizes is the
Christian body or " body of CHRIST "—and every sect is
a second body ; they actually call themselves Christian
" bodies."   No man, in other words, can be a Dissenter
without saying, as some Dissenters *do* say, openly, that
S. Paul's beliefs and ideas are now out of date.   They
say the founders of the sects have been inspired as well
as he. [2]   If we are to be Dissenters we must think and
say the same, and that we are not prepared to do.   Now
I come to my last reason :

6. *We dare not be Dissenters, because we dare not weaken or
discredit CHRIST'S religion.*   We have always understood
that " union is strength "—that division must mean
weakness and loss of force.   We observe too that our
Dissenting brethren are of exactly the same opinion,
wherever religion is not concerned ; it is only in the
Church that they see virtues in dis-union.   Not only so,
but however energetically they defend divisions in the
Christian body, and defend them on the ground that
" competition is a good thing," and promotes the work
of GOD, they all deplore divisions in *their own* bodies as
disastrous and ruinous.   But if their body is injured by

[1] Eph. iv. 4 ; Chap. i. 22, 23.
[2] *Review of the Churches,* iv., p. 305.

secession, why not CHRIST's body? If their work is impeded, why not CHRIST's work? And it is easy to show that Dissent *has* injured religion. People often point to the great work Dissenters have done, to the souls they have won and the like, as proofs of the value of Dissent, forgetting that all this work might have been done just the same without any separation. It is not secession saves souls, but Christianity. Yes! the work might have been done and the frightful injury and loss would have been avoided. For is it no injury that Christians are all at sixes and sevens? Is it no loss that they are fighting against each other, instead of the common foe? Are not the strifes and jealousies, the heartburning and bitterness, the waste and overlapping which our divisions engender, and in the nature of things must engender—are they not terrible hindrances to religion? do they not cause its enemies to blaspheme? Not only do they "silence the voice of the Church," so that it cannot speak with any authority; not only do they impair its energies and arrest its activities, but they make it contemptible to those outside its pale. "It is a matter of merriment"—so a Hindoo writes in the *Times* —"to see the different sects of Christians keeping up an incessant warfare with each other." "My sons," said an African chief, "want me to be baptized. But I say to them, 'Christians here won't speak to Christians there. When one of them has converted the other, it will be time to come to me.'" All over the Mission Field our divisions block the way. A venerable Presbyterian Missionary exclaims that "in our present

o

divided state we shall never Christianize China, never!" The late Primate of Australia testifies that "the Christianity of our outpost settlements is simply being destroyed" by them. Indeed, how could it be otherwise? "A house divided against a house falleth."

You understand, accordingly, "Why we are not Dissenters," and cannot be. Not because we think them bad men—some of them are much better than we are—but because the Church is GOD's society, the visible institution ordained and founded by Him to carry on His work, and therefore, however corrupted it may be, we cannot separate from it without going counter to GOD, without disobeying CHRIST, without slighting His example, without denying Him His prayer, without contradicting the fundamental principles of His religion, without hindering its advance among men. We dare not do—what we conceive to be—"this great wickedness." We must not do evil that good may come. We must not leave GOD's great Society for man's little societies because we think the latter will do the work better.

One word more. If these are valid reasons—and you will find it difficult to disprove them—for our not becoming Dissenters, then they are equally valid reasons why those who are Dissenters, and who perhaps became such under the firm but mistaken conviction that this was their duty, should return to our communion. Not because it is *our* Church, for it is not, or because it is a *pure* Church, for it is not, but because, in spite of its impurities, it is still GOD's Church. They left it because of its supposed errors or imperfections, but I have proved (as I believe) that such errors or such imperfections, however real, afford us no warrant whatsoever for deserting it, or for standing aloof from it. If it is a Church, it is GOD's Church, and it is GOD's, I cannot, I dare not, renounce it.

WHY WE CANNOT COUNTENANCE DISSENT.[1]

I COR. III. 4.

"While one saith, I am of Paul, and another, I am of Apollos, are ye not carnal?"

IN my last sermon I tried to tell you why it would be sinful in us to leave the Church and join the Chapel. But there are Churchmen who, whilst they adhere to the Church, see no harm in going to Chapel occasionally, and who consider it only kind and neighbourly and Christian so to do. But some of us do see harm in it—I do for one. And thinking it wrong, we owe it to them to say so, and to say *why* we think it wrong, with all plainness of speech.

But still more do we owe it to Dissenters. If we cannot conscientiously go to their Chapels, or if we cannot subscribe to their funds, then we are bound by every dictate of charity and brotherly love to tell them why. It is our bounden duty to state our reasons, if for no other cause, for this—that our attitude is constantly misunderstood, and that this misunderstanding breeds

[1] The argument of this sermon is embodied in a tract, entitled, *Why we cannot go or give to Chapel.*

much resentment ; it is a fruitful source of that bitterness
which, unhappily, so often exists between us. For Nonconformists, with rare exceptions, cannot understand
why Church people, for the most part, stand severely
aloof from them. To them it seems to be monstrous
that those who believe in the same GOD and, as they
often say, are "making for the same place," cannot or
will not join with them. It wounds them deeply, because
it looks like a reflection either on their piety or their
intelligence. If they were bad men, or if they met for
an unworthy purpose, they say they could understand it,
but as it is, it amazes them, and they set it all down to
pride of place, or bigotry and intolerance, and many of
them *think*, and some of them *say*, that it all proceeds
from the exclusiveness and arrogance which are bred by
what they call a " State Church."

And it only confirms them in their suspicions that
there are *some* Churchmen, as I have already remarked,
who have no scruples whatever about making common
cause with them ; who will subscribe to their funds, give
sites for their sanctuaries and attend their meetings.
Many of these are devout and honourable men, and their
action makes a deep impression on Dissenters, who
naturally ask why, if one Churchman can do this, others
cannot, and who see in the very sympathy and help
which they receive from such Churchmen convincing
proof that all the rest, who will have nothing to say to
them, are actuated by no considerations of principle or
conscience, but are under the influence of envy or of
pride, if of nothing worse.

It may, therefore, I think, be useful if I set down here some of the reasons which compel us, most sorrowfully and unwillingly, to make this stand ; some of those beliefs which lead us, rightly or wrongly, to the conclusion that *for us* it would be distinctly wrong, it would be sinful, to go to Chapel or to join forces with Chapel people.

But before I do this, I should like to remark that, whatever pain *our* attitude may cause to Nonconformists, the pain and the surprise are not all on their side.   It does not seem to occur to them that if *they* are wounded by our refusing to go to Chapel, *we* must be no less afflicted and humiliated by their declining to worship at Church.   And the more so, as this separation, this going to different sanctuaries is, as I shall show presently, not of our making.   If we and they do not join in worship, it is not because we have withdrawn from them, but *because they or their forefathers withdrew from us*.   If anybody, therefore, is entitled to complain, it is we, not they. All that we do is merely to say that we cannot *follow* those who said they could not *stay* with us.   All that Dissenters can accuse us of is that we take up a position identical with that which they have taken up already, and held for centuries ; we say there are religious reasons which prevent our joining with them, just as they said there were conscientious reasons which forbade their remaining with us.   For if we ask them, even now, why they left us or why they cannot rejoin us, they reply at once that they have conscientious scruples which make it impossible, or that their religious convictions will not allow of it.   But if they were actuated by these *high*

motives in separating, then why must we be governed by
base motives in remaining separate? It seems never to
occur to some of them that Churchmen may have consciences as well as they; that we may have just as pure
and just as powerful reasons for *shunning* their assemblies
as they had, or believed they had, for *deserting* ours. Why
should it be principle in their case, and mere prejudice
and bigotry in our case? I think it well, therefore, to
point out to our Dissenting friends at the outset that, if
we do decline to go to Chapel, we are only taking a leaf
out of their book, only following their example in refusing
to go to Church or to continue in its fellowship; and
that really they ought to be the very last persons in the
world to blame us for doing what they constantly pride
themselves on having done, for conscience sake.

But, even if Dissenters *ought* not to be pained by our
attitude, the fact remains that they *are.* And, therefore,
it becomes our duty to render them, most patiently and
most affectionately, our reasons, which is what I now
proceed to do. Or, rather, I will in the first place say
what are *not* our reasons. It seems to me quite as necessary to do this as to do the other, because it is in our
supposed reasons that the offence mainly lies. I say, then,
that it is not—

1. *Because Chapel people are nothing to us.* How could
they be? Are they not men and brethren? Are they
not, many of them, Christian men? It may mean very
little to them that they have been christened, but it
means a great deal to us, just because of our belief about
baptism. Our belief is that all Chapel people who have

been duly baptized are in a sense Churchmen ; they are
" members of CHRIST, children of GOD, and inheritors of
the Kingdom of Heaven." We do not say that they,
any more than we, are all *sound* members or *good* children
—but members and children nevertheless. How, then,
could we scorn them ? Especially when we remember
how many of them love our Sacred LORD in sincerity,
and, according to their lights, are doing the will of our
FATHER in Heaven. Nor is it, secondly,

2. *Because they are less religious or less devout than Church
people.* Please observe that I do not pronounce any
opinion as to the comparative piety of Churchmen and
Dissenters. No, I make no comparisons—though they
have been made on both sides. What I say is that our
standing aloof from them is *no reflection on their piety*, for
if they were ten times as good as they are, and if Churchmen were ten times as bad as they sometimes are, we
should maintain our attitude of isolation. And as little
is it, in the third place,

3. *Because their ministers are less able or less learned than
the clergy.* Again, I repeat, I make no comparisons.
But I say that neither learning nor ability has anything
to do with it. Dissenters *do* take up this ground ; we do
not. I have often heard it alleged as a conclusive reason
for leaving the Church that the clergyman was such a
feeble creature—not half as smart as the Chapel minister.
But that is not our reason for shunning the Chapel. If
all the ministers were as eloquent as Robert Hall, or as
able as Dr. Dale, or as saintly as Dr. Doddridge, we
should be just as far from Chapel-going. Our refusal is,

therefore, *no reflection on the ministers.* **Nor is our reason**

4. *Because the* ministers do not preach **the** gospel. To tell the truth, we **are** sometimes afraid that **they** do not— **just** as Mr. Spurgeon was. What with **one** thing and another, things which I need not specify here, **we cannot** but have our fears. But it is not because of those fears that we stand aloof. We know that it is made a reason for not attending Church that the pure gospel is never heard there. **If it were** always heard **at** Chapel and **heard in its** integrity, **we** should **be** just **as far from** showing our **faces there.** Nor is it, again,

5. *Because the ministers have* **not been** *episcopally ordained.* **True, we** do believe in episcopal regimen—and small **blame to us; a** leading Wesleyan, **Mr. Price** Hughes, has admitted that for fifteen centuries no other rule was known in the **Church.** Still, it **is not because** the Chapel ministers are destitute of such orders that we are prevented from recognizing them, for many of them, in fact, have absolutely no orders at all. **Many of** them scoff at **the** very idea **of** orders—the *Nonconformist* newspaper **does.** Many of them have preferred—Mr. Horton, of Hampstead, has—to be set apart by the shaking of hands rather than by the laying-on of hands. But none **of** these thing decide us. If they had *all* been episcopally ordained, as **some** ministers of the so-called " **Free** Church of England " **have,** we should still decline to give them one farthing or to go near **the place.** And it is not, lastly—

6. *Because* we think that Dissenters have done **no good.** **For we** cannot help seeing, and we readily allow, that many

of them have done *much* good. We do not say that it is
good unmixed with evil—perhaps no good ever is—but
good it is. They have changed some lives; they have
transfigured some homes; they have elevated some
neighbourhoods. There are few religious bodies, whatever their views, but have some such trophies to show.
But none of these things reconcile us to the Chapel.
Partly because, whatever good Dissenters have accomplished, they have accomplished not *qua* Dissenters, but
as Christians. It is Christianity, not Nonconformity,
that changes the heart and life. Partly because, as I
have already observed, whatever good they have done
might have been done just the same, if not indeed better,
without a secession. Partly because such success proves
nothing, either as to moral character or to soundness
of view. Good work is often done—it is "one of the
mysteries of GOD's kingdom"—by men who are altogether in the wrong. Judas Iscariot cast out devils, yet
he was himself a "devil." No, we do not deny and we
do not depreciate the good they have done, but we say
that that success of theirs proves nothing whatever as to
the wisdom or lawfulness of their course.

And now, it may be said to me, "These are strange
confessions. You allow that baptized Dissenters are
your brethren in CHRIST. You admit that they may be
every whit as religious as Church people; that their
ministers may be as able as the clergy; that these ministers may have preached the gospel, and that their
preaching has done good; then what more do you want?
How can it be wrong for you to join in acts of worship

with good men, and Christian men, who have done a
good work ? "

The answer is : We cannot, we dare not, go to Chapel
just because *it is against God's will that that Chapel exists.*
The members may be good, the ministers good, the
doctrine sound, the service reasonable, but the *place itself*
exists in defiance of God's design. We cannot go or
give to it, because we should thereby countenance and
support a state of things which, as we believe, Almighty
God disallows. I do not now say that these views are
right—that remains to be proved—but I do say that
these *are* the views and convictions which compel us to
act as we do. And I now proceed to set forth the
considerations which conduct us to this conclusion.

But, first, I must ask you to consider how, as a matter
of fact, these Chapels, one and all, Romanist and
Protestant, came into existence. They all began in the
same way ; they all owe their existence to a division, to
a separation. I do not suppose this will be disputed ; it
can only be disputed in the teeth of obvious facts, and in
disregard of English history. For once on a time, and
probably not so long ago (most of our Chapels have
been built within the present century), there were no
Chapels in our parishes. Once there was nothing but
the Church. What public worship of God there was,
what ministry of the word and sacraments of CHRIST,
was at Church. How, then, has the Chapel come into
being ? By making a division amongst the Church members ; by diverting some professed Christians from the
Church, and collecting them into a rival communion.

Even if all the Chapel members were persons who had seldom, if ever, attended Church, or persons who had been neglected or repelled by the clergy, still that Chapel owes its existence to a division amongst Christians. For how can there be in any parish or city or country two separate altars, two pulpits, two denominations, and yet no division ? If there is no division, how is it that they are not united ? On the contrary, so long as this state of things lasts, both Church and Chapel are monuments of division. Monuments of division with this difference —that the separation was *on the part of the Chapel from the Church, not on the part of the Church from the Chapel.* Why, the very stones and structure of the building, in the vast majority of cases, show which existed first ; which was the original and which the seceding community. So does the very name of " Dissenters " and still more the name of " Separatists," which they bore at first. " Separatism," said Dr. Mackennal, at the Grindelwald Conference, " is really none other than the old word for what we now call ' Congregationalism.' " And he well added that " separatism has become the most formative and constructive Church doctrine in England of to-day," for we cannot discover any denomination that has been " formed " or " constructed " in any other way.

I pass over for the present the grounds—they were many and varied—on which these separations have been made. All that I am now concerned with is that every Chapel witnesses to a *dichostasia*, or standing-apart, amongst Christians, and it shows that the Chapel, not the Church, has made the *dichostasia*. I have still to prove that all such *dichostasia* is hateful to GOD.

And the proof is extremely simple. For it so happens that this very thing, *dichostasia*, or, what is much the same thing, *schisma*, a division amongst Christians, a rent in the body, is expressly and repeatedly condemned in Holy Writ. I may refer you to my text, which denounces even parties and party cries as "carnal"; to the first chapter of this Epistle, the 10th verse, where the Apostle "beseeches them, in the Name of our LORD JESUS CHRIST, that there be no divisions among them"; to the 11th chapter, the 18th verse, where "divisions" are again condemned, as a schism is in the 12th chapter, the 25th verse. I may also point you to Rom. xvi. 17, and Gal. v. 20. And these Scriptures should settle the question. The Chapel exists by doing what they forbid and condemn.

Yes, but I am much afraid that they will not settle it. I shall be told that the Epistles were written so long ago, or that things have changed since the Apostles' days. Something more than a string of texts will be required, if we are to show that the City Temple and the Metropolitan Tabernacle were built in defiance—*unconscious* defiance, of course—of GOD's will, and I therefore proceed to observe—

First, *that it must be against* GOD'S *will that men should divide His Church.* There is no getting away from this. If this or that community is GOD's—if GOD is its founder, owner, governor, head, then it cannot be right that men should leave it. He cannot will that they should forsake, for any reason whatsoever, a society which is His. If

He is *for* it, they must not be against it. So long as He remains, *they* must remain also.

Secondly, *it is also against GOD'S will that men should make a breach in GOD'S Church.* For it may be said that Dissent is not a departure from the Church, but a division within it. Be it so! Still, we come to the same conclusion. If this or that society be GOD's, then I must make no rent or rupture therein, because I must not weaken or injure the society of GOD.

And now, I must pause to ask a question, which I have often asked before. Is the Church of England, or rather, let me say, are our parish congregations in England, Churches of GOD or not? I do not ask whether they are *pure and incorrupt* Churches : I am quite prepared to allow that they are not. All I want to know is whether they are Churches *at all ;* whether they have existed all these years and have never been " Churches," or whether they *once* were Churches but now have forfeited the name? Have our errors and abuses been so flagrant as to take away our Church *status ?* Dissenters say, "No": they freely allow that the " Church of England " is a *Church,* or at least that our congregations are Churches. Most of them would say that it is a great Church, and a historic Church, and a zealous Church, and a learned Church, and so forth. They are extremely kind and flattering in many of the things they say of us. They complain that we " unchurch " them, whilst they do *not* unchurch us. With hardly an exception they allow that we form a Church, if an impure one. Then, if so, we form a " Church *of the living* GOD." We must do this, because there is no such thing as a Church which is not GOD's. What distinguishes the Church from other societies and institutions is precisely this— that it is *GOD's.* Such a thing as a " Church of England," or a " Methodist Church," which is not also a Church of CHRIST, is an impossibility. I can well believe that it is not a " church," but only a " private Christian club "; but what we cannot believe is that, if it is a Church, it is not GOD's. The Church at Corinth was GOD's, as I have reminded you on a former occasion, despite the shameful incest which defiled it. The Church at Sardis was CHRIST's, although it was " dead." Then the Church of England is GOD's, whatever its errors and abuses, its lethargy and its Erastianism have been.

But, if this is so, then we have a conclusive reason for not going or giving to Chapel. We dare not desert the society of GOD already planted in the parish, and join an opposition society over the way. GOD has put us into *His* society, and there we must remain. We dare not go to Chapel, just because there is a Church of GOD and the Chapel is a split from it.

But I dare not for another reason, namely, that Almighty GOD has *told us in His Word that every Chapel in the land is against His will.* I am not left to inferences such as I have just drawn, however sure they may be ; we have Scripture teaching on this question. All separatism is forbidden by the Old Testament, forbidden in the Gospels, forbidden in the Epistles, and forbidden, lastly, in the Apocalypse. I cannot, of course, give detailed proof of this now ; I can only mention a few particulars.

But first I must refer for a moment to the *reasons* which have impelled Dissenters to make their separation from the Church. Now, I have little hesitation in saying that whilst *some* of our denominations have had their origin (as everybody knows) in strife, in quarrelling, the great majority owe their existence to a belief that it was a solemn duty to GOD to make a secession. Men thought that (the abuses of the Church being what they were) they would be guilty in the sight of GOD if they remained, and so, for the greater glory of GOD, as they honestly believed, they withdrew from the Church, and built the Chapel.

I refer to their motives, because it is not difficult to prove from Holy Scripture that secession *even for such reasons as these*, even for the sake of starting a purer communion, or for the sake of being presumably free to do GOD's work more effectually, is distinctly forbidden. I appeal, in the first place, to the *Old Testament.* Was ever the Church of England, even in its darkest days, *worse* than "the church in the wilderness," or the Church of the Judges, or the Church of the Prophets? No reasonable man pretends that it was. Then why may men withdraw from *it*, when they might not withdraw from the flagrantly corrupt Church of the Jews? The Jews might not, on any account, leave GOD's Church *then ;* why may Christians leave it now? I appeal, secondly, to the *Gospels.* For I observe that, at the time of the Incarnation, that Jewish Church was, if possible, worse than ever ; it was honeycombed with formalism and hypocrisy ; its scribes and teachers were " vipers " and " children of hell." Yet our LORD CHRIST, knowing this, joined it, remained in it, worshipped in it, died in it. He no more deserted the synagogues (though they were centres of corruption) than He did the temple. His example is conclusive against all secession. So, by the way, are His precepts, and His prayers, but of these I cannot treat now. I appeal, in the next place, to the *Epistles*. Some of the Churches to which S. Paul wrote were far, far worse than the Church of England has ever been. However low we may have sunk, we have never been *worse*, either doctrinally or in practice, than was the Church of Corinth. Yet the Apostles never talked of separation, never counselled it, as they *must* have done, if it had been the right thing to do. On the contrary, as my text shows plainly, they forbade all divisions, even *within* the Church—how much more, therefore, separations *from* it ! I appeal, lastly, to the *Apocalypse*. The Church of England has not been worse, it has been nothing like so bad as some of the Churches of Asia. Yet our LORD, much as He had to say to them, never said one word about separating ; never counselled good Christians, even at Sardis, where the Church " had a name to live and was *dead* " to come out of it and start a purer denomination—no, not even as a last resource. Unless, therefore, we have entirely misread our Bibles, our main reason for not going or giving to Chapel is a most conclusive one, " We dare not do this great wickedness and sin against GOD." We do not say that it is a wickedness in all Dissenters to go to Chapel—many of them are acting in perfect good faith, and have no sort of idea that schism is a sin—but

P

we do affirm that *for us*, knowing what we do, and believing what we believe, it would be a sin against GOD in any way to assist in breaking up the Body of CHRIST— the "*one* Body" of which so much is said to us—into so many "bodies" or denominations, and it would also be a sin in any way to countenance or encourage the breaches which have been made. Dissenters may be better men than we are; their preachers may be cleverer than our clergy, but still the fact remains that the Bible, as we read it, says as plainly as it can say, that it is against GOD's will that there is a sect, a split from GOD's Church, in the land. The Bible suggests that the way to reform the Church of GOD is to remain in it; not to secede and set up brand-new "churches," formed by art and man's device, by its side, to the weakening and discredit and discomfiture of our religion.

WHY WE CANNOT SUBMIT TO THE POPE.[1]

S. MATT. XV. 13.

" Every plant which My heavenly FATHER hath not planted shall be rooted up."

THE Bishop of Rome, the Pope, claims, as you are all aware, to be the Supreme and Infallible Head of the Church upon earth ; he claims to be the " Vicar "—that is to say, " the substitute," " the vicegerent " of CHRIST. He " holds the place," according to the Roman Canon Law,[2] " of the Redeemer Himself upon the earth," or (as a Roman pontiff[3] puts it) he " bears the authority . . . of the true

[1] This Sermon was preached in S. Andrew's Church, Plymouth, on Sunday evening, March 8th, 1896, and Sermon **XVIII.** on the Sunday following. An able and estimable Jesuit Father, whom I may not name, has done me the favour to look over the proofs, and has furnished me with a considerable number of criticisms. I have endeavoured to give them their due weight, and have in some instances modified the text to meet his objections. But I cannot pretend that he has in any way shaken my convictions. The proofs that I ask for he has not attempted to supply. He has confirmed me in the belief that they do not exist.

[2] *Corp. Jur. Can.* Joan Gib. ii. 6, quoted in Bishop Boyd-Carpenter's *Christian Reunion.*

[3] Innocent III. " Veri Dei vicem gerit in terra." Phillpotts' *Letters to Butler*, p. **143.**

GOD upon the earth."[1]   And he, and many others, call upon us to recognize his claims and to submit ourselves to his sway.

Nor are we altogether disinclined, or *some* of us are not, to submit.   We are by no means insensible to the strong and subtle attractions which cluster round the see and the system of Rome.   It is a grand and inspiring conception, that of one spiritual prince ruling over universal Christendom.   And it would save us so much trouble, so much inquiry and uncertainty, if we could only accept that spiritual autocrat as our teacher and pastor.   It would put an end, too, to those bitter and unseemly disputes and divisions which are the reproach of our English Christianity, if we could all agree to take the law from his lips.   We can quite understand, consequently, the powerful fascination which Roman ideas have exercised over men like Manning and Newman— and such minds there will always be.   If, therefore, we do *not* submit to the Pope, it is not because we are altogether impervious to the attractions of the Papal system.

But we do *not* submit ; we have no intention of so doing.   No, and I hope that you who hear me will never submit.   I hope that, come what may, you will never

---

[1] Fr. B—— asks me to explain that the " Catholic claim for the Pope is that he stands to our LORD in much the same relation as a Viceroy of India to the Queen—*mutatis mutandis.*"   I answer that this may be *his* idea, but it is not that of others.   In his book, *Le Christianisme et les Temps presents,* the late Bp. of Laval wrote that " the Pope is the second form of the Real Presence of JESUS CHRIST in the Church," and the Bp. of Bayonne, preaching in his Cathedral on May 24th, 1896, spoke of the Pope as " the visible personification of the SPIRIT of GOD " and as " the incarnation of the HOLY GHOST."—*Guardian,* June 17th, p. 934.

bend your neck to the Papal yoke, a yoke which our fathers were not able to bear. And I propose in this sermon to tell you *why;* why, anxious as we are for peace and unity, and for reconciliation and communion with all who bear the Christian name, we cannot, we dare not take the Pope at his word.

Now, Roman writers demand our submission, they claim that we should recognize this spiritual supremacy, mainly on the following grounds. They say—

1. First, that S. Peter was *appointed* by our SAVIOUR CHRIST *to be His* "*vicar*," to be "supreme head and ruler and pastor and teacher" of the visible Church. This is their *first* claim. They affirm—

2. Secondly, that this same S. Peter in due course, by the Divine ordering, *became bishop of Rome*, or in any case "nominated that see as the inheritor of his supremacy." This is their *second* contention. The third is

3. That by the will of GOD all S. Peter's privileges and prerogatives, his authority, his infallibility and the rest, *descended to his successors* the bishops of Rome, so that, as touching the Church, the Popes are, each in his day, what S. Peter was in his, and what our SAVIOUR CHRIST was in His.[1]

Or, to put the self-same argument in another shape: the Pope demands our submission,

1. First, because he is the lawfully elected and divinely appointed bishop of Rome.

2. Secondly, because, as such, he sits in the chair of

---

[1] Fr. B—— asks me to expunge this last clause. He has omitted to observe that it is based on Fr. Lyons's assertions, quoted below, p. 239.

S. Peter, and is the inheritor of his unique authority.

Lastly, because S. Peter was by GOD invested with *supreme* authority to teach and govern the whole visible Church.

These are, in brief, the Roman claims, so far as the Pope is concerned, and these are the claims which we conceive ourselves bound to resist. We say, and say distinctly, after calm and careful examination, that these prodigious pretensions *have never been established*, and that, unless further and very different evidence is forthcoming, *they never can be*. We say that Papal Supremacy appears to us to be a plant of purely human growth, one which " our Heavenly FATHER hath not planted," and one, therefore, which, some day shall be rooted up. We reply that we cannot but conclude, from the evidence before us, that the Papacy is not " from Heaven," but is " of men." And for *this* reason—because the Pope has thrust himself, or has been thrust by others, into the chair of CHRIST, the Church's Living and Acting Head, and has usurped HIS authority—we cannot, we may not submit. Our answer, our respectful answer, to the Pope is—

First, we have *no sufficient proof* that S. Peter was ever constituted CHRIST's Vicar or the Church's head, or anything like it.

Secondly, that, even if we had such proof, we have none—certainly, none that would satisfy an impartial historian[1]—that he was ever bishop of Rome, or desig-

---

[1] Fr. B —— reminds me that "Lardner writes, ' None denied the bishop of Rome to have *what they called* [the italics are mine] the chair of Peter,'" and that Archbp. Bramhall wrote to much the same effect. He also fur-

nated the see of Rome as the seat of authority ; and, lastly,

Even if he was both Vicar of CHRIST and bishop of Rome, we have no proof, and certainly none of such a character as this portentous claim demands, that he did or could *transmit his authority* to each and all of his successors in the Roman see.

I say that we have no proof of any of these propositions *such as these colossal* claims require. For they are colossal claims ; they alter our whole conception of Christianity.[1] In that case our place in the Church depends, not on our communion with CHRIST, but on our communion with the Pope. In that case, the whole belief and regimen of the Church rests with one man. In that case, whatever the Pope decrees as " of faith," I must accept as the voice of GOD. " Disobedience is at the peril of salvation."[2] I say the doctrine of Papal Supremacy changes the whole complexion of our religion, and therefore I am justified in requiring the most convincing proof.

nishes me with a list of Protestant divines who affirmed that S. Peter was at Rome. But this I have never denied : I am not even concerned to deny that he was *bishop* of Rome : what I say is that we have no adequate proof of his episcopate. For I cannot regard the beliefs of a much later age as proofs.

[1] They really require a new article in the Apostles' Creed, between " I believe in the HOLY GHOST " and "the Holy Catholic Church." " In the present Roman Church, the whole body is made perilously and unnaturally to stand upon its head."—Jenkins, *Privilege of Peter*, p. 12.

[2] " The whole question of reunion therefore lies within a nutshell. It is not a question of examining and accepting a long list of Catholic doctrines. It is simply a question of the fundamental and essential constitution of the Church [previously explained to mean that " the Pope has received by Divine right authority to teach and govern the whole Church "]. Settle this matter and everything falls into its proper place and becomes easy."—Cardinal Vaughan—see *Guardian*, Sept. 11th, 1895.

If this doctrine is true, then it will be clearly, not obscurely, revealed. In mercy to my soul, God will have written it large, so that he that runs may read.[1] Yes, if the doctrine is true, then we shall have, not merely guesses or dubious inferences, but ample proof. And so far we have no proof at all; we have nothing that is worthy of the name.

I. I turn to the first proposition. I say that so far it is "not proven" that S. Peter was appointed to be the supreme teacher and governor of the Early Church. The Romanists say that it *is;* they further say that the main proof may be found in the pages of the New Testament. And they appeal in the first place to the GOSPELS, and to the language of our LORD recorded therein. They cite three texts—"*the* three texts," as they are often called. Let us calmly and honestly examine them.

But, first, let me express my regret that a recent Roman controversialist[2] should have allowed himself to speak of these as texts " which Anglicans dislike "; to which we give a " wide berth," and which, instead of explaining, we "explain away." I regret such language, not merely because I dislike all insinuations, but because it is untrue—I will not say that the writer knew it to be untrue. But he either knew it to be untrue, or he did

---

[1] " Can we doubt that if GOD had intended us to hold our faith on such a tenure as the continuousness and legitimacy of a succession to a visible monarchy like that of the Roman Pontiffs, He would have given us the clearest possible proofs and directions in a matter of such supreme importance."—Jenkins, *Privilege*, p. 181.

[2] The Rev. Sydney Smith, S.J., in his tract on *Papal Supremacy and Infallibility.*

not know our writings—one or the other.   For he cannot
name a single Anglican theologian **of any** repute, **who
has** shirked their examination **or** manifested any reluct-
ance to discuss them.[1] **We are** simply amazed **that**
anybody should think that we want to shirk them.
Anyhow, we will, if you please, consider them now.
And the first is

I. S. Matt. xvi. 18, "Thou art Peter *(Petros)*, and **upon**
this rock *(petra)* I will build **my Church,** and the gates of
Hades shall not prevail against it.   **And I** will give unto
thee the keys of the kingdom **of** Heaven, and whatsoever
thou shalt bind on earth shall **be bound in** Heaven, and
whatsoever **thou shalt loose on earth shall be** loosed in
Heaven."   This is their "charter-text"; it stares you in
the face as you enter S. Peter's, in Rome: some of them
say that it is, by itself, "decisive."   They **bid** us observe
"First, that Peter *alone* received a new name.   Second,
Peter *alone* was made *petra ecclesiæ*, **the rock** of the Church.
Thirdly, **Peter** *alone* received the keys, the symbol **of**
supreme authority."[2]   **To this we** reply,

First, It is *not true* that "S. Peter *alone* received **a new
name."**   A similar name was **given to** James **and John,**
"the sons of thunder."[3]

---

[1] Mr. Smith's reply to this challenge is that we all do it—I am myself, he
says, a conspicuous **instance.   I certainly am,** if to examine at length is the
same thing as to shirk an examination.

[2] Lyons, *Christianity and Infallibility,* p. **122.**

[3] **Nor is it true,** as Lyons says, that the name of "Simon" was
"changed."   He was *surnamed* "Peter," but he was **called** "Simon" to
the last.   Our LORD often addressed him **by** this name, and only once
calls him Peter (S. Luke xxii. 34), and then at the very moment when He
forewarns him of his approaching denials.   I regret to have to add that

Secondly, that it is *by no means certain* that S. Peter was the rock on which our CHRIST would build His Church. Roman Catholics speak as if it were, but there is so much *un*certainty about it that more of the ancients *dis*believed than believed it. A learned French Romanist, Launoy, as is well known, cites *seventeen* testimonies from ancient writers, "the Fathers," as they are called, identifying Peter with the rock. But then he cites *forty-four* which interpret "the rock" of *the faith* which S. Peter had just confessed—"Thou art the CHRIST, the SON of the Living GOD"— and *sixteen* which see in "the rock" our LORD Himself—"that rock was CHRIST." It is quite clear, therefore, that the ancients did not all or most of them find in these words what Roman Catholics do, namely, the promise of future supremacy over the whole Church to Simon Peter.[1] No, they *differ* in their interpretations, differ widely.[2] But if these words had

---

Fr. B—— finds an instance of "shirking" in what I have just written. He insists that the name Peter was a name of *office ;* that of Boanerges one "indicating personal *character."* That *may* be so—I do not discuss the point now—but still the fact remains that Fr. Lyons has affirmed what is not true, and it is one of his cardinal contentions. I think Romanists sometimes forget that the name Peter was not first bestowed in S. Matt. xvi. It is first found in S. John i. 42.

[1] For example, Tertullian, "the earliest writer quoted as interpreting 'the Rock' to mean S. Peter," did not. He "contends vehemently (*De Pudic*, 21) that the privilege conferred by our LORD on that occasion was exclusively personal, and was fulfilled by the part Peter took in the first formation of the Church."—Salmon, *Infallibility of the Church,* p. 341, note. Edit. 1890.

[2] This fact ought to estop the Roman clergy from building on this text, for they have vowed "not to interpret Scripture otherwise than in accordance with the unanimous consent of the Fathers." "I do not know of a single early Christian Father, who in a single passage indicates an approach to the idea that the primacy of Rome was to be the fulfilment of these

really made S. Peter the universal Pastor, they would have been agreed ; the meaning of this text in that case could never have been forgotten, for it alters the entire constitution of the Church. We observe, thirdly, that the gift of the keys, which was here undoubtedly peculiar to S. Peter,[1] did not necessarily convey supremacy, but primacy, stewardship, oversight. In Isaiah xxii. 22, the " key of the house of David " is given to Eliakim, the son of Hilkiah, but that did not make him supreme in the kingdom of David; it merely made him "treasurer" in the place of Shebna. It is to be remembered too that this key is now in our LORD'S hands (not Peter's or the Pope's), as we are told in Rev. iii. 7. We further remark that the next and corresponding words, " Whatsoever thou shalt bind on earth shall be bound in Heaven," here addressed to S. Peter, are in this same Gospel, in chapter xviii. 18, addressed to *all the Apostles*, thus showing that they shared these powers with Peter. And we observe, lastly, that five verses lower down, the

divine words. And yet the passages (S. Matt. xvi. 18 and S. John xxi. 17) have received very careful treatment at the hands of such men as Origen, Chrysostom, Hilary, Augustine, Cyril, Therdoret."—Bp. G. F. Browne, *On what are Modern Papal Claims founded*, p. 76.

[1] But here only. Origen (*in* Matt. tom. xii. 11, quoted by Gore, *Rom. Cath. Claims*, p. 87) says, " In this place the words, ' whatsoever thou shalt bind on earth,' etc., seem as if they were spoken to Peter. But in the Gospel of John, the SAVIOUR, giving the HOLY SPIRIT to the disciples . . . says, Receive ye the HOLY GHOST. Whosoever sins," etc. So Theophylact on this text. "Though the ' I will give thee,' was spoken to Peter alone, yet the gift has been given to all the Apostles. When ? When He said, ' Whosoever sins ye remit,' etc. For this ' I will give ' indicates a future time—the time, that is, after the Resurrection." Benedict XIV., according to Jenkins, allows that the *potestas clavium* was given to the Apostles generally in the words of S. John xx. 23.

" rock," if such S. Peter was, has already become a
stumbling-block, a " rock *of offence*," and Simon is
addressed by our LORD as Satan,[1] and the future " vicar
of CHRIST " is told to get out of His sight, for he
" minded not the things of GOD, but the things of men,"
which, to say the least, does not promise well for his
future infallibility.

Let us allow, however, as many Anglican and other
divines do, that S. Peter was the rock and none else ;
still, he was not the sole, nor yet the main foundation
of the Church.   Not the *sole* foundation, for the Church
is expressly said by S. Paul to be " built on the foundation of the *apostles and prophets* "[2]—the city of GOD, as
we read in the Apocalypse,[3] has twelve foundations, and
" on them twelve names of twelve apostles of the
LAMB."[4]   Not the *main* foundation, for " JESUS CHRIST
Himself is the chief corner stone."   Still, a foundation,
a rock, Simon Peter was, and on him, with others, the

---

[1] A remark of Wiclif's is worth quoting here : " As it does not follow,
because Peter was personally called ' Satan ' by our LORD, that therefore
he was made *lower* than any of the apostles, so it does not follow, because
certain privileges were given him personally in the words, *Tu es Petrus*,
that therefore He was made Pope and head of the Church after our LORD's
Ascension."

[2] Eph. ii. 20.   [3] Rev. xxi. 14.

[4] Fr. B—— insists, as Romanists constantly do, that " the rock is quite
a different thing from the foundation laid upon the rock."   I cannot recognize the distinction.   S. Peter tells us himself that CHRIST is the " living
stone " (1 Peter ii. 4) ; Peter was but a stone laid, as were the rest, on
that rock—*prima petra in fundamento posita*, to borrow Card. Pole's
phrase (*De Concil.* quaest ii., in Jenkins).   The foundations of the Church
were laid before there was any privilege of Peter.   And as it was *prior in
tempore*, so also was it *potior in jure*.   Its authority and jurisdiction were
established by our LORD, as Jenkins observes, in the calling and mission of
the Apostles.

Church was built—that is to say, these words were fulfilled in *Peter's own person*, in what he did and what cannot be repeated. He preached on the day of **Pentecost**, and three thousand Jews were added to the Church ; he preached in the house of Cornelius, and Gentiles are admitted to CHRIST's fold. **The two** walls of the temple of GOD, the Jewish **and the** Gentile, thus rest on S. Peter —S. **Peter amongst others.** But that foundation once laid cannot be relaid. **No man can** do Peter's peculiar work again [1] any more than CHRIST's foundation work, **or** the apostles' and **prophets'** foundation **work.** Peter, therefore, may be " the **rock**," but **it by no** means follows that the Popes are [2]; **we** do **not dig up old** foundations every **few years, and put** others in their place. So, again, with the **power of the keys. He opened the door to** Jews, he opened **it to** Gentiles, **but that work is** *done ;* no Pope can repeat it ; **the door** stands **open ;** CHRIST **has the key, and** " **no man can shut it.**" You see, then, that **we may allow** almost everything that the Romans **claim** for S. Peter, **on the strength of** these words, **and** still **be as** far as **ever** from believing that *every Pope* is " the rock," or that *every Pope* has power to **open and** shut the Church's **gate.** I pass, accordingly, to the second of the three texts, namely,

2. S. Luke **xxi. 31** : " Simon, Simon, behold **Satan**

---

[1] " We may as well draw water out of a pumice stone as *power, government,* or *dominion* out of this word *rock*, which hath relation only to solidity, firmness . . . or something of that kind."—Bp. Patrick.

[2] " Of all the Fathers who interpret these passages (S. Matt. xvi. **18**; S. John xxi. **15**) **not** a single one applies them to the Roman bishops as Peter's successors."—Döllinger, *Pope* **and Council,** p. 91.

asked to have *you* (the word is plural : it points to *all* the
Apostles) but I have prayed for *thee* (singular) that thy
faith fail not, and do thou, when thou hast turned again,
stablish thy brethren." "Who does not see here," says
a Roman writer, "the pre-eminence of Peter in the mind
of our LORD." Undoubtedly, but it is a pre-eminence in
danger. The words do speak of special care and special
prayer—and Peter needed both ; he was about to be
tempted, as the others were not, and to fall, as the others
did not. The special prayer was because of the special
peril ; there is absolutely nothing here to import that
S. Peter, let alone his local successor, was to be
appointed Vicar of CHRIST, or even the teacher of the
other Apostles. We may be reminded that he is charged,
after his conversion, to "stablish his brethren." Precisely, because of the sharp lesson which he had learned
as to human frailty and instability. Besides, *that* work
is no more than every Apostle had to do, and was what
every Apostle did. The very same word is used of
S. Paul,[1] of Judas and Silas,[2] and of Timothy,[3] and a
similar charge is given to the "angel of the Church in
Sardis."[4] If stablishing the brethren, consequently, is a
proof of supremacy and infallibility, then S. Peter was
not alone in his glory. No, the more we try to weigh
this Scripture honestly and dispassionately, the less do
we discover in it of any testimony to "the privilege of
Peter." It is nothing of the kind, nor did any one early

---

[1] Rom. i. 11 ; Acts xv. 41 ; xviii. 23.   [2] Acts xv. 32.
[3] 1 Thess. iii. 2.   [4] Rev. iii. 2.

Christian writer regard it as such,[1] and I understand that some Romanists do not think it prudent to rely upon it. They would, in my humble opinion, be well advised if they dropped it altogether. I now turn to the *third* text,

3. S. John xxi. 15-17: " He saith unto him, Feed My lambs. . . He saith unto him, Tend My sheep. . . JESUS saith unto him, Feed My sheep." This, according to Roman writers, was " the occasion when our LORD formally appoints Peter to take His place on earth, and to be to His Apostles and the Church what He Himself was to them during His public ministry."[2] They say that what He only *promised* in S. Matthew's Gospel, He now *bestows*, the supremacy. But we cannot help observing, first, that " feeding " or " tending " the flock of CHRIST is not a duty or a privilege peculiar to S. Peter, any more than confirming the brethren is, for we find S. Paul charging the elders of Ephesus to " feed " or " tend "—the very same word—" the Church of GOD,"[3] and we find S. Peter himself exhorting the elders of the dispersion to tend—again the same word—the flock of GOD which was among them[4]; we observe, in fact, that this is a duty which devolves on *all* the ministers of CHRIST. We shall be told, perhaps, that this charge was given to S. Peter *thrice.* But the obvious answer is,

---

[1] " So far as I know, no one suggested such a meaning, till Pope Agatho pressed the passage into his service about the year 680 "—in " the unsuccessful attempt to shield from public condemnation his heretical predecessor, Honorius."—Bp. G. F Browne, *Modern Papal Claims,* p. 76.

[2] Lyons, *Christianity and Infallibility,* pp. 104-5.

[3] Acts xx. 28.   [4] 1 Peter v. 2.

" Yes, because S. Peter had denied our SAVIOUR thrice."
Many of the Fathers connect this triple commission with
the triple denial.   They do see in the words the rehabili-
tation of S. Peter in his office of *Apostle*[1]—which office
he had compromised by his denials—but they do *not*
discover anything here which " solemnly installed him
as supreme pastor and ruler."[2]   Nor does S. Peter himself appear to have so understood our LORD's words—in
that case he would hardly have been " grieved."   Nor
can I believe that if CHRIST now made S. Peter the
monarch over His Church on earth, He would have
passed on, without another word, to speak on a topic of
comparative insignificance, of the manner of his death,
and still less that He would have openly rebuked His
Vicar's curiosity, when he inquired as to the fate of
S. John—" What is that to thee; follow thou Me."[3]   No,
if ever plain speaking as to the Supremacy was needed,
it was now, and this language was *not* plain ; there was
nothing in these few words to convince the Apostles that
S. Peter was henceforth to be their absolute ruler and
infallible teacher—there was nothing to convince *them*,
and there is nothing to convince *us*.

And these are *all the texts*, apart from those which
show that Simon took the first place among the twelve—

---

[1] " Peter's offence, which was given *to* all, and which corresponded to
the public warning given *before* all, could be properly and fully forgiven
only by a *public* word of reconciliation."—Stier, *in loc.*

[2] Lyons.   " Observe, he does not give him the office of *ruling* but rather
of *confirming* them."—Card. Cajetan, *Comm. in Luc.*, c. xxii., quoted by
Jenkins.

[3] This rebuke must have compromised the new Vicar from the first in the
eyes of his fellow Apostles and of the Church.

the first in a band of brothers and equals, a leader, but not a ruler; I find nothing in the position which he sustains which cannot be accounted for by his age and force of character and fidelity—these are all the texts which the Romanists can allege out of the four Gospels. And I submit to you and to them—I respectfully and affectionately submit to them—that such evidence is altogether insufficient. If this is all they can show from our LORD's lips to prove that He constituted Simon Peter His Vicar, then I can only say that it is not proven. The evidence, such as it is, is altogether inadequate and inconclusive.

Does, then, the rest of the New Testament afford any firmer and broader foundation on which to rest these stupendous claims? Does it show, for example, that S. Peter *enjoyed* this dignity? That is a question the consideration of which I must defer till next Sunday evening. I shall then, GOD willing, hope to put before you the teaching of the *Epistles* and the *Acts of the Apostles*, and I shall hope to show that while the Gospels do not prove Papal supremacy, the Epistles *dis*prove it. Indeed, there are some passages in the *Gospels* which prove clearly that, up to the night of the betrayal at any rate, the Apostles never recognized any supremacy or promise of supremacy to S. Peter. On two occasions,[1] one of which was on that last sad night, there was strife and disputation amongst them as to " which should be accounted the greatest." But they *could not* have disputed thus had they believed what Romanists do, that the supremacy

[1] S. Matt. xviii. 1 ; S. Luke xxii. 24.

Q

over the rest was already promised to S. Peter. On another occasion [1] James and John ask that they may sit, one on CHRIST's right hand and the other on His left, in His Kingdom. But they *could* not have asked this had they known that the chief place in that Kingdom was already given away.[2] These are difficulties, however, which I merely mention in passing. My main contention, so far, is that there is nothing, absolutely nothing, *in the Gospels* to prove the Roman claims. That there is nothing in the remaining writings still remains to be shown.

And if I should succeed in proving that the Acts and Epistles know as little of "the privilege of Peter" as the Gospels do, then the entire Roman claim as to the Papacy falls to the ground. If it cannot be proved that *S. Peter* was supreme, it cannot be pretended that the Popes are.[3] There is really no need to debate the second question—whether S. Peter was Bishop of Rome; or the third—whether the present Bishop of Rome has succeeded to his powers, if it cannot be shown—and it cannot—that S. Peter had supreme authority in the Church of his day.

All the same, I think it well to discuss them. I think it well, because they are often put forward in a very specious way, and they may possibly have troubled your minds. I shall now, therefore, assume, for the sake of argument, that you are still doubtful as to this first proposition. Or rather,

---

[1] S. Matt. xx. 21.   [2] Salmon, p. 334.

[3] " The principality of Peter is the real and only source of the dignity of the Roman Church."—Archbp. Kenrick, *The Primacy of the Apostolic See*, p. 95.

let me assume that it is clearly proven **that S. Peter** *was* the **head of the** visible Church and **the** Vicar of Christ in **his day.** Still, I am as far as ever from submitting to the Pope, for, in the second place,

II. We have **no** historical proof—this is **a matter of** history rather than of doctrine—that S. Peter was Bishop of Rome **or** founder **of** the Roman Church. There **is** certainly **no such** proof in the **Bible,** though, **as that** contains **a** history of the early Church, an Epistle to the **Roman** Church, and an Epistle of **S.** Peter, we might fairly have expected to find some there. But whilst there **is no** *proof,* there **is** what looks **very** much like *disproof.* For the New Testament shows us pretty clearly either that **S. Peter was not bishop, or that he was nearly** always non-resident at **his see till just** before his **death.**

Roman Catholics **affirm that S.** Peter **became** bishop **of Rome in the year 42, and was** bishop **for** 25 years, 7 months, **and 8 days. As to** which we observe, **first, that it is** extremely doubtful whether there *was* **any** organized " church " at Rome—anything more, **I mean,** than congregations like that in the house of Prisca **and** Aquila, not only in A.D. 42, but **even** in the year **58,** when the Epistle to the Romans was penned. **It is** noticeable that S. **Paul** does **not** speak **therein of any** "*church* at Rome," **as** he does of the " church at Corinth," or the " churches of Galatia." Anyhow, **no one** can prove, men can only *assume,* **that** there **was** then a **church at** Rome. Still less can they prove **that** at that **time, or,** indeed, at **a** much later **date,** there **were any** diocesan bishops. **There were no** *bishops* because there were the *Apostles*—" the episcopate then slept in the apostolate"; moreover, the office of local bishop is hardly compatible with that of an Apostle—the one is stationary, the other is itinerant.[1] When our Roman brethren say, consequently, that S. Peter became bishop of Rome in A.D. 42, we may remind them that they cannot prove that either church or bishop then existed. Suppose we allow, however, that there *was* a church, and that Peter was its bishop. Then he was not resident some two years later, for 44 is set down as the year when Herod sought to slay him, and he was then in Jerusalem. Nor was he resident about A.D. 51, for that is, roughly speaking, the date of the Council of Jerusalem, which Peter attended. Nor about the year 52, for then all Jews had to depart from Rome; moreover, it was about this time that S. Paul " withstood him to the face " at Antioch. Nor was he resident, if indeed he had ever been at Rome at all, by the year 58, for that, as already observed, is the date of the Epistle to the Romans, which Epistle affords us the strongest reasons for believing that, up to this moment, S. Peter had never set foot in the eternal city. For, observe, S. Paul says he " longs to see them that he may impart unto them *some spiritual gift.*" But what *could* he give them, what could he *do* for them, that Peter, the Prince of the Apostles had not done already, if he was their bishop ? Nay, what does S. Paul mean by writing a letter to the Romans—it was

---

[1] " A locally established supremacy in any single apostle was inconsistent with the missionary character of the trust (" Go ye into all the world," etc.), and would render its execution impossible."—Jenkins, p. 31.

a piece of presumption in him, if they had as their bishop the supreme head of the Church ? You remember how **careful S. Paul was, as** he **tells us in** this very Epistle, " not to build on another man's foundation ; " **is** it likely, then, that he would address this long letter and give these manifold instructions to a church over which S. Peter presided, **and** for which S. Peter alone was responsible ? Above all, is it credible that he could have written this long letter—the longest **of** all the Epistles— to a church **over** which S. Peter had presided for **sixteen years,** or, **for the matter of** that for **sixteen** months, **and** *never have* **made** *the faintest reference to* **him** or to his labours ? **To me it is absolutely incredible.** I cannot believe that S. Paul could mention so many names as he does, and give so many directions, **and** yet consistently ignore the bishop, if that bishop **were S. Peter.** I know what Roman Catholics say, namely, that **S. Peter's** name **is** suppressed **because** it might have involved him in danger to mention it, it might have told adversaries where to look for him ; but **it is an** excuse hardly worthy of serious notice. For, first, this letter **was not** addressed to adversaries, nor was it likely to fall into their hands ; it was addressed to Christians. Besides, we may be quite sure that if Peter *was* bishop, the fact must have **been so** well known that the mere mention of " Simeon " or " Cephas " **in a letter** could have made no difference. **In** addition **to** which **I** must remind you that **it** was quite possible to refer to S. Peter and to recognize his work without any mention whatsoever **of his** *name.* And lastly, S. Paul has no hesitation in

speaking about the saints of Cæsar's household; he has
no fear of injuring them; why, then, should he fear to
refer to the bishop of these saints ?   I repeat, therefore,
that this Epistle is practically decisive as to any episcopate
of S. Peter up to the year 58.   But as little was he
resident in Rome in the years 61, 62, for that is the time
of S. Paul's first imprisonment, and it is inconceivable
that, had S. Peter then been there, the historian would
not have mentioned it.   What he does mention is that
S. Paul addressed the Roman Jews as men who had
never heard the gospel before,[1] which they must have
done had Peter, the Apostle of the Circumcision, been
bishop.   Nor was he at his post, apparently, in 63, for
that is about the date of S. Peter's first Epistle, and
that Epistle is dated from " Babylon."   Roman Catholics
will tell you, no doubt, that this is a mystical name for
Rome, and so some of the fathers taught, but it is a
settled rule of interpretation to take a word—and especially an *address*—literally when the literal interpretation
will stand.   And here it *will* stand : we know that there
was at this time a large colony of Jews at Babylon on
the Euphrates—a " great multitude," Josephus says—
and we also know that Peter was the Apostle of the
Circumcision.   So that he was *then* far from Rome.
And he was still non-resident about 67 or 68, for that is
the time when S. Paul wrote his *second* Epistle to
Timothy, and he wrote from Rome where, as he tells us,
" only Luke was with him."   If, therefore, Peter became
Bishop of Rome, as they pretend, in the second year of

---

[1] Acts xxviii. 20-22.

Claudius, he was constantly away from his see till close upon his death, for 68 is the date of Nero's death, and S. Peter is supposed to have been put to death by Nero: he was away, therefore, almost to the last. Not only so, but he "never wrote a letter to his Church while he *was* away, or if he did, they did not think it worth preserving."[1]

There is nothing, therefore, in the New Testament to show that S. Peter was Bishop of Rome, whilst there is much that looks the other way. Is there any proof—*proof* as distinguished from *conjecture*—from other sources? Again I say that we have something like disproof. I will mention two facts—I have no time for more. First, no single writer, for a century after his supposed martyrdom, refers to any residence of S. Peter in Rome, neither Clement, Bishop of Rome, nor Ignatius, S. Peter's successor at Antioch, nor Justin Martyr, who lived at Rome for some years. The first mention of it is found in the Clementine Homilies, a fictitious work of the latter part of the second century. Secondly, Irenæus, about the year 180, gives us a list, the earliest extant list, of the Bishops of Rome, and in that list S. Peter's name does not appear. These are his words: "The blessed Apostles"—*i.e.*, S. Peter and S. Paul, S. Paul as much as S. Peter—"having founded and built the Church, committed the episcopal office to Linus. To him succeeded Anencletus. After him Clement suc-

---

[1] Salmon, *Infallibility*, p. 350. *The Times*, of June 30th, 1896, commenting on the Encyclical *De Unitate*, draws attention to the "remarkable absence of evidence on the most critical point of all—S. Peter's alleged connexion with the Roman see."

ceeded in the *third place* from the Apostles." But if so, where does Peter's Episcopate come in ? It comes in nowhere; no place is found for it. I now turn for one moment to the last proposition. I say that

III. Even if S. Peter was supreme in the early Church, and was also Bishop of Rome, we have so far no proof that he could or did transmit his supremacy to the Popes. This may be dismissed in a sentence. Of this proposition we have no proofs—proofs as distinguished from *assertions—except perchance those which have been proved to be forged.* It is a sad thing to have to say of any Christian doctrine, but I only borrow the words of a great Roman Catholic, a priest of the Oratory, when I say that this question of Papal Supremacy and Infallibility is one which is " completely gangrened with fraud."[1] I do not accuse Roman Catholics of conniving at these frauds, but the fact remains—that the power of the Popes has been cemented, has been in part created, by a tissue of audacious forgeries. This, then, is why we cannot submit to the Pope. He has not proven, he cannot prove, any one of the propositions on which his prodigious claims are based. If he could not prove *one*

---

[1] Fr. B—— reminds me that Père Gratry recanted these words shortly before his death. I was well aware of it, but such recantation does not invalidate his testimony. I can quite believe, with Canon Bright, that "his submission may have been obtained under threat of refusal of sacraments." Fr. B—— is indignant at such a suggestion, but I venture to remind him of the recent funeral of Grignani, one of the few Italian priests who protested against the dogma of the Immaculate Conception, and renewed his protest in his will. "He was denied Church burial, and . . . a censure was pronounced on those who carried the coffin to the grave with a cross in front."—*The Guardian*, June 17th, 1896.

of them—one of the three—that would be fatal. He cannot prove *any one* of the three.

And so we conclude that the Papacy is not "from Heaven." More than that, we can see that it is "of men." We can trace the gradual rise of the Papal pretensions; we can mark their growth in the page of history. The see of Rome has come to be what it is mainly because the city of Rome was what it was. It was the seat of empire, the metropolis of the civilized world; who can wonder if its "political consequence during the first four centuries . . . gave to its bishop the primacy amongst all bishops."[1] That primacy "grew naturally out of the precedence accorded to the bishop of the first city of the empire."[2] No doubt other causes helped, such as the steadfast orthodoxy of the Roman Church, its great liberality, and the like, but all these causes were human. Imperial Rome was the centre of the world; what wonder if Papal Rome became the centre of Christendom. "The fathers"—so it was laid down at the Council of Chalcedon in 451, and with this I conclude for the present—"properly gave privileges to the throne of old Rome *because it was the imperial city.*" Precisely, it was the imperial city! Papal supremacy is is not from Heaven but of men; it is a plant which our "heavenly FATHER hath not planted."

[1] Curteis, *Dissent and the Church of England*, p. 162. [2] Salmon, p. 370.

THE PETRINE CLAIMS IN THE LIGHT OF THE PAULINE POSITION.

1 KINGS VII. 21.

"And he set up the pillars at the porch of the temple; and he set up the right pillar and called the name thereof Jachin; and he set up the left pillar and called the name thereof Boaz."

N Sunday last I endeavoured to show, and I believe I *did* show, that Papal Supremacy is a plant of human growth; that this gigantic institution of the Papacy, which dominates a great part of Christendom,[1] is not "from heaven," but is "of men." I submitted to you that, so far, no sufficient evidence has been produced to establish any *one* of the three propositions on which the Roman claims rest. They cannot prove—or, let me say, they *have* not proven so far—first, that Simon Peter was invested by our LORD with any supremacy over the other Apostles and the early Church. Still less have they proven, or can they prove with the materials now in their possession, that he was founder or first bishop of the Church at Rome.

[1] It may be as well to remark here, as Roman Catholics are apt to identify themselves with Christendom, that there are at the present moment more baptized Christians who reject than who allow the Papal claims.

And least of all can they prove, lastly, that if he was supreme in his day, and bishop of Rome in his day, his powers and privileges have descended to his successors in the see down to the present day.

And this argument, I should like to point out, is complete in itself. It is quite true that we have not yet examined the Acts of the Apostles or the Epistles—we are to examine them to-night. Still, neither the Acts nor the Epistles can add to or alter the "three texts." The Roman claim is that our LORD Himself *promised* the supremacy to Simon Peter in the words recorded in S. Matt. xvi., "Thou art Peter," etc., and *invested* him with it in the words of S. John xxi., "Feed My sheep." Well, we say that we have read these texts and studied and weighed them no less than Roman Catholics have, and that we cannot persuade ourselves that there is any *promise* of ecclesiastical principality in the first, or any *bestowal* of it in the second. We cannot bring ourselves to believe that if our Sacred LORD had intended to instal one man in His place, to wield his authority and be to the Church what HE had been to it, He would have said no more than this. Nor can anything that we find in the Epistles or elsewhere shake this conviction. It is not as if the Acts or Epistles contained *additional* words of our CHRIST; no, all they can do is to illustrate, to throw light on "the three texts." They may show, for example, that S. Peter *exercised* a supremacy in the early Church; they may show that he was *recognized* as CHRIST's Vicar, in which case, no doubt, they would immensely strengthen the Romanist interpretation; they

may also show on the other hand that they contain no
traces whatever of any supremacy on his part, in which
case they will strenuously confirm our view, but they
can do no more.   The premier argument of last Sunday
night—that we have no sort of proof in the Gospels of
any principality of Peter conferred by CHRIST—was
complete in itself.   I only appeal to the Acts and to the
Epistles to clench that argument, to prove to you that
we have not misinterpreted our SAVIOUR's words, and
that our Roman brethren must have done so.

Now, the testimony of the Acts, which is a brief
history of the early Church, and of the Epistles, which
are so many letters to the local churches or to the officers
of churches, may be conveniently arranged under the
three following heads :

First, there is nothing in these writings to show that
S. Peter *acted* as CHRIST's Vicar, or was *recognized* as
such by the infant Church.

Secondly, there are passages which prove that he was
not CHRIST's Vicar, or—what is the same thing—passages
which prove that, if he *was* CHRIST's Vicar, he and others
were quite unconscious of it, and acted accordingly.

Thirdly, that if he *was* CHRIST's Vicar, if he is to be
regarded as such on the strength of the position which
he occupies in these writings, then our LORD must have
appointed *two Vicars,* for the position assigned in Holy
Scripture to S. Paul is in no wise inferior to that occupied
by S. Peter.   These are the three propositions which I
shall hope to establish to-night.

I.   I begin with the first.   I have undertaken to prove

that S. Peter is nowhere recognized in the Acts or the Epistles as supreme over the early Church, and as standing to it in the place of our Redeemer. The Romanists say that there *is* such recognition.[1] They point us, for example, to the election of Matthias, to the day of Pentecost, to the council of Jerusalem, to S. Paul's visit to S. Peter, and the like. They say that on these occasions S. Peter acted as Pope, or was recognized as such. Let us see whether this is so. Let us begin with the appointment of Matthias, of which we read in Acts i. 15-26.

Now what did the Vicar of CHRIST do on this occasion? CHRIST appointed the Apostles Himself; for one, he appointed Judas Iscariot. But S. Peter *did not appoint the successor to Judas;* he did not even designate the *two* men out of whom "one must be chosen." All that he did was to *address* the assembled disciples on the question —somebody must do it, and who so likely as "Simon Peter, the first." No doubt this shows a certain primacy, but it does not point to any supremacy; he did nothing more than any other Apostle might have done. If he had *designated* the man himself, as our LORD did, it would have been quite another thing[2]—but he does not; he

---

[1] "It appears from the first twelve chapters of the Acts that S. Peter exercised a supremacy over the other Apostles and over the whole Church."— Di Bruno, *Catholic Belief*, p. 110. But Romanists are much divided as to the relations of S. Peter to the other apostles. See Gore, p. 78. Fr. B—— claims for each of them "the right and power of universal jurisdiction." The question is, What were their relations to *Peter*—not to the Church? Were they *over* him, *equal* with him, or *under* him? Of course they were *under him*, in the belief of every Roman Catholic.

[2] Chrysostom mentions this as one possible method of making the appointment. See Gore, *Rom. Catholic Claims*, p. 88, Note.

merely refers the appointment to the Church and to GOD.
We are told that CHRIST speaks in Peter, and yet Peter
must needs have recourse to the lot. Besides, why this
haste (we may ask) to secure an Apostle at all, if the
Church was really governed by one man? The very
anxiety they betray to make up the number of the twelve
shows that the Church was to be under the regimen of
the twelve. And now, as to the day of Pentecost. Well,
it is indisputable that Peter stood up as the spokesman
of the band—he " stood up *with the eleven*"—but there is
nothing to show that he was anything more—more than
GOD's instrument among the Apostles for admitting believers to the Church. And here let me remark in passing
that, whilst a sharp line of distinction is ever drawn
between the Apostles and the rest—" of the rest durst
no man join himself to *them* "—no such distinction is
drawn between the Apostles and S. Peter. They are all
apparently on the same level; S. Peter is one of them,
and no more. It was "in the *apostles'* doctrine and
fellowship "—not *S. Peter's*—that the first Christians
continued so steadfastly[1]; it was the *apostles* that
" wrought signs and wonders among the people "[2]; it
was the *apostles* gave witness of the resurrection[3]; it was
the *apostles* ordained the seven " deacons "[4]; it is the
apostles that always appear as the rulers and teachers of
the Church. I pass on to the council of Jerusalem—for
brevity's sake (and *only* for brevity's sake) I omit some
passages of minor importance. A Roman Catholic
writer says that this council "is perhaps the most con-

[1] Acts ii. 42.   [2] Chap. v. 12.   [3] Chap. iv. 33.   [4] Chap. vi. 6.

vincing proof in the Scriptural evidence of the exercise
of the Primacy."[1]   I hope I may be allowed to say that
if this is their strongest point, no Protestant need despair.
For observe, in the first place, Paul and Barnabas were
not sent to Jerusalem to consult S. Peter ; they were sent
" to the apostles and elders."[2]   But why to *them*, if both
supremacy and infallibility—in matters of faith and morals
—resided with S. Peter ?   How is it, again, that nothing
is said here about the head of the Church, if head (under
Christ) S. Peter was ?   Now was the time, if ever, to
insist upon his principality.   But no ; the " apostles and
elders " are mentioned four or five times to his once.   We
are reminded, however, that " after there had been much
disputing, Peter rose up," and we are asked, " Why is it
said that *he* rose up, rather than the others ? "   The
answer is, " Because he *did* rise up then, and the others
rose up later ; the historian simply relates what actually
happened."   It is affirmed, too, that S. Peter settled the
question there and then, because, after he had spoken,
" the multitude kept silence."[3]   But why did they keep
silence ?   It was partly because his words gave food for
reflection, and partly to " *hearken unto Paul and Barnabas*
rehearsing what God had wrought among the Gentiles
by them," which is in itself a proof that Peter's pro-
nouncement was *not* regarded as final and conclusive.

---

[1] Lyons, p. 117.

[2] Acts xv. 2.   "Though every controversy and every question in the
early Church might have been terminated in a moment by a simple appeal
to the judgment of S. Peter, this obvious remedy was never resorted to."—
Jenkins, *Privilege*, p. 16.

[3] Verse 12.

Besides, if Peter had settled it, why did James interpose
with further arguments ? No, it was James settled it,
rather than Peter. He spoke last, and his words are,
" My judgment is." But what business has *he* to pronounce any judgment at all, or to have any opinion at
all, after CHRIST's Vicar has decided the question authori-
tatively, after CHRIST has spoken by Peter ?[1] Why,
again, does the decree proceed from " the apostles and
elders," without any mention of S. Peter, if the latter had,
and the former had not, " the authority of the true GOD
upon the earth "? It seems to us, therefore, that this
council is decisive *against* the Papal claim. If Peter was
Pope, both apostles and elders appear to have been
profoundly unaware of it. I turn in the last place to
S. Paul's visit to Peter, recorded in Gal. i. " After
three years I went up to *visit*"—or, as the Margin explains
it, " to *make the acquaintance* of Cephas." But a *visit*
proves nothing. Is it surprising that S. Paul wanted to
know Peter ?[2] Nay, the surprising thing is that, if Peter
was Pope, was CHRIST's own *substitute*, S. Paul should
have waited *three years* before going to see him, and then
should have learnt nothing from him, as he says was the
case.[3] No, I cannot find any proof of Petrine supremacy,
cannot find any instance of its exercise, either in the

---

[1] Cyril of Alexandria (*Ad Nest.* Ep. iii. 5)—in Gore, p. 87—speaks
of Peter and James as " of equal honour " as apostles and disciples.

[2] S. Chrysostom (*in Gal.* i. 18), who says that S. Paul went up to see
Peter, on account of the latter's primacy, adds, " Not as needing anything
of him or of his voice, but as *being his equal in honour.*"—Quoted by Gore.
Rom. Cath. Claims, p. 88.

[3] Chap. ii. 6.

Acts or the Epistles. I have tried to be fair, to follow the truth whithersoever it leads me, but I cannot find a single passage in these writings which proves that S. Peter was the first of the Popes. The passages alleged to prove it are singularly inconclusive.

II. But that is not all. I find a considerable number which show that he was *not accepted*, and did not *act* as Pope. I come now to my second proposition, which is, that the Acts and the Epistles furnish us with conclusive *disproof* of the Roman claim; they show plainly that if S. Peter was CHRIST'S Vicar, he and others were entirely unaware of it.

I say, first, that if Peter was CHRIST'S Vicar, and the infallible head of the visible Church, *the other Apostles* were unaware of it. Not merely because they act and speak as if they were his equals; not merely because they nowhere recognize any distinction between him and them, but because they actually *dispatch him on a mission.* "When the apostles . . . heard that Samaria had received the word of GOD, they *sent unto them* Peter and John."[1] Roman Catholics say that Peter was greater than all the other Apostles put together, but our LORD flatly contradicts them—"Neither," He says, "is he that is sent greater than he that sent him." I respectfully commend this difficulty to candid Romanists; I venture to think that they cannot get over it. Certainly, so far as my reading extends, they have not done so hitherto. I should also like to ask them whether the bishops or even the cardinals ever send the Pope on any mission nowa-

[1] Chap. viii. 14.

R

days; can you imagine any conclave dispatching the " Holy Father" to Samaria or anywhere else? They would soon be told that they did not know their proper place, if they suggested it. Are we to understand, then, that the *Apostles* did not know *their* proper place when they " sent Peter "? They certainly did not know that he was Christ's Vicar, and " held the place of the true God upon earth."

Nor, in the second place, did the Christians of the circumcision know it, for we are told in Acts xi. that they "*contended* with Peter." But they *could* not have contended with him had they believed, as the Romans do, that he held the place of the Redeemer—fancy any Romanist contending with the Pope, and on such a fundamental question, too, as circumcision !

Not only so, but I observe, thirdly, that S. Peter himself did not know that he was Pope, for observe ! he did not answer these objectors by pleading his supremacy and infallibility : on the contrary, he stands humbly on his defence ; he "rehearses the matter from the begining," as any ordinary person would do ; he pleads a *special* revelation. Here is a second difficulty for our Roman fellow-Christians to solve. Shall I tell you how some of them have solved it ? They have said that this must have been some other Peter !

Fourthly, S. James did not know, as we have just seen.

Finally, S. Paul did not know. Had he known that Peter was our Lord's substitute, surely he would have said so somewhere in one or other of his many Epistles. He is constantly talking about the Church, and Church order, and the Church's Head, yet he never mentions any head but CHRIST, never drops the slightest hint that that Church had a visible head in the person of Peter. Nor does Peter himself, by the way, in his epistle, say anything about his own headship. He calls himself an " apostle " and an " elder,"[1] but says not one word about being CHRIST's Vicar. Perhaps you say that it was modesty, it was profound humility on his part. But the Pope has no such humility. *He* never hesitates to assert his position and to magnify his office. Nor can I blame him for so doing. If he is what he professes himself to be, it is his bounden duty to say so; it is no charity to us to keep it back. No, I do not blame *him*, but I must blame S. Peter and all the sacred writers, in that, if he was Pope, and CHRIST spoke in him, they have not plainly said so. Their silence may cost many of us dear; it may cost us our souls, for partly on the strength of that silence we are resisting the Pope. But let us return to S. Paul. I repeat that he cannot have known that our LORD had invested S. Peter with supreme authority over his Church, or, writing as he does about the Church, he would have said so. As it is, he says something incompatible with this. On two occasions he speaks of the Church's hierarchy; and what are his words? " GOD hath set in the Church, first apostles, secondly prophets, thirdly teachers."[2] But according to Roman Catholics, this must be all wrong : he should have said, " first a Pope, secondly apostles, thirdly prophets, fourthly teachers." I see no escape from this con-

[1] 1 Peter i. 1; v. 1.   [2] 1 Cor. xii. 28; Eph. iv. 11.

clusion : if they are right, then S. Paul was wrong ; he
was either very ignorant or very uncharitable. But that
is not all.   If he nowhere describes S. Peter as Pope, he
is not silent as to his position. According to him, S.
Peter was reputed to be a pillar.   Yes, but only as James
and John were " pillars " [1] ; he allows of no difference of
rank ; he puts the three on the same level. Nay, he
mentions S. James *first* ; he puts Cephas *second* [2] ; he
could not have done this had he known that Cephas held
the place of the Redeemer.   Again I say, if the Romans
are right, S. Paul was wrong, and his writings are not
to be trusted ; he is misleading us.   But I have something more to say to you.   So little did S. Paul know
that Peter was CHRIST's Vicar, that he " withstood him
to the face " [3] ; he accused him of shuffling and dissimu-
lation.   Peter "stood condemned" already by the Church
at Antioch ; he was publicly blamed.   S. Paul administers
to him a public rebuke—and why ? Because he "walked
not uprightly"—mark the words—" according to the
truth of the gospel." [4]   So that, if Roman Catholics are
right, the head of the Church was " blamed " by the
Church, and the infallible teacher was resisted to his
face, was openly rebuked by a subordinate, and that for
compromising " the truth of the gospel," and misleading

[1] Gal. ii. 9.   It is significant, as Jenkins observes, that S. Paul does not
say, as a Romanist would do, " When Peter the rock perceived." etc., but
" When James, Cephas and John who were reputed to be pillars, perceived," etc.

[2] Some Romanists have laboured hard to have these positions reversed.
But the MSS. defy their efforts.

[3] Gal. ii. 11.   [4] Verse 14.

the Church.[1] I say, then, that S. Paul did not, could not, know of S. Peter's supremacy. So that we who do not recognize that supremacy are in good company; our ignorance or our obstinacy, whichever it is, was shared by the Apostles, shared by the first Christians, shared by S. Paul, shared by S. James, shared by S. Peter himself.

III. I now come to my last proposition. I affirm, thirdly, that if I am to recognize S. Peter as Vicar of CHRIST because of the position which he occupies in the Acts and the Epistles, then I must recognize *two* Vicars of CHRIST, for S. Paul, from the time he began his missionary work, is in no respect inferior to S. Peter.

And in proof of this position it should almost suffice to cite S. Paul's own words. He tells us, not once but twice,[2] that "in nothing was he behind the very chiefest apostles" — "not a whit behind those pre-eminent apostles."[3] But he was behind S. Peter in almost every respect, if the Papal claims are well founded. S. Peter was then head of the Church; he was under the head; S. Peter stood in the place of the Redeemer; S. Paul occupied a much humbler position. S. Peter

---

1 " S. Paul's resistance was nothing less than an appeal against Peter to the whole Church, which if Peter had resisted, he would have been condemned by the Church." **Gerson,** quoted by Jenkins, who asks, " Why was not Peter's privilege asserted then? Because it did not exist. No other answer is possible."

2 2 Cor. xi. 5; xii. 11.

3 I give both renderings, that of the Revised Version in the text and that in the margin. The Revisers evidently preferred the former, according to which S. Paul asserted his equality with the foremost of the twelve Apostles. Romanists will no doubt insist on the latter, according to which he is referring to false apostles.

was infallible when he spoke *ex cathedra* on faith and morals; S. Paul had no such prerogative. Romanists say—their creed compels them to say—that S. Paul in *many* things came behind the first of the Apostles. S. Paul says himself, if our Revised Version gives the true meaning of his words, that he came behind in nothing. Obviously they cannot both be right, for they flatly contradict one another.

I do not lay any great stress on this statement, however, because its meaning is disputed. But I still believe that S. Paul " was in nothing behind " S. Peter, because of the relative proportions which these two Apostles assume in the sacred writings. I submit to you that in the pages of S. Luke—in the Acts—and in the Epistles, S. Paul is every whit as lofty and august and influential a personage as is S. Peter. I contend that if the latter unmistakably "acts the Pope" (as a Roman writer[1] says he does) in the first days of the Church, the former does the same in its later days. In other words, that we have either *no* Vicar of CHRIST or we have *two* Vicars. I shall aim at showing that there was *no* Pope in the early Church, but two colossal "*pillars*," S. Peter and S. Paul, each, like *Jachin* and *Boaz*, the great columns which stood before Solomon's temple, each the counterpart of the other, similar in height, in girth, in materials, in structure, and in dignity.

1. Let us begin with their *Names*. And this because a Roman controversialist[1] asks us to observe that S. Peter's name occurs fifty-three times in the first twelve chapters,

[1] Lyons.

whilst the names of all the rest put together only occur twenty-three times. He has omitted to notice, but you will not omit to notice, that S. Paul's name is found some seventy-five times in the next nine chapters, whilst there are only two mentions of S. Peter, two of S. James, and none of the rest. So that if such numbers are to decide the question of supremacy, the decision must be in favour of S. Paul. I may also remark in passing that " Paul," no less than " Peter," was a new name.

2. I pass on to their respective *Miracles*—for miracles are " the signs of an Apostle."[1] Here, again, I find S. Paul at least the equal of S. Peter. Am I reminded that the latter healed the impotent man at the gate of the temple ? the former healed a similar impotent man at Lystra—in each case a man lame from his birth. Am I told that S. Peter raised Dorcas to life ? in the same way S. Paul raised Eutychus. Is it surmised that S. Peter had *extraordinary* powers because they brought the sick into the streets that his shadow, as he passed by, might overshadow some [one] of them ?[2] it is expressly *stated* that " GOD wrought *special* miracles by the hands of Paul," insomuch that handkerchiefs or aprons were carried from his body to the sick, and they were healed.[3] Again I say, if there is any difference between the two it is in favour of S. Paul, who says he will not dare to speak of the signs and wonders which GOD wrought by him. Let us turn to their

3. *Revelations*—I mean the revelations made to them. S. Paul appeals to these to establish his position, so we

---

[1] 2 Cor. xii. 12.   [2] Acts v. 15.   [3] Acts xix. 11, 12.

may do the same. We have it on the testimony of our
LORD[1] that Simon Peter was not taught his confession
of CHRIST's divinity by "flesh and blood," but by the
FATHER. But S. Paul was taught *his* gospel in the
same way. He, too, " conferred not with flesh and
blood."[2] The GOD Who separated him, from his
mother's womb, "revealed" His SON in him. His
message was given him "by revelation of JESUS
CHRIST."[3] Even his account of the Holy Communion
he had from the LORD.[4] Once again, we find that
Peter has no advantage over Paul; if anything, it is
the other way. For we never read that S. Peter received such " abundance," " such exceeding greatness,"
of revelations that he must needs have a thorn in the
flesh to buffet him, lest he should be exalted over-
much[5]; we never read that *he* was "caught up into
Paradise, and heard unspeakable words which it is not
lawful for a man to utter."[6] In the matter of *revelations*,
S. Paul is at least S. Peter's equal. And the same may
be said of their spheres of work and

4. *Labours.* Was S. Peter the Apostle of the circumcision ? S. Paul was every whit as much the Apostle
of the uncircumcision. Was the former intrusted by
GOD with the gospel of the circumcision ? the same GOD,
as he tells us himself, wrought in the latter unto the
Gentiles. S. Paul speaks of himself here as on a footing
of perfect equality[7] with Peter. If they were *not* equal;

---

[1] S. Matt. xvi. 17.   [2] Gal. i. 16.   [3] Ver. 12.   [4] 1 Cor. xi. 23.

[5] 2 Cor. xii. 7.   [6] 2 Cor. xii. 4.

[7] " There is no sort of dependence of S. Paul on S. Peter, which these
words do not exclude."—Gore, p. 84.

if Peter was the substitute of CHRIST, and Paul an altogether inferior servant, then he has used most misleading language. The Vicar, he says, has the smaller whilst he has the larger half of the vineyard. But from the *departments* let us turn to the *work done.* Am I told that Peter "went throughout all parts" of Palestine?[1] I am told of S. Paul's travels in two continents, and he tells me himself that "in labours" he was "more abundant" than other ministers of CHRIST. Is S. Peter charged with the oversight of the "elect of the dispersion"?[2] on S. Paul fell "the care of *all* the churches"[3]; yes, and he ordained customs in *all* the churches.[4] And here I will ask you to observe that, in so doing, S. Paul took a great deal too much upon himself and greatly exaggerated his own importance and exceeded his powers, if S. Peter all the time was universal Pastor. In that case S. Peter had "the care of all the churches," and none else. In that case S. Paul was building on another man's foundation and intruding into another man's province. It is of no use to protest, as he does,[5] that he never did this; if Peter was charged by CHRIST with "the care of all the churches," what can S. Paul mean by taking that care on *his* shoulders, and "ordaining customs" in Peter's place? And, finally, I submit that no impartial person can read his New Testament without seeing that, as far as the record goes, the Apostle of the Gentiles accomplished quite as much for the extension of CHRIST's Kingdom as did the Apostle of

[1] Acts ix. 32.   [2] 1 Peter i. 1.   [3] 2 Cor. xi. 28.
[4] 1 Cor. vii. 17.   [5] Rom. xv. 20.

the circumcision. Of S. Peter's labours very little is
said—very little about his sufferings and persecutions,
his stripes and imprisonments; it is of S. Paul that
these things are recorded, and it is S. Paul who tells us
that "from Jerusalem and round about, even unto
Illyricum," he has "fully preached the gospel of
CHRIST."

5. But a principal part of the work of an Apostle was
his *Teaching*. We are told that S. Peter was the supreme
and (within certain limits) infallible teacher of the
Church. But who, I must ask, has taught the Church
most? who teaches it most at the present day, S. Peter
or S. Paul? Well, here is one fact for your consideration—that S. Peter wrote one, or at the most two,
Epistles, as against thirteen or fourteen written by
S. Paul. It is the Pope writes all the Encyclicals *now*,
but it was not S. Peter who wrote them then: his con-
tribution to the New Testament is just one twelfth part
of S. Paul's. And these Epistles still teach the Church—
that is why we read them Sunday by Sunday, but S. Paul's
voice speaks to us and instructs us much oftener than
S. Peter's. Why, it was S. Paul who even wrote the
Epistle to the *Romans*, the Church over which, according
to Roman Catholics, S. Peter had for sixteen years presided as bishop! If, therefore, S. Peter enjoyed the
dignity of supreme teacher, it was S. Paul did most of
the *work*. And I think it not unworthy of notice that
whilst S. Paul's Epistles are mentioned in the second
Epistle of Peter with commendation, S. Paul mentions
S. Peter in one of *his* Epistles to condemn his conduct.

I should not think this of any consequence but for the extraordinary and overpowering claims which have been made by the Romanists for S. Peter and his so-called successors.

And I might pursue this comparison at much greater length, were it necessary or profitable so to do. I might show that, according to ancient writers, they were not only equal in their lives, but in their death they were not divided. Irenæus, for example, as I reminded you last week, ascribes to them an *equal share* in the founding and organizing of the church at Rome—he is often cited by disingenuous Romanists (and I must sorrowfully include Cardinal Wiseman and Fr. Bernard Vaughan under this category)[1] to prove that Peter was bishop of Rome, whereas he represents Paul just as much or just as little bishop as Peter. Dionysius of Corinth, again,

---

[1] Cardinal Wiseman, *Lectures on the Catholic Church*, Vol. 1, p. 278 (quoted in Salmon's *Infallibility of the Church*, p. 353) says, "I presume it will not be necessary to enter into any argument to show that S. Peter was the first Bishop of Rome [N.B. 'A controversialist who has ventured on an assertion which, when challenged, he finds himself unable to prove, has no better resource than to protest loudly that the thing is too evident to need any proof.'—Salmon.] . . . 'To S. Peter,' as Irenæus observes, 'succeeded Linus, to Linus Anacletus, then in the third place Clement.'" But why "to S. Peter"? That is precisely the point at issue. Irenæus says "the Apostles"; he does not say S. Peter. What he says of S. Peter, the same he says of S. Paul. Fr. B. Vaughan, a writer, by the way, of a very different order, is guilty of the same prevarication in his *Free Trade Hall Lectures*, and this after Dr. Wiseman's dishonest quotation had been exposed and denounced. "Perhaps there is nothing which gives to the minds of intelligent and truth-loving men so invincible a prejudice against the Ultramontane system and temper—nothing which so radically convinces them that it is not Divine, as the certainty that Ultramontane writers will always be found manipulating facts and making out a case."—Gore, *Roman Catholic Claims*, p. 112.

in the second century, mentions it as a fact universally known . . . that Peter and Paul *both* taught in Italy, and suffered martyrdom there, about the same time.[1] Their equality as the two great pillars of the Church was maintained to the last. In no particular did S. Paul come behind that pre-eminent Apostle, S. Peter. The one is the *Jachin*, the other the *Boaz* of the Church.

In fact, I have sometimes thought that these two names were in a way prophetic, as they are certainly descriptive, of the respective powers and functions of Peter and Paul, the two great " pillars in the temple of our GOD." For the meaning of the word *Jachin* is " He shall *establish*," and the meaning of *Boaz* is " In him is *strength*." Could there be a more apt description of their particular work and their place in Church history ? S. Peter was connected with the first setting up of the Christian Society; his it was to erect it in CHRIST's Name on a firm basis; S. Paul was identified with its growth and extension. The one began, the other continued ; the one " stablished," the other " strengthened," the temple of the LORD. Neither was greater or less than the other.

And now, bear with me a moment whilst I sum up what has been said. We are importuned, we are urged, we are summoned to submit to the Pope. We are required to recognize in him the Vicar of CHRIST and to own his authority as that of the Redeemer Himself. We say, say respectfully and in a sense *regretfully*, that

[1] Tertullian speaks to the same effect, *De Prescrip.*, 20, 21. Quoted by Robertson, *Growth of the Papal Power*.

we *cannot* do it. We *dare* not do it, because the Popedom seems to us to be no creation of CHRIST, no development of *His* will, but the creation of circumstances, the product of human frailty and ambition. And we reach this conclusion on the joint testimony of Holy Scriptures and of ancient writers. We submit that neither from the Scriptures nor from the early Fathers can the Romanists prove what they affirm. Neither from the one nor the other, and still less from both, can they show—if they *can*, it is high time that they *did*—either that our SAVIOUR appointed S. Peter to be His substitute, or that, if He did, S. Peter became by His appointment first bishop of Rome or that, if he was first bishop, the present bishop of Rome has, by CHRIST's appointment, succeeded to His powers. We are open to conviction, but so far we have no adequate proof of any one of these positions. On the contrary, we have what we cannot but regard as *disproof*—disproof at least of the *first* proposition—and if *that* falls, the others fall with it. We think it can be proven that the Apostles, the first Christians, S. James, S. Paul, and S. Peter himself were all entirely ignorant of his principality. We think it can be proven that if *S. Peter* was Pope, S. Paul was no less; proven that either CHRIST had two Vicars or none; proven that the Petrine claims will not stand in the light of the Pauline position.

SERMON XIX.

THE RELIGIOUS ASPECT OF DISESTABLISHMENT.[1]

S. JOHN XVIII. 36.

"My kingdom is not of this world."

THE question, and the only question which I now propose to consider is this—whether the disestablishment of the Church (about which we hear so much, and which is sometimes advocated on religious grounds) is demanded by GOD or would be pleasing to GOD. I have nothing to do now with party politics and nothing to say about them—I want to lift this question above the level of politics: besides, this is not the place to consider *them*. But it is the place, and perhaps it is the best place, to consider dispassionately whether there are any real *religious* reasons for disestablishment: whether establishment or any essential feature of it is against the will of our LORD CHRIST. It is often assumed so to be, and some sincere Christians, some Churchmen even, have persuaded themselves that the connection between Church and State in

---

[1] This Sermon was preached in Truro Cathedral on February 4th, 1895. It has since been printed as a tract, bearing the title, *Does Christ call for Disestablishment?* London: C. Taylor.

this country is irreligious and adulterous. Well, if it is, the sooner it is put an end to the better : as to that, I think we shall all be agreed. *But is it irreligious ?* Is it in any way contrary to Christianity ? I shall hope to give you some plain reasons for thinking that it is not ; for holding that such " establishment " as we have here in England is according to the will of CHRIST, and that *dis*establishment would be as distinctly against His will and pleasure.

But if these reasons of mine are to have any value, we must first endeavour—it is not always an easy thing to do—to rid ourselves of misconception ; we must take pains to understand what the (so called) " Establishment" of the Church consists in. The phrase is constantly on men's lips, but I hardly know a word that is more misleading. Not one person in a thousand can tell you what it means ; the politicians, as a rule, cannot, and they are hardly to blame for it ; the word itself has led them astray. It has suggested to some minds that the Church was *set up by the State*, that the State *planted* it or *adopted* it here in England. The State did *not* plant it, or in any way begin it. It *could* not do it, if it tried ; it could not, because "the Church is a *Divine* institution"; there is no Church but GOD's Church. And it never tried to do it ; if it did you would be able to tell me *when* and *where*, and you cannot. You cannot point to any Act or ordinance which professed to begin the Christian Church (or, if you like, the *National* Church) in this country. I do not deny that some early Christian princes may have fostered and encouraged it, as surely they had a perfect right to do; what I deny is that they in any way *founded* or *started* it. That is not the case, and history shows that it is not the case in a very conclusive way. It shows that there was a Church, and *one* Church, in England under the Heptarchy, 155 years before there was any realm of England, and 592 years before there was any effective Parliament of England. The Church was organized in the land by Archbishop Theodore, Theodore of Tarsus, in the year 673. But there was no King of England until 827, and no Parliament until 1265, and when Parliament first met it was indebted to the Church for its Council-chamber, and it sate for years in the Chapter House of Westminster Abbey. Nor did the State, finding the Church in the country, formally *adopt it.* " There was no moment," says Mr. Freeman the historian, " when the nation or its rulers made up their minds that it would be a good thing to have an established Church." "The establishment of the Church in England," writes Lord Selborne, " grew up gradually and silently in an early stage of society, not as the result of any definite act, compact or conflict, but so that no one can now trace the exact steps of the process." And as there was no compact at first, so there has been none since—there was none, for example, at the Reformation. The State has never made any *Concordat* with the Church such as Napoleon made with the Pope. If it has, it will be easy to say *when* this was done, but no one can say. Nor has the State *endowed* the Church. It is often supposed that kings or parliaments gave it its present resources, its lands and tithes, but they did not. No doubt kings sometimes gave grants of land out of their own demesnes, just as our Queen might give a site for a Church, or even a sum of money towards building a Chapel, but that was all. "The whole of the present endowments of the Church," says a Dissenting lawyer, Mr. Toulmin Smith, " *were voluntary endowments.*" In the year 1818 Parliament voted a million of money for the building of Churches, as a thank-offering for the restoration of peace, and in 1824 another half million, but that is about all ; if it has been given more, it will be easy to trace it in the Acts of Parliament, or in the accounts of the Treasury. So that "established" does not mean *endowed.* Nor does it mean, lastly, that the Church is *managed* by the State. No doubt it is, to a certain extent, controlled and regulated by the civil power, but so is the Chapel, so is every similar institution. Everything in England is subject to law ; other religious bodies are as well as ours. Laws have no doubt been made from time to time for the Church, but similar, if fewer, laws have also been made for the Chapel—I could give you a list of them if it were necessary. But the State no more appoints our rites or ordains our ministers than it does theirs ; you cannot tell me of one dogma which it has decreed or modified, or of one humble deacon whom it has ordained. Its tribunals have sometimes been invoked to *interpret* our formularies, but they have also decided what the Chapel doctrines are as well as ours : the Court of Chancery, for example, has held that " Baptism is not indispensable among the Baptists." It is urged against us that we cannot alter our standards

s

without having recourse to Parliament, but as little can Dissenters alter theirs. Why, Mr. Wesley's *Deed of Declaration*, which is the charter of the Wesleyan body, is enrolled in Chancery, and at this very time there is some talk of an application to Parliament to alter it. There is no established Church in the United States, but the Presbyterians cannot change their creed, as some of them desire to do, without going into the law courts. We greatly err, therefore, if we think, as many people do think, that " Establishment " consists in this, or in any of the things just mentioned. In all these respects the Church and the sects stand on the same level. And the same remark applies to the other meaning of this word, the only sense in which it can be rightly used of any religious communion in its relation to the State, namely, in the sense of *confirmed in its position*, settled and "established " in the enjoyment of its rights and revenues. The Church does owe thus much to the State, recognition and protection and confirmation, and if you choose to call this " Establishment," then the Church *is* established ; yes, the Church is established, and so is the Chapel ; each is *legibus stabilita*—stablished by laws, and neither is established in any other sense. And this is why some lawyers speak of Dissent as "established" ; this is why Lord Mansfield held that " the Dissenters way of worship is established," and this explains Speaker Onslow's words, that " the Dissenters are as truly established as is the Church of England."

But if this is so—and it is so—then you will observe that the very term " disestablishment " is entirely mis-

leading. " The word," as Bishop Westcott has remarked,
" conveys a suggestion of something which is absolutely
false. If we speak of *disestablishing* a society, it is implied
that there has been some previous *establishment* of it.
But the student of history knows that the Church never
has been established in this country."

Do I then, you will ask, contend that there is no
difference between Church and Chapel in this respect?
By no means. I allow that the relations of the Church
of England to the State are very different, and especially
different in *degree*, from those of other religious bodies;
you can see for yourselves that there is a difference.
But why is it, and how has it come to pass? Not, as
some persons would fain persuade you, not because the
State has taken one sect out of many and heaped favours
and privileges upon it, but because, till comparatively
recent years, *there were no sects;* there was nothing but
the Church; it was the only religious community in the
land, the only representative of Christianity, and every
English Christian belonged to it. The Church stands in
a different position to the State from what the Chapel
does, because the entire State formerly believed, as many
of us do still, in *one Church and no more;* because this was
the historic Church, which existed before the State, and
helped to shape and consolidate the State, whilst it is
only of late years that the Chapel has had any existence
at all. Take the county of Cornwall, for example. The
Churches were built, with few exceptions, centuries ago,
as their very architecture shows, whereas in 1725, according to Defoe, there were only *four* meeting-houses in all

Cornwall. It is this that accounts for the difference. The Church was when the Chapel was not; the Church was when the State was not. Can you wonder that Church and State should touch at so many more points and have so much closer relations than Chapel and State? Both have a connection with the State; both *must* have, but the institution which has been for over 1,300 years in the country, and which for over 1,000 years had no rival in the country, will naturally occupy a very different position in Parliament and in the statute book, from an institution which began 100 or even 300 years ago. It is this, coupled with the old and true belief in *one* Church of GOD, which accounts for the difference.

But *in what respects* do they differ? They differ in the following particulars, and, so far as I know, in these alone.

1. The King and the Lord Chancellor, who is "the keeper of the King's conscience," must be members of the Church of England. This is to prevent their being Romanists.

2. The Church has, and has had for a thousand years, its ecclesiastical courts for the trial of ecclesiastical causes, and these courts have a coercive jurisdiction.

3. The bishops are nominated for their sees and some of the clergy are chosen for their cures by the crown or its ministers.

4. These bishops are, for the most part, peers of Parliament; they sit in the House of Lords, and can speak and vote on the questions of the day.

5. Many of the clergy are maintained, wholly or in part, by a tithe rent-charge.

6. **The** clergy, as they are not appointed **by** their congregations, **so** they are irremovable **at the** pleasure or caprice of their congregations. They **are only remov-**able by legal process, after cause shown.

7. Convocation, the Parliament of the clergy, requires the consent of the Parliament of the country, in order **to** ratify its decisions.

8. The State, having always been, **since it** existed, **a** commonwealth **of** Christians, professes the Christian religion and the ancient historic form of that religion.

And now, I proceed to ask, which of these things, **the** things that constitute what is called " Establishment "— which of these things furnishes **a** *religious* reason **for** disestablishment? **Let us examine them in order. And** I say that

1. It cannot be against GOD's will that **king or queen** should be a member of His Church, the historic church of the country—provided of course that they believe in it—unless it **is** against His will that *anybody* should belong to it. If GOD has left **that Church, no** doubt **He would** wish the king and everybody else **to do** the same, **but if He has** *not* left it—and **I do not know** any intelligent Dissenter who maintains that He has—then **it cannot** be against His will that the **King** and the Chancellor, who have been admitted **into it at** their baptism, should *remain* in its **communion.**

2. Nor, secondly, can it be against GOD's will that the Church should have its own tribunals. **No, we** are some-times reproached because we have to submit to the State courts—Dissenters **have** to do the same—but it cannot

also be a reproach that we settle some disputes amongst ourselves. We only do therein what S. Paul enjoined.

3. But perhaps you say that it must be against the mind of CHRIST that the King or the Prime Minister, who may be an atheist, should appoint the Church's bishops. I answer unhesitatingly, No. Let me remind you, in the first place, that this Prime Minister, if he *is* an atheist (we have had no atheists at the head of our affairs so far) is nevertheless the " minister of GOD "—he is so described in the Book of GOD. For him, therefore, to nominate a bishop, is for one minister of GOD to nominate another minister of GOD—that is all. I say to " nominate," for all that he can do is to *choose* a qualified man for the post. He cannot *make* any man bishop or priest—only ordination can do that ; he cannot prescribe his functions or duties or doctrines, nor can he appoint a man who is not already a " priest "; all he can do is to choose a man already ordained and so far qualified out of a number of men ordained and qualified ; the *very worst* he can do, that is to say, is to appoint an inferior, but still qualified person. You say that he is unfit to do even this ! Then he is certainly unfit to rule GOD's realm— and the blame rests with those who have made him Premier. They had no right to put a man at the head of GOD's England who cannot be trusted to fill up a vacant post in GOD's Church. Or you say that he ought to be a Christian. Well, we say the same, but we also say that if he is *not*, that does not make his appointments unchristian, or against CHRIST's will. And for this reason : the Roman Emperors or their procurators or the

Herods, at the time of our LORD, appointed the High Priests, and He and His apostles recognized and respected their appointments, and so taught us to treat such appointments with respect. We do not say that this is the **best** possible arrangement, though as a rule it **has given us** excellent men, but we do say that it does not contradict any principle **of CHRIST. Nor can the** Liberationist prove that it does.

4. **Is it, then,** against **CHRIST's will that the** bishops should **have any voice in the senate of our country?** I **will answer** that **question by asking another. Is it a** disqualification in a legislator **that he is a** Christian **or a** Christian pastor? **Observe, I am not pleading for the** presence of bishops **in the House of Lords; I do not even** say that **it is** desirable, **though I have my own opinions** on that point; **what I do say is that there can be nothing** wrong, nothing **unchristian in their presence there. You** cannot expect **me to believe that a** man is unfitted either to have an opinion **or to express it in** Parliament or to enforce it by **a vote,** just **because he is** an ambassador of CHRIST. Neither Christianity **nor the** ministry destroys our interest in our **country or our common sense. Nor** do I find that Dissenters object to the **presence of their** ministers on **School** Boards **or on** County Councils; **in** fact, they are extremely proud of it, and sometimes make heroic efforts **to secure it. Yet the** principle is precisely the same. If **it is** unchristian in the former **case,** it is unchristian in the latter also. **It cannot be** pretended, therefore, that this feature, this **accident of** "establishment" is against the will of **GOD.**

5. And as to the next incident, tithes, why, every Christian knows that tithes were instituted by GOD, or were approved by GOD. They were an essential feature of the first dispensation; to withhold them was to rob GOD. But if they were right then, right in *principle*, they cannot be wrong now. GOD does not change *His* principles from time to time; it is the privilege—or the dishonour—of our politicians to do that.

6. I proceed to notice another feature, what has been called the parson's freehold. In the first place, the clergy are not appointed by their flocks—for we do not find in Scripture that the sheep are to choose their shepherds —and, secondly, when they are appointed, it is for life, or during good behaviour. So long as they do nothing to forfeit their position, the State maintains them in it, as it maintains other officials. Yes, and it maintains Dissenting ministers in their pastorates, as the *Stannard* case proves, if the Chapel has an endowment. Wherever there is property the State protects it, protects " vested interests "; you would not wish it to do otherwise. Now, I am very well aware that this sometimes works badly, as our best arrangements are liable to do; sometimes it maintains a clergyman in a post for which he is entirely unfitted; but I submit to you that the *principle* is nevertheless a sound one, for the principle is that CHRIST'S minister should be independent of his congregation; independent in the sense of being able to deliver his soul without fear of consequences. " How can a minister "— I quote the words of a Wesleyan minister printed recently—how can a " minister, however good he may

be, speak all the things in his **heart under the voluntary system ?** " The Bible speaks, too, of " the elders which rule "; it cannot, therefore, be GOD's will that such men should be in a position to be *ruled* by their flocks, **or** gagged, or frightened, as they must be, more **or less,** when they are removable by their flocks.

7. And as **for** Convocation, of **course I** could **wish** for it greater liberty, but all the same **it** is not in any unchristian bondage. **It** would not **have liberty to do** just as it liked if we were disestablished; no Dissenting community can **do just as it** likes; **all experience** the restraints of law. And **we need not make** a great trouble of it so long as **we** have *this* liberty—to **preach CHRIST's** gospel and minister His sacraments **and do** all the good in our parishes that we *can* do, without **let or** hindrance.

8. I now come to the last feature of " Establishment," namely, that the State, **as a** State, makes public profession of the Christian religion, or, let us say, one form of that religion. **It has not** selected one form **out of many;** it professes the **form of** Christianity which has been handed down **and recovered in this country.** Perhaps **it** is this that you really object **to ; you want** to sever the connexion **between** the **realm, as a realm, and its** religion. For this **is** what Disestablishment involves; **if it is to** be thorough and consistent it cannot profess any one form of religion more **than** another — **not** Christianity more than Mohammedanism or Buddhism; **if it** does, it **to** that extent " establishes " that form of religion. Very good! **Here, then, we join** issue. **I say** that it *cannot* be the will of CHRIST that a State composed

largely of Christians, a State, too, which at the present moment professes Christianity, should repudiate that profession, or should discontinue it—should say that, as a State, it has henceforward no religion at all. And this, let me say, is why we dread disestablishment—because of the dishonour which, as we conceive, would be done to *CHRIST*, because of the blow which would be dealt at His beneficent religion. We hold that that religion is the very best thing in the world, the only thing, indeed, that we are really and truly to live for, and we cannot bear that our country, or the government of our country, should dethrone it from the place which it has so long occupied in England, and bid it take a back seat. We affirm that it is distinctly *against* the Divine will that any such deed should be done. For consider, first—

1. You say that the State is to have nothing to do with GOD or with religion, and yet *the State itself is an institutution of GOD!* We often hear men speak as if the Church belonged to GOD and the State to the devil, whereas He Who founded the one ordained the other also. "The powers that be are ordained of GOD." We talk again of some things being "sacred" and others "secular," whereas there is really nothing secular in GOD's world, *nothing but sin.* I repeat, the State is GOD's—GOD's institution as much as the family; the kingdoms of this world are His, and His CHRIST's, that is one main lesson of the Old Testament—and if it renounces GOD, He will not release it from its obligations to Him. You cannot disestablish the King of nations, or tear Him from His throne. Some of you may remem-

ber the warning that was uttered during the troubles of the Commonwealth, " If you gentlemen begin to say that you have nothing to do with GOD or religion, He will soon show that He has something to do with you."

2. You say the State, as such, should have nothing to do with religion, and yet the Bible tells us that GOD *entrusted His religion to the keeping of a State !* People forget that the connexion between Church and State in England is nothing like so close and intimate as was that connexion between Church and State which GOD Himself ordained ; they forget that we have in the Old Testament the history of a Church which GOD Himself established. Even the Liberation Society allows that " there was an established religion amongst the Jews," and that it was "established by GOD." Precisely so. But if GOD willed to have an established Church then, how can it be against His will now ? The *principle* is the same. If it was a valid principle then, why must it be a vicious principle now ? I entreat you, therefore, always to remember that we *find an Established Church in the Bible,* a Church *much more established* than ours is, and that this establishment was GOD'S *own work.*

3. But perhaps you object that, whatever the Old Testament may say, " established Churches are against the spirit of Christianity." Then I must remind you that the Founder of Christianity *joined* an established Church ; He became a member of it ; He lived and died a member of it, and He recognized its laws and rites and ministers. For the Church which our LORD joined at His circumcision, the Church whose temple and syna-

gogues He attended, and whose Passover He celebrated the last night of His life, was in close connexion with the Jewish State and with the Roman. Why, its chief priests were sometimes appointed by Pagans, by the Roman procurators or the Idumean Herods. Yet our LORD CHRIST joined it and continued in it to the last. And yet they want us to believe that an established Church in any shape is against the spirit of His religion —in other words, that CHRIST's action was inconsistent with CHRIST's religion.

4. But this is not all. Our LORD not only joined the Jewish State Church or Church State—whichever you like to call it, so close was the connection—but He foresaw that the Churches of Europe would be "established" Churches. Such they have been for many centuries; such most of them are still. And foreseeing this, He never breathed one word to put us on our guard. Not one word; if He did, you will perhaps tell me where to find it. You say perchance that He told us that His "kingdom" was "not of this world." I answer, "Undoubtedly He did, but what has that to do with disestablishment?" And here, I must remark in passing on the singular fact that there are only two texts in the whole Bible which the Liberationists cite in favour of disestablishment, and that neither of these has any bearing on the question. The text just cited certainly has not: you will perceive this if you will study the context. Remember that our LORD had been denounced to Pilate as a pretender to a throne, as a possible rival to Cæsar, and as claiming to be the King of the Jews. Hence it is

that Pilate asks, " Art Thou the King of the Jews ? " And it is to this charge that our LORD replies, " My kingdom **is not** of this world "—not **like Herod's,** not like Cæsar's ; they have nothing to fear from Me. And that this is His meaning is **clear** from the next **words,** " If My kingdom were of this world, *then would* **My servants** *fight* "—"they would not leave Me helpless in your hands : if I were seeking **an** earthly throne, they would do battle in My behalf." Yes, *this* **is** His meaning, and yet this ' text is industriously alleged, year after year, in favour of disestablishment, **as** is **also that** other saying, " Render **unto Cæsar the** things **that are** Cæsar's, and unto GOD the things **that are** GOD's." They want **us to** believe that Cæsar's province and **GOD'S** province are utterly and entirely *distinct*, and **yet** Cæsar **himself, S. Paul** says, was " the minister of GOD." No, our LORD foresaw that the churches **of** Europe **would be** " established " and— **He** left men to " establish " them.

In fact, of religious reasons for disestablishment there **are none,** unless we may **call our** *religious divisions* a religious reason. **That is the real reason** why this irreligious measure is advocated. **If** Christians had not been so divided, and if they **were not** so bitterly jealous **of** each other, we should have heard **very** little about it. But for this, Christians would have striven to *remedy the abuses* which have arisen in connection with " establishments," as they arise in all human institutions, instead of clamouring for confiscation and destruction. **No, there** is **no** religious argument for disestablishment, **or if** there is, it **has** not yet been alleged. The religious argument **is all** the other way. Religion is hardly likely to suggest that the first thing the State has to remember is that it must have no religion at all. We want to make the State more and not less religious, more than ever GOD's organ and domain ; can it be that the way to do this is to inflict on England " a moral blow "—I borrow the words of Bishop Lightfoot—" under which it would reel and stagger for many generations to come"? But I trust that you who hear me will do nothing of the kind. I hope *your* answer to the Liberationist will be, " Destroy it not, for a blessing is in it." I ask you honestly and prayerfully to study this question, and from the Christian point of view ; the more you do so, the better for the Church. We are not afraid of the light ; what we are afraid of is ignorance and prejudice and jealousy and statecraft. Study it, and we believe you will reach the conclusion of Mr. Gladstone : " If there are those who consider that national establishments are opposed under all circum- stances to the principles of the Christian religion, we are not of the number of such persons."

THE RELIGIOUS ASPECT OF DISENDOWMENT.[1]

MALACHI III. 8, 9.

" Will a man rob GOD ? Yet ye rob Me. But ye say, Wherein have we robbed Thee ? In tithes and offerings. Ye are cursed with the curse, for ye rob Me, even this whole nation."

WHATEVER differences of opinion there may be amongst us, and whatever we may think about Disestablishment in particular, on one point we shall all be agreed—that the Church of GOD cannot do its work, cannot fulfil its mission in the world without money. Though a spiritual institution with spiritual aims, it must have material resources, just as much as any other institution. This is why we have our perpetual offertories and collections ; this is why we are reduced to subscription lists and sales of work. The Church *must* have money, and I believe that all religious bodies will tell you that if they only had more money, they could do more work. How often do we hear of this good cause and that which is languishing simply for want of funds !

[1] Preached in Truro Cathedral on February 18th, 1895, and since printed (in substance) as a tract, entitled, *What does Disendowment Mean ?*

And I think that we shall be further agreed that if the Church or other religious community has any *endowments*, any funds to fall back upon, so much the better for its work. It must have endowments, if it is to work well, if only for these three reasons :—

First, that otherwise the most necessitous districts, the districts which need money most and are least able to provide it, will be starved, as you may see for yourselves in the East of London and elsewhere.

Secondly, because the least showy and attractive agencies, those which make the least noise, though they sometimes do the most work, are so liable to be over-looked, and

Lastly, because voluntary contributions vary so much from year to year; because they are so precarious, so dependent on trade, on the weather, on the popularity of the preacher. I do not say that endowments are to take the place of voluntary contributions, but I do say that they are valuable as an *additional* resource, and that they are indispensable where there are few other resources. But I need scarcely argue this question, for I feel sure that there is no one here who would resolutely refuse an endowment if it were offered him, and if investments are so good for the individual, it is difficult to see why they should be so needless or so pernicious to the community. If you find it good for your family and its needs that those who preceded you provided for it a modest endow-ment, why should a similar endowment be bad for the household of GOD and its needs? No, CHRIST's Church must have *some* endowments, if its work is to be evenly and methodically done, and only fanatics can want us to dispense with them altogether.

Now, the Church of England, most happily, most providentially, as I think, has and has had for many centuries certain possessions for the purposes of religion in England. I say "the Church" has; it would be more correct if I said that the *parish churches* have, for there has been no endowment of the Church *as a whole*, none whatsoever. "People talk," says Mr. Freeman, "as if Church property were the property of one vast corporation called the Church. In truth, it is simply the property of the several local churches. The Church of England, as a single body, has no property." Gifts of land or money have from time to time been made to our parish churches and clergy, but that is all. Some of these were given long ago, when the Church was under Papal domination; others have been given quite recently. They were not given by the *State*—"every parish church in England was founded" (these are the words of a Dissenter, Mr. Toulmin Smith) "*not by the State, but by individual donations*"; they were not given by the *King*, except in comparatively rare instances; they were given, and given freely, by private Christians for religious purposes. And having been so given, they *belong* to the churches. "Every lawyer and historian," says Sir Richard Webster, "who has examined the question, has come independently to the conclusion . . . that the property of the Church belongs to the Church in the same way that the property of every private individual belongs to that individual." It may be well if I

T

cite some few of these lawyers. I will take four. " The clergy" (says Blackstone) " have precisely the same right to the tithes as the heir-at-law has to his ancestor's estate." " No lawyer can prove "—these are the words of Lord Eldon—" that the revenues of the Church belong to the State." " I think the right of the Church in the property it enjoys as sacred as the right of individuals in their estates and freeholds "—so said Lord Brougham. "As a matter of law," said Baron Wilde, "the funds of the Established Church are as sacred as private property." So that if right is right, and if churches are not to be treated differently from individuals or from non-religious bodies, the resources of the Church belong to the Church, and do not, and never did, belong to the nation. " Church property," writes the historian Freeman, "is not national property, except in the sense in which all property is national property."

Let us suppose, however, for the sake of argument, that the property now held by the Church was given by the *nation*. Still, that does not prove that it belongs to the *nation;* it rather proves that it belongs to the *Church.* The estate which you have given to your neighbour you do not consider yours, but your neighbour's; nor do you think yourself entitled to have a thing restored to you because you once gave it away. If all the property now held by the Church was given by the people, still it was *given*, and it was given *to* GOD; it was consecrated to His service, and it is being used in His service ; it is used mainly for the support of His ministers. So that if we allowed that every penny that we possess came to us from the public exchequer—which it did not—we are still entitled to ask what right the State has to resume possession of it.

And it is now proposed that the State should take possession of it ; **that** it should take *all* the property **of** the Church, save the churches and parsonages and the endowments which have accrued since **the year** 1662. **It is not yet** settled **to what** precise purposes this property shall **be** applied. Some have spoken of baths and washhouses ; some of allotments and asylums or of museums and galleries of art ; some of old age pensions or elementary schools—on this point there has been the greatest diversity of opinion. But on one point **they are** all agreed—that *it shall not be for* CHRIST'S *religion in* **any** *shape whatsoever.* Though these endowments were given for the purposes of that religion, and though that religion, or the Church form of **it, has long enjoyed** them, and is now using them **for the** purposes for which they were bestowed, **it** is agreed that neither **that nor** any form of religion is to have them, or **any of** them ; they are to be *secularized ;* **to be applied to** uses which, whatever else they are, are non-religious. They are to **be** taken **from** GOD and given unto Cæsar. **This is** a point upon which, I believe, all Liberationists are agreed.

Now **the** question which I have to submit to you is this—whether this would be *right ;* whether **it** would be *honest ;* whether it **would be** *acceptable to* **GOD.** I am concerned exclusively with the *moral* and *religious* aspects of Disendowment, and **I** affirm—and I shall hope to prove —that it would *not* **be** just ; that it would be *dis*honest and

displeasing to our Maker ; that it would be robbing Him
and His religion and our country and the poor.

But before I enter upon this proof, it may be well to
remind you that Disendowment is the *real*, the *practical*
question before the country. I need hardly say that
there is no *necessary* connection between Disestablishment
and Disendowment. It is not necessary to take our
money because you put the bishops out of the House of
Lords or do away with the ecclesiastical courts, and if
people were really concerned for CHRIST's religion, you
would expect them to contemplate one measure without
the other. But they never do ; on the contrary, they tell
us that they care very little for Disestablishment in
comparison with Disendowment. " Disendowment,"
says a Dissenting organ, the *British Weekly*, " Disendowment is the great matter for which we are fighting. By
its side Disestablishment is the merest trifle." That is
to say, though it is the " establishment " of religion which
from their point of view is so unspiritual and so irreligious,
and though endowment is neither the one nor the other—
how can it be when they have endowments of their own ?
—still it is Disendowment, not Disestablishment that
they are aiming at. Now, we could understand this
perfectly if their object was to *injure* the Church, but
when their one idea is, as they repeatedly assure us, to
purify it, to liberate and elevate it, this causes us some
surprise. But let that pass. Disendowment is *for us*
the practical thing. I do not mean that Disestablishment is not, in its way, a very practical matter, for it
raises the question whether the State should repudiate

all profession of religion; whether, as a State, it should know CHRIST no longer; still, this would make nothing like the *felt* difference to our country that Disendowment would. Disestablishment we have to a large extent already; it has been brought about piecemeal; there is little, except the recognition of religion left for . our legislators to take. But with Disendowment it is quite another thing. That *would* touch the Church and the country at every point; it would cripple religious work for generations to come; its effects would be felt in almost every parish and household in the land. I repeat: *Disendowment* is what they are fighting for, and the sooner we understand it the better.

But before I begin to argue either for or against this step, there are three observations which I wish to make, and then there are three objections which I have to meet. And the first observation is this—that

1. If it was not religion, or a religious community that was possessed of these resources, no one would dream of taking them away. Let us suppose that the lands and tithes of the Church belonged to educational or charitable institutions, say to our schools and colleges, or to our hospitals and dispensaries. In that case we should never have heard one word about confiscating them; why, one proposition is to take our funds and give them to schools and colleges. No, there would have been no talk of Disendowment *then*, and certainly no one would contend in that case that it was for the *good of the institution* that it should be stripped of its resources. Why, then, is the Church to be disendowed when schools and hospitals

are to be endowed? Is religion altogether inferior to education? does it do harm whilst hospitals do good? The first point, then, for Christian men to remember in connection with this project is this—It is proposed to disendow the Church *because it has to do with religion.* If it had not to do with religion no one would speak of disendowing it. Moreover,

2. If it was not a form of the *Christian* religion that was in possession of these revenues, we should hear nothing about secularizing them. If the monies given to the Church—centuries ago, it is true, but I do not know that that makes any difference; it is generally held that the longer an institution has been in possession of its estates, the stronger is its title—if, I say, the monies given to the Church had been given to the Jews, either anciently or recently, say by the Rothschilds or the Montifiores, then no statesman would propose, and no constituency would demand their confiscation, so long as the Jews were making a good use of them. Nor would they secularize them, even if Jews were divided into as many sects as, unhappily, Christians are. Men would say that they had no right—it would be unjust—to divert them to baths and washhouses. Well, is Christianity inferior to Judaism, or is it entitled to less consideration and fairness? A second point for you, therefore, to bear in mind is this: Disendowment is only contemplated because the Church teaches a form of Christianity; because its funds are used for the furtherance of CHRIST'S religion. If they had been given and were being used for the *Jews'* religion, your conscience would forbid

you to touch them. My third observation is this:

3. If it were not for the divisions and jealousies of Christians, no Christian would advocate Disendowment. No doubt infidels and secularists might desire it, but Christians would not ; it is the very last thing they would think of. No, it is just because, for one reason or other, some of CHRIST's followers could not agree to worship and work with others of His followers, but left them, and then became jealous of them, that Disendowment has been agitated for ; it is born of "our unhappy divisions." Dissenters, as the very name shows, left the Church ; they virtually said that we were **not fit** for them to worship with any longer—and GOD knows **that** we had our faults !—they said that conscience compelled **them to** separate. And now, having separated, they demand, not a *share* of the endowments—we could understand that, and there might be some show of reason in it —but that *the Church should have none.* Though they have endowments of their own, and very naturally mean to keep them, yet they insist on secularizing ours. Just because we are not **Jews or** Turks, but Christians, Christians who **only** differ from them **on** some few points, but Christians who belong to a communion which is in competition with theirs, they press for Disendowment. This is a third thing to remember, that if religion **is** stripped **of** its resources, resources which it must have, if its work is to be done, it will be purely and entirely because CHRIST's disciples could not agree amongst themselves ; because some left the old society, and then suddenly discovered that its possessions must

be appropriated by the State. And now I proceed to deal with the three objections.

1. The first is that some of the revenues of the Church once belonged to the Roman Catholics, and that, as the State took them away from *them*, so now it may fairly take them away from us. To which I reply. First, there might be some force in this argument if it were proposed to *restore* these funds to the Romanists. But that is the very last thing which the Liberationists dream of doing. What they propose to do, if this view of the case is correct, is, to *take Roman Catholic money* and *to apply it to secular uses*. But I observe, secondly, that this view is not correct. In the first place, the Romanists, or their leaders, lay no claim to these endowments; they say that they are not theirs. I quote the words of the Roman bishops of England in the year 1826. They said, " We regard all the revenues and temporalities of the Church Established as the property of those in whom they are settled by the laws of the land. We disclaim any right, title, or pretension to the same." But even if they *did* claim them, we should still deny their right to them, and this because the monies were given to the English Church for purposes of religion, and therefore they belong to that Church. " Not one ancient endowment now held by the Church of England, not one building for her worship was conveyed to her on any condition, express or implied, that she should be subject to the authority of the Pope, and should forfeit it otherwise. They were all given for ecclesiastical uses; in each place for the benefit of the Church of England, not

of the Church of Rome **in** England." You may remind
me that large monies were given in ancient times for
procuring masses for the dead, and no doubt that is so ;
but then, as the Dissenting lawyer whom I have already
quoted points out, all such property, that of the chantries
and monasteries, was confiscated by Henry the Eighth.
No, our endowments were not given to the Pope or any
foreign prelate, but to religion, the religion of the
Catholic Church, which religion our Church, to the **best**
of its knowledge, holds and preaches still.

2. The second objection is this—that since **these**
monies or estates were given to the Church, half the
people of this country have become Dissenters from it.
But I observe, first : This, again, might possibly be **a**
valid argument, if it **were** proposed to *share* these monies
between Churchmen and Dissenters, but that is **not**
proposed ; Disendowment does **not** mean *sharing*, but
stripping and *secularizing*. And in **the** second place, those
who left the Church left it of their own free will. You
have heard it said, I daresay, that they were "kicked
out," but there is not one word of truth in it. No one can
produce a case, not one person, who has been thrust out of
the English Church. The Pope has excommunicated us,
not we him ; the Dissenters left us, not we them. **And**
when they left us they left at the same time the possessions of the Church. This, at least, is the rule observed
amongst themselves. When the Wesleyan Reformers
left the old body, did they take the funds with them, or
did they claim a share in them ? If they did, they did
not get it. There is a chapel in Wales, again, to take a

more recent case, where there was a split some five years ago. The seceders asked to have the monies which they had contributed towards the building of the chapel restored to them, but they were answered, " Not so ; when you left us you left the funds." But what is fair in the one case is fair in the other. Why is one rule to prevail when Dissenters leave Dissenters, and another when they leave the Church ?

3. Here is a third objection—that some of the revenues of the Church, preserved to it at the Reformation, are being insidiously used for the propagation of Romanism. To which I reply that, if this is so—and at present we have bare assertions, not proofs—if it is so, and I do not deny that some of the clergy are indiscreet, and do not always distinguish between what is Catholic and ancient and what is Roman and modern, any more than the laity always do ; perhaps what you call Roman is really Christian ; if it is the case, how many of the twenty thousand clergy of the English Church are chargeable with such perfidy ? Why, not one in a hundred ; perhaps not one in a thousand. Think of the districts you know, and you will see that this is so. Then, I ask, are the ninety and nine to be sacrificed because of the one ? I have read of a city that GOD would have spared for the sake of ten righteous men—only ten out of thousands— but now GOD's own city is to be despoiled because of ten traitors. Is this your idea of justice ? I repeat : the charge is made, but it is not proven, and if it were proven, then it is an argument for reform, not for revolution or confiscation.

But I must now begin my brief examination of the reasons for and against Disendowment. In its favour it is urged—

1. **That it** would promote religious **equality.** As to which I observe, first, that we find it difficult to recognize any equality in a measure which would confiscate Church endowments whilst it leaves Dissenting **endowments** untouched. Secondly, **that we have** religious equality already. If there is any inequality, it is that Churchmen are not treated **so well by the** State as Dissenters are. What **we have not, and** what we never shall have, is social equality. **Disestablishment would not give us** that; it has not **secured it** in the United States. **And I say, lastly, that if** Disestablishment is necessary to ensure religious equality, Disendowment is not. I may add that " religious equality," desirable **as it** may be, is not to be secured, **if it** would be secured, by robbery. Altogether, **it is a** strange argument for devoting Church money to **secular** uses that other Christians **make it a** grievance that we should have more than they. **The** next thing will be that private property must be confiscated **in** order to promote *material* equality. A second reason **is**—

2. **That some Dissenters and** many secularists insist on Disendowment, and will not **rest** content without it. No doubt that is so; they **will** not vote for candidates who are not pledged **to** disendow the Church. And this plea is constantly put forward **in** Parliament and elsewhere. Wales, **we** are told, wants Disendowment; therefore it must have **it.** And it is natural enough that

politicians should regard the question from this point of view. But we are Christians, and we have to consider, not merely whether the measure is demanded, but whether it is *just*. And this is not just. Neither secularists nor Dissenters gave the money; why, then, should it be taken away to please them? Is it right to secure their votes at the price of sacrilege? Now I come to a third reason, namely,

3. That the monies taken from the Church would do much good to the country; that they can be more usefully employed, in fact, than they are at present. Here we join issue. I observe, first, that much of the money when confiscated would be frittered away—it always is—in the course of "conveyance." Neither lawyers nor commissioners will do their work for nothing—why should they? The leakage would be tremendous. Secondly, that much would, especially if we may judge from the precedent of the Irish Church, be applied to doubtful purposes; it is a very doubtful purpose to restore evicted tenants to their holdings. Thirdly, that a blessing does not seem to rest somehow on the secularization of Church revenues. The spoil of the abbeys and monasteries did not bring much profit to the receivers, any more than it did to the thief:

" They tell us that the LORD of HOSTS will not avenge His own,
  They tell us that He careth not for temples overthrown ;
  Go, look through England's thousand vales and show me, he that
    may,
  The abbey lands that have not wrought their owners' swift decay."

It will hardly be contended, again, that Disendowment

has brought peace or prosperity to Ireland. **And I** say, lastly, that whatever good art galleries and the like might do, they will not do so much for our country's true weal as preaching CHRIST's gospel will, His religion of **charity** and purity. **If that** religion were a delusion, it **would** still be a question whether Church monies could be more usefully employed than **in** disseminating its teachings, which certainly make for righteousness and happiness, but if it **is *true*,** you cannot hold that they can be put **to** a better use—no, not if Parliament gave the tithe to the tithe payers, which it will never **do.** Besides, however good art galleries or asylums may be, they can easily be built without plundering the Church. Ours is **a** rich country, **the** richest **in** the world. Think of the sums we spend on our army and navy, on our civil list, on our pleasures, our **dress, our** drink bill. I say it is an opulent country; it has "exceeding many flocks and herds." Why then, if **it wants** museums, must it **take** the poor man's lamb, **yes, take** the bread of the poor clergy to build them with?

But **I must now** turn to the reasons *against* Disendowment. They are these in brief :—

1. It would be a sin against GOD. **For** whether Church property has been given to the **Church** or not, one thing is certain—that it has been set apart for GOD; it is also certain that it has been used in His service for centuries, and is so used still. It is therefore stealing, and stealing *from* **GOD,** to take it away and secularize it. You may call this strong language: I answer that it is *Bible* language. **If it** was robbery in the Jew—and the prophets called it

such—to *withhold* tithes and offerings, why is it less robbery to *alienate* them? And Dissenters have called it "robbery" in their day. "To take away," said Dr. John Owen, "the public maintenance provided for the public dispensers of the gospel . . . is in plain terms downright robbery." "For the State to take away what it never gave," said Dr. Pye Smith, "is downright robbery." And that it is robbery is also evidenced by the fact that no one proposes to touch the tithes which are in lay hands. Though the lay rectors do no duty in return for their endowments, whilst the clergy do, yet the latter are to be stripped and the former are to be secured. And why are the lay impropriators to escape? Because of the rights of property! The squire's property, that is to say, is to be respected; it is his; he can do what he likes with it. But Church property must be confiscated because it is *not* the clergyman's, because it only belongs to CHRIST's Church. Yes, this is the main argument against Disendowment—"Will a man rob GOD?" But secondly, if any second reason is needed,

2. It would be an injury to religion—it would deprive it of material resources necessary for its maintenance and extension. We have seen that religion cannot do without money, and we know that Disendowment means taking it away. No doubt, voluntary contributions would fill up part of the gap, as in the case of the Free Kirk of Scotland, but then you must remember there had been no Disendowment in Scotland; its possessions had *not* been filched away from the Kirk. Here it would

be different; some would **argue that those who** have
confiscated *once* may confiscate again. Once bitten, twice
shy! **I** ask you, then, to pause before you deal this blow
at the religion of your LORD. That religion has a life and
death struggle before it; it has to face the assaults of
secularism and socialism. Then why **rob it of its**
resources? If you do, rest assured that you will **rue**
the day. When the secularists turn again and rend you
and perhaps **use** Church monies against you, you may
vainly wish that **you had** not played **into their** hands.
Thirdly,

  3. **It would be a calamity to** our country, and especially **to our poor.** For these endowments—to mention
one thing only—provide a clergyman in every parish.
That clergyman is the servant of all and at the call of
the poorest; his ministrations are free to all. I do not
pretend that **all the** clergy are learned and devout and
discreet—it would be strange if they were; still, it is
allowed that **they** compare favourably with any similar
body of men; it **is** allowed, too, that the great majority
are faithfully and laboriously discharging their duty,
especially towards the poor. Why, then, should you
disendow them? Why take away their slender means?
No one alleges that they are overpaid; the average value
of the 14,000 livings of England and **Wales** is less than
£200 *per annum.* **You may** say, perhaps, that they should
be paid by their congregations. Yes, if no other pro-
vision had been made for them; but other provision
has **been** made, **a** provision which you want **to** take
away. **It ill** becomes you first **to** despoil them and then

insist that others should support them. Besides, how can congregations, say in the East of London or in our scanty and sluggish villages, maintain their clergy? The voluntary system breaks down in such cases. "You gave me thirty shillings last week," said a Dissenting minister to his flock, "how can you expect me to live on that?" I ask you, then, to pause before you wound our country in the persons of its poor clergy, and before you deprive our poor of their friends and helpers.

But enough of these reasons against Disestablishment —I could easily give you more if necessary. I return for a moment to the supreme reason—one which, I venture to say, you cannot meet or overthrow. I say, again, that the revenues of the Church, by whomsoever given, were given to GOD, given for religious purposes, and that it is robbing religion and robbing GOD to secularize them. And so strongly do I feel this that I would rather, if we must have Disestablishment, that you gave our endowments to the Methodists or Romanists, or some form of Christianity, than that you should "do this great wickedness and sin against GOD." It is sometimes said that if the Church is disendowed we ought to agitate for the secularization of Dissenting endowments. I earnestly hope that you will do nothing of the kind. "Two wrongs do not make a right." I hold that these Dissenting monies have been given to GOD, just as our tithes and lands were, and that it would be sacrilege to touch them. No, we will have no part in robbing GOD in any shape. We will resist to the utmost of our power, by every legitimate means, the confiscation of Church property—not because it is *ours*, but because it is GOD'S; because we hold it in trust for His religion and **His poor.** **But** if we are **overborne,** as we may be—the **bribe** dangled before the eyes of our voters is a very substantial and a very tempting one—if **we** are overborne, we **will** still go on to the best of our power; we will still cling to the old religion **and** the old Church; will still be "**the friends of all and** the enemies of none," and **will** still **pray** GOD **to** bless **our** country, **and not to** smite it with His **curse.**

v

RELIGIOUS EQUALITY.[1]

ROMANS II. 1 *(Revised Version)*.

" Thou art without excuse, O man, whosoever thou art that judgest ; for wherein thou judgest another, thou condemnest thyself."

THERE are few things in this world, I imagine, more powerful than *phrases*. Not only is the *pen*, as Napoleon confessed, much stronger than the *sword ;* the phrase is more powerful than either. I question whether the whole press of England exerts as much influence on public opinion and action as a striking proverb or a biting epigram. The politicians know this well ; hence the strange cries and absurd shibboleths which still do duty at election times.

And the power of a phrase is not unfrequently in *inverse ratio* to its soundness and wisdom ; the less of right reason there is in it, the more effective it sometimes proves to be. It may beg or misrepresent the entire question ; it may divert attention from the real point at issue, but if it only *sounds* well, if it has the right ring, it is sure to tell ; it is only one person here and there who

[1] This sermon was preached in S. John's Church, Truro, on Sunday, June 23rd, 1895.

stops to ask whether the sense is equal to the sound. The phrase is sometimes powerful, just because it misses the point.

To give you one example. The early Methodists were constantly pursued, as other men have been since, with the cry of " No Popery." There were really no men who had less in common with Popery than the Wesleys, but all the same the cry procured for them much rough usage. It caught the ear of the mob ; it roused their prejudices ; most of them did not know what *was* Popery and what was not, but that did not matter in the least ; it was an excellent stick to beat the Methodist dog with ; it served its purpose, and then it was thrown away. Its *power* was in inverse ratio to its *propriety*.

Now such a phrase, one equally influential and equally unreasonable, circulates amongst us at the present day— I refer to the cry for " Religious Equality." I believe that these two words have done and are doing as much for Disestablishment and Disendowment as all the multifarious efforts of the Liberation Society. With many persons they seem to settle the question. They are but *two* words, it is true, but they imply a great deal. They imply that we have in England, at the present moment, religious *in*equality ; they convey the idea that men are suffering on account of their conscience and their religion ; what wonder if thousands of unthinking persons jump to the conclusion that this wrong must be remedied, and that only Disestablishment can do it. In fact, you will find that the demand for Disestablishment is constantly based on this assumption. It is

assumed—thousands never pause to ask whether it is
really the case—it is *assumed* that Churchmen and Dissenters have not equal rights and privileges; it is
assumed that the latter are injured by the relations of
Church and State in this country; it is *assumed* that
Disestablishment would remedy this evil; it is forthwith
concluded that nothing else remains to be done. It is
only a phrase, but there can be no question as to its
power. Whether its power is equalled by its pertinence,
it remains for us to consider.

I begin by admitting that there has been, and for
many a long year, distinct and undeniable religious *in-*
equality in England. There was religious injustice and
oppression under the Tudors, under the Stuarts, under
the Commonwealth. In those days, whatever party was
in power, it dealt out a large measure of intolerance and
persecution to those who presumed to differ from it. It
is constantly assumed, and it is widely believed, that all
this persecution was on the part of the Church; it is *so*
widely believed that I must spend a few moments in
proving that this was not so. And I offer this proof
not to accuse other Christians, but simply to show that
Churchmen were no *worse* than other Christians; to
show that religious persecution was a vice of the *age*, and
not of any one body only. I begin by reminding you
that Calvin, the real parent of Nonconformity, colossal
as was his mind and sincere as was his piety, roasted
the Unitarian Servetus to death over a slow fire; that
the Long Parliament beheaded Archbishop Laud for no
crime but his religious views; that the Westminster

Assembly condemned John Bidle to death for Socinianism; that "during the Protectorate"—these are the **words of** Skeats, the Dissenting historian—" five **thousand one** hundred and seventy-three Quakers were imprisoned, two of whom died in confinement. Their persecutors," he continues, " were for the most part Presbyterians and Independents." I go on **to** say that in New England, **under** the rule of the Pilgrim **Fathers,** who left **this country for** conscience sake, **things** were even **worse. The code of laws** drawn **up in** 1650 for the **State of** Connecticut began thus : " Whosoever shall worship **any other** god but the LORD shall be put **to death."** By a law of Massachusetts, passed on October **14th,** 1656, it was enacted that any Quaker landing on the coast should **be** seized and whipped. **Every** Roman Catholic priest who returned **after one** expulsion was **to be put** to death. In fact, history abundantly illustrates the truth of Oliver Cromwell's **words :** " Every sect saith, 'O give me liberty.' **But give it to him,** and to his **power, he** will not yield it to anybody **else." "** The Presbyterians," says Skeats, " who pleaded with tears for liberty of con- science, denied it to the first Anabaptist they met." Elsewhere he says **that** " Gouge and Manton, Calamy and Spurston "—the earlier Nonconformists—" believed at that time that toleration was a doctrine born of hell," and he reminds us that **even** the Quaker Penn was against the toleration of Romanism. I will mention one further fact—that during **the** Commonwealth it was made a penal offence to use the Book of Common Prayer **in** public worship—to show, not only that there *has* been gross religious intolerance in England, but that all the intolerance and all the persecution have not been, as some would have you think, on one side.

But I now proceed to admit that since open persecution ceased amongst us there has been distinct religious inequality. It is impossible to deny that Dissenters have laboured under severe disabilities, and that within living memory. We may have little doubt in our minds that, had they been in power, Churchmen would have been placed under similar if not severer restraints (just because this was so when Dissenters had the power), but that is not the point—"two wrongs do not make a right" —and we have to confess with sorrow that they have not had, until late years, the full enjoyment of their civil rights. It was not until 1828 that the Test and Corporation Acts were repealed, and not until 1871 that they were admitted on equal terms to the Universities. There *have* been inequalities, and it would be dishonourable to deny it.

But I say that *such inequalities exist no longer*—there are none worth mentioning or none that cannot easily be remedied. There is one small matter, I may freely allow, which I think ought to be attended to, and that is the presence of the Civil Registrar at marriages in the Chapel, whilst no such officer is required at weddings in the Church. It may be said that this is a purely *sentimental* grievance—that nobody is one bit the worse for his presence. That may be so, but then it must be remembered that a large proportion of our grievances are sentimental ones, and if there *are* those to whom this seems to be any indignity, by all means let it be removed. **If** a minister may be trusted to *solemnize* a marriage, **it** is a poor thing if you cannot trust him to *enter it* in the book provided for the purpose. It is also possible **that** Dissenters have a grievance in the matter of burial fees. Well, I say again, if there *is* any injustice, by all manner of means let it be rectified ; we do not want to retain .any privilege or **any** payment to which **we** are not entitled. **But as little do we** want to be humiliated or plundered to gratify **sectarian pique** or enmity.

But apart from these small matters, will you tell me, **will** anyone tell me, what real religious inequality exists at the present day, or what inequality that Disestablish-ment would remedy ? This is the question which I beg **you to face.** **We are** asked by some to make a funda-mental change in the British constitution ; **we are** asked to displace and degrade a part of the Church of GOD, which existed before the realm and which has grown with the growth of the realm ; we are invited to secularize its property, and we are required to do this on the ground of " religious equality." Then we want to know where is the religious *in*equality, the religious disability (except perhaps on *the part of the Church)* which Disestablishment is going to cure ? Where is it, for example, in your own parish ? **Yes, let us** fix **our** attention **on** this parish. We know the state **of** things here, perhaps better than we know them elsewhere. **And** your own **parish** is a fair specimen ; it is not unlike other parishes. The law which prevails here, prevails elsewhere. I think, there-**fore, that it** may help to clear the ground, it may put the

question before you in a more practical and concrete
shape, if we consider what inequality there is, *here and
now*, amongst ourselves.   If there is little or none here,
then there will be little or none elsewhere.   I will ask
you, therefore, to consider calmly what equality Disestablishment will ensure to the Dissenters of this city which
they do not enjoy already.   But in the first place, I will
ask you to remember—

*That if the Church here or elsewhere has any privileges,
any privileges of any kind whatsoever, Dissenters are free to
share them, as free as Churchmen, and on the same terms as
Churchmen.*   They are free to belong to the Church ;
there is no one to prevent it but themselves ; in fact,
both Church and State regard all baptized men as
Churchmen and entitled to a place in the Church.   So
that if we Churchmen are in any way *more* privileged
than they are, it can only be because they have renounced
and still renounce these privileges.   If they do occupy
an inferior position, it can only be because, by their own
act and deed, they have put themselves into that position.
Not only are they free to belong to the Church, but they
are by law regarded as belonging to it ; yes, and they
are regarded as in some sense belonging to it, even after
they have left it ; they have a voice, for example, in its
vestries ; they can even serve as Churchwardens.   This
is the first point to be observed—*If there is any inequality,
it is because they have themselves created it.*   It is hardly fair,
therefore, to complain that they have not this or that
privilege, when they have cut themselves off from it.   I
wonder what would be thought of a Dissenter who, after

leaving one **Nonconformist body for another, complained**
that he had not **the full benefits of the body** which he
had left, as well as of that which he had just joined, or
lamented that he no longer enjoyed perfect equality **with**
those who remained? What would you think of **the**
Wesleyan Reformer, for example, who having gone out
in 1849, now made it a hardship that he had no part, since
the split, in the institutions or investments of the Wesleyan Methodists? **What** would **you say** about the cry
of " Religious Equality " on *his* lips? Especially if the
old body could turn upon him and say, **" We have never**
expelled you, never cut **you** adrift; to this day your
name is retained on our list of members; the privileges
which you say you are deprived of are yours **as** soon as
ever you care to claim them. **You can have** them on
the self-same conditions **on** which we enjoy them."
Why, you would laugh to scorn the demand for " religious
equality " **in** such **a case** as that. And **yet** that **is**
precisely **the case of the** Dissenter who has left **the**
Church.

But perhaps **you tell** me that *Dissenters* **have left the**
Church for conscientious reasons, and that this makes all the
difference. Does it? If one man leaves one chapel for
conscientious reasons and joins **another,** it never occurs
to him or to others to plead his conscience as entitling
him to share in the privileges, whatever they may be, of
the community which he has **left;** you would all **cry**
shame on him if he did plead it. You would say to him,
" We honour you for acting **up to your** conscience, but
you must really have a little conscience as to your claims.

You cannot expect to have both your conscience and your convenience ; to have at the same time the privileges of Conformity and of Nonconformity.   Yours must be an elastic conscience, if, after compelling you to secede, it permits you to claim the privileges which were designed for those who stay."   Yes, this is what you would say when Dissenter leaves Dissenter.   But when he leaves the Church, then it is quite a different thing !   Then, whatever his reasons may be, he has not "religious equality" if he is not allowed at the same moment to repudiate his obligations and yet retain his privileges !

But something more must be said here.   It is not the case, except in rare instances, that Dissenters have left us for conscientious reasons ; it is not the case with one in a hundred.   You have only to talk with them, and they will assure you that it is so.   Most of them will speedily inform you that they are Dissenters because they were born such, or that they go to Chapel, not because they have anything against the Church, but because they "got their good" at Chapel, or prefer its services or its minister.   Besides, you can see for yourself how little conscience has to do with it.   Is it conscience that makes the upper classes Churchmen, and the middle class Dissenters, and the lowest stratum Salvation Army?   Any one who reflects can see that social considerations have much more to do with the denomination a man belongs to than conviction or religion ; if it were not so, we should not have so much *class* religion as we have.   But if it were *all* conscience and nothing else, still that gives no man the right, at one and the same time, to separate from a religious body and to claim a share in its benefits.

So that if the **State** secured to every Churchman in your city—and every Churchman in the land—a hundred or a thousand pounds a year (as a matter of fact, it takes good care not to give us one penny) no Dissenter would have any right to complain, as long as no portion of it came out of his pocket. **If** every Churchman had honours and dignities heaped upon him, instead of (as sometimes happens) misrepresentation and abuse, still no Dissenter would **be wronged. Not** wronged, because these things were meant **for *him* ; they are there for** him, and if he does **not have** them, it is because **he** will not take them, though in the vast majority of cases he **cannot** tell you *why*, cannot assign any adequate reason for renouncing his birthright.

But I now proceed to observe that the Churchman enjoys no such favours, no privileges in fact, of any kind. You say we have not religious equality. Then we ask you again to tell us **in** what the inequality lies. Is it that we have a superior religion, **for** " *religious* equality " means properly equality *in religion ?* Why no ; Dissenters tell us that their religion is superior to ours ; some of them say that they left the Church because they got **a** better form of religion elsewhere. Is **it, then,** that they cannot be *equally religious ?* **that** they cannot serve GOD as truly **as we can? On** the contrary, some of them maintain that they can and **do serve** Him better. Is it, then, that we have not equality **in** *all religious matters*, in the things which *pertain* to religion ? Yes, most of them

would say that *that* is where the inequality lies; they
contend that we have not *denominational* equality; they
say that their denominations are at a disadvantage, as
compared with the Church, at a disadvantage in many
respects, because the latter is more connected with the
State.   Let us discover, then, if we can, where the
disadvantage lies.   We shall find, I think, that we
certainly have *not* equality in religious things, and nothing
like it ; and we shall also find that the inequality, the
injustice and the hardship are on *our* side, not theirs.
We shall find that, on their own showing, or on the
testimony of admitted facts, Dissenters are better off, are
treated better by the State, than Churchmen are.

Let us begin with the Parish Church. I need not
remind you that the Nonconformist is free to attend it—
as free as he is to stay away from it—nor need I say that
they do attend our Churches in considerable numbers.
They are quite within their rights in so doing, and we
are very glad that they should, if only *sometimes*, worship
with us; it is *their parish Church ;* all the seats are free—
free by law; they can occupy one whensoever they
please, without any payment, whether they give to the
offertory or subscribe to Church funds or not.   If they
are Dissenters, it is still their parish Church.   *But their*
Chapel is not our parish Chapel; we have no rights *there ;*
it is a private building ; if we want a seat there, we must
pay for it.   No, they are quite right : we have not strict
equality ; in this respect at least they have a distinct
advantage over us.   The Church is theirs as well as
ours ; the Chapel is theirs and it is not ours.

From the Parish Church, let us pass to the Parish Priest. And first, let us speak of his appointment. The minister of the Chapel is chosen by the congregation or by the members; sometimes, I understand, by one or two rich men in the congregation. The clergyman is not so appointed; sometimes he is appointed by the Prime Minister or the Lord Chancellor, sometimes by the Bishop or the Dean and Chapter; in any case, it is but seldom that the congregation is consulted. Now, Dissenters leave us in no doubt as to which system they prefer; of course, they much prefer their own; they think ours indeed little short of sinful. The deacons or the Chapel members, they say, are the proper persons to appoint; the Prime Minister is not the proper person. So that, on their own showing, they are *better off, better treated by the State*, than we are. They can choose their minister and can dismiss him; Churchmen can do neither. Yes, and in the few cases where the Incumbent is chosen by the parishioners, Dissenters have votes as well as Churchmen; that is to say, they have a voice in the election of our pastors, whilst we have none in the appointment of theirs.

But it is not only in the matter of *appointment* that, on their own showing, we are unequal; there is a similar inequality as regards their and our *ministrations*. Every Dissenter is legally entitled to the religious offices of his parish priest; he can claim, for example, to be married at Church, or buried by the Church—in other words, the parish priest is *their* parish priest. But we have no such claim on the Nonconformist pastor—he is not our pastor.

The disability, therefore, is on our part, not theirs. They have advantages which we have not.

I pass to another point. Once a year the Church-wardens, who are the representatives of the Church laity, are appointed. Their duties are now restricted entirely to Church matters. Yet Dissenters, as already remarked, can take part in the election, and sometimes they do; they can themselves be elected, and sometimes they are. *But we cannot take part in the choosing of their officers; still less can we serve as Chapel stewards or deacons ourselves;* they would soon tell us to mind our own business if we sug- gested it. Here, then, is another inequality, but it is not Dissenters who are the sufferers: it is Churchmen.

And the same remark applies as to our religious *structures*, and even to our *services*. They can build Chapels much more easily than we can erect Churches; that is to say, there are conditions and restrictions in our case, restrictions imposed by State law, from which they are exempt. They can freely sell their buildings again, whereas we cannot sell our Churches—I am glad to believe that it is not often that we want to sell them. They can use the Chapel, again, for purposes for which we cannot use the Church—for political meetings, for example. Well, are they wronged because they have more liberty than we? Is it a proof of religious inequality that they can do what we cannot?

And they can do what we cannot in the matter of their services. They can invite anybody they please to conduct the service; we cannot. They can have almost any sort of service which approves itself to them; we cannot. They can read what lessons of Holy Scripture they like, or no lessons at all ; we cannot ; we must read two lessons, and those the lessons for the day. They can have forms of prayer or no forms, Bibles or no Bibles, ministers or no ministers ; we have no such liberty. I am not complaining of these restrictions—very far from it ; I should be sorry to see them relaxed ; I am only showing that we Churchmen *have not equal liberties with Dissenters*. They themselves insist that we have not. In fact, the very persons who complain the loudest that they have not " equality " with us are constantly boasting of their *superior* freedom, of their *greater religious liberty*. And they are quite right ; so far as the control of law goes they *have* greater liberty ; whether that is any real gain is another thing ; anyhow, they have it. Not only can they avail themselves of *our* rites and ministrations, and at the same time enjoy their own ; but *in* their own ministrations, and in all that appertains to them, they have facilities, and they *boast* of having facilities, which we have not. They have gained this advantage over us—if it *is* an advantage—by virtue of their Dissent. They can share our good things and keep their own to themselves.

But it may be said here—it is often said—that it is a reproach to the Church that its liberties should be thus restricted. I reply, " No." The Church is not a sect, and you must not narrow it to the dimensions of a sect. The sects (I do not mean the word offensively) only have liberties which we have not, because they are sects, and not the old historic Church of the country. Besides, I

beg you to observe that if there is a reproach at all, it
lies at the *door of the State, and not the Church.*   I
observe that *we* are constantly blamed for what the State
has done, for its aggressions or usurpations.   It is sometimes asserted that we are " bound hand and foot by the
State." Well, if that is so, the more shame to the State !
If it has robbed us of any of our liberties—though it
seems to me that we have more true freedom than any
communion in Christendom—then it is the State has
reason to blush, not we.   I will ask you to remember
this, for it is a conclusive answer to many of the acid
and ill-natured taunts that are levelled at us.   We are
taunted with the Erastian encroachments of the civil
power on the Church's province.   Such gibes should be
reserved for those who made the encroachment.   So long
as we do not submit to conditions which are unchristian
we shall take no blame to ourselves, whatever the
State's usurpations may be; we shall rather take credit
to ourselves for submitting to " every ordinance of man
for the LORD's sake."

   But let us return for a moment to our question of
" religious equality."   We have seen that in many
matters pertaining to religion Dissenters, on their own
showing, are more than equal with the Church.   " Yes,"
but they will say, " you cannot deny that the Church, by
reason of its ' establishment ' (so called)—its ' State
trappings,' as some call them—has a position and a
prestige and a social repute which the Chapel has not."
They say that these things give it an air of distinction
and respectability, and so secure for it an unfair advan-

tage over **other communions. Ah, now we** begin to understand each other ; **at** last **we** reach **the real griev-ance ;** what **you** mean when you say that you have not *religious* equality is that you have not *social* equality. And there we **are with you** ; we freely allow that, **for** one reason or other, **the** Chapel is *not* supposed to **be so** respectable or aristocratic as the Church. **Yes,** for **one** reason **or other, but not for the** reason **you imagine ; not because of its "** establishment.**" And here is the proof of it.** The **Roman Catholics are not established, but they** have an equal social *prestige* with the Church. **Society** receives their ministers **just as** readily **as it does** the clergy. Here is another **proof.** There is no established Church **in the United** States, but **the** denominations there are just as unequal, socially, **as they are here ;** the Romanists **and the Episcopalians (so called) take the lead there as here.** Besides, just ask yourselves : **Is there anybody in** this parish who thinks any **better of** the Church because **of its** relations **to the State ? Can** you mention anyone who has joined **it** on that account ? I know **a** number **of** persons who think **the** worse **of it** for its " Establishment " ; **I** do not **know one who** belongs to it for **that reason.** If, therefore, we have any **sort** of *prestige* **which** the Chapels have not, we certainly have not the State **to** thank for **it.** Nor will Disestab-lishment, if it comes, rob **us of** that prestige. How could it do **so ? It** cannot take away our history ; cannot **rob us** of our antiquity ; cannot strip us **of our** associa-**tions ;** cannot deprive us **of our** scholars and divines. **No, if** there *are* **any** people so weak as to prefer **the**

w

Church because of its "State trappings," such persons, I imagine, would still adhere to it because it once wore them. It would be enough for them that it *had* been the National Church in its day.

We see, then, that there is really no *religious* inequality in England—except that all forms of religion are not, and never can be, equally good, and that all people are not, and never will be, equally religious; that there is no *denominational* inequality—except that we have not the sort of liberty that the denominations have, and the denominations have not the antiquity and history that we have; that there is no *political favouritism*—if the Church differs from the Chapel, it is not because the State has preferred it to the Chapel; not because it has chosen one body out of many; it is because it is ancient, and the Chapel is modern; because for many centuries there was nothing but the Church to deal with; no, there is only a social difference. It is really *social* equality that is meant and aimed at under the name of religious equality. And this "Establishment" did not give and Disestablishment will not take away. And yet we are about—or it seems as if we were about—on the score of equality, to recast our constitution, to root out of its place the oldest institution in the land. For this you are asked to take away the moneys given to GOD and to apply them to museums and art galleries. And when you have done it, you will find that you are as far off from both religious and social equality as ever; you will find that you can no more coerce society than you can coerce conscience, and that whatever the State can do, it cannot make all religions or all denominations equal.

THE REUNION OF THE CHURCH.[1]

PSALM CXXII. 6.

"O pray for the peace of Jerusalem ; they shall prosper that love thee."

IT is a common observation amongst us that "Reunion is in the air"—the reunion of Christian men who have now, in England at least and her dependencies, been for so long split up into sects and denominations. It is said to be one of the signs of the times. Not only so, but a measure of reunion has been here and there achieved. I do not know that any fusion of all the different denominations into one body has anywhere taken place, but in some of our colonies religious bodies of *the same order* have of late coalesced—the different sections of Methodism have in Canada, and the various types of Presbyterianism in Victoria. And in England, many and deep-seated as are "our unhappy divisions," there has been some approach — some efforts have been made for reunion. Within the last year or two, for example, we have been invited to pray for it, and sermons have been preached on the subject. But a short time ago, even so much as

[1] Preached in St. Austell Church on Whitsunday, 1895.

this would have been impossible. But a short time ago, thousands of Christians gloried in division; they loved to have it so; there are some, unhappily, who do this still. But the devout prayers which have been offered that GOD would "open the people of England's eyes" have not been in vain, and men everywhere are fast awakening to the sinfulness and shamefulness of our divisions. They are beginning to see—what but a few years ago we should hardly have dared to hope for—that all division is in itself an evil; that there cannot be estrangement between Christian and Christian without sin somewhere. They are also beginning to see that our divisions, as represented by our endless sects and denominations, even if they are lawful, are not expedient; that they are a reproach to our religion and a barrier to its progress. And I ascribe this altered attitude (as does the Archbishop in his pastoral) to the prayers which have been offered without ceasing unto GOD in this behalf. You can only account for the yearnings after peace and reconciliation, which of late years have filled men's bosoms, to the secret power of the HOLY GHOST. What else can have moved the Pope on the one hand, and the Nonconformist leaders on the other—men so utterly unlike in other respects—to beg for the prayers of Christians for Christian oneness? We may thank GOD that we have lived to see this day. Believing as I do that reunion is what our Christendom needs at the present moment above everything; believing that nothing else can do so much for morality and piety, it would be strange if I did not rejoice. No doubt we are still a long, a very long way from corporate reunion, either with our Roman brethren on the one hand, or with our Nonconformist fellow-Christians on the other; still, we are going the right, and the only right way to work in praying GOD to grant it. For this is *CHRIST'S* way; He prayed, and prayed importunately, that last night of His life for the oneness of His followers. And in so doing He has required us to do the same; He has "left us an example that we should copy" His *prayers*. The Christian who does not pray for unity, in one respect at least, is not Christlike.

But whilst I beseech you to unite your prayers, your daily prayers, to that stream of supplications which from so many hearts and so many lands ever flows towards the heavenly throne, I have to say to you that something more than prayer is needed, if unity is ever to be regained. You know the saying, "*Qui laborat orat*"—"He prays who works": we must do our part as well as pray GOD to do His. We must be "fellow-workers with Him." There are obstacles—and some perhaps of our creation—to be removed; there are prejudices to be encountered; there are errors to be combatted; there are mistakes to be repaired. We ourselves have much to learn, and others perhaps have no less. And, therefore, I propose to speak to you to-day of the measures which it remains for *us* to take to promote the reunion of Christendom—the preliminary steps which must precede all overtures and negotiations. For at present we are not at all prepared for reunion. If it came at this instant it might be but a dubious blessing; all we could do at this moment would be to patch up a hollow and tempo-

rary peace. No, there is much to be learned, and much
to be done before our prayers for reunion can ripen into
proposals. It is to this preliminary work that I would
fain commit you. I want not only to infect you with an
enthusiasm for reunion, but to enlist your help in making
the crooked straight and the rough places plain, and in
building in the desert a highway for our GOD. I shall
therefore speak, first, of what we have to *learn*, and,
secondly, of what we have to *do*. And the very first
thing which we have to learn is this—

1. *That our present state of division is in direct opposition to
the revealed will of GOD.* We are so accustomed to disunion,
are so surrounded by it; we breathe such an atmosphere
of sectarianism that we have come to acquiesce in it, to
apologize for it, if not to approve of it. But GOD does
not, cannot, approve of it. It must be hateful to Him,
the sight of these sanctuaries of so many sorts; hateful,
not because those who worship there are none of His, or
because they are not sincere, but because the buildings
are so many monuments of division. For GOD is One, and
GOD is Love—He is "the author of peace, and lover
of concord," and here are conspicuous confusion and
open discord. He has revealed Himself as "our FATHER,"
has taught us that "all we are brethren"; what must
He think of His children, brothers and sisters who
cannot endure to worship under the same roof? According to CHRIST'S purpose, the visible Church was to be
one great association, united by the closest of bonds.
S. Paul bids us "love the brotherhood," and S. John
says "we ought to lay down our lives for the brethren."

What must He think, then, of a brotherhood which is all at sixes and sevens, and the members of which too often envy and hate and loathe and oppose one another? It was one main object of **His** coming that He might *unite* men—that He might "gather together into one the children of GOD that were scattered abroad"[1]; what grief, humanly speaking, it must cause His gentle heart to see that His religion is constantly made the means of *separating* them—of separating them as perhaps nothing else under the sun separates them. No doubt they plead in their defence that they have conscientious objections to this doctrine or that usage. Yes, but dislike of this blemish or that in the Society of GOD can be no excuse for breaking it up; breaking up the community which CHRIST has founded for carrying on His work! Division *must* be displeasing to GOD, and if for no other reason for this—because "a house divided against a house falleth." I repeat, therefore, that the first thing we have to learn and to lay to heart, both Churchmen and Dissenters, is, that all our splits and sects and cabals are simply hateful to the Most High. It is not necessary that we should know exactly *who* is to blame; it is enough for us to know that *somebody* is—in all probability there is blame on both sides—but learn we must that, however this may be, as long as this state of things lasts, it lasts in defiance of GOD's will.

2. And a second point that needs to be rooted in our minds is this—that these divisions, even if they are *not* positively wicked; even if they were made and can now

[1] S. John xi. 52.

be maintained without sin, *are nevertheless ruinous to the cause of true religion.* We want to be clear as to the infinite waste and loss and mischief and misery which they entail. It used to be contended that they were good for our " common Christianity "; it was often said that competition was as good in religion as in railways or in business—one American divine has stated that " in every decent-sized town there ought to be five or six denominations *at least.*" Well, we need to learn that this religious competition is simply eating the life out of our religion ; is compromising and degrading and para-lyzing it. Surely anyone who reflects, anyone not blinded by prejudice, must see this for himself. He will observe the envy and jealousy, the heart-burning and the positive hatred, which it occasions—if you have any doubt about it I commend you to the (so called) religious newspapers, or I ask you to study the speeches made on questions of Church and Dissent at " Conferences " and " Unions " and in Parliament. They are for the most part steeped in gall and bitterness ; you would think, from the language used, that the speakers were attacking their deadliest enemies, and the enemies of all righteousness. But no, it is only their Christian brethren, Christians who differ in a few particulars from them, or are supposed to have a few minute advantages over them ! I say that if there were nothing more than the mean and contemptible passions, and the utterly unchristian tempers which division creates, to condemn it, that would be condemnation enough. But you must also consider the effect which these same divisions, and the malice **and** uncharitableness **which** they ever **beget have, and must** have, upon the **world.** That world is not exactly prejudiced in favour of **our religion ;** on the contrary, it is intensely hostile to **it.** You may imagine, therefore, how rejoiced it is when its professors **cannot** agree, when they **are** at daggers drawn and worry one another instead of warring against vice and ignorance. Think what **a fine** excuse these divisions afford, both **at home and** abroad in **the** mission field, for rejecting Christianity altogether, **and it** is often **rejected for** this reason. Even a Hottentot has observed that Christians here **will not** speak to Christians there, and Hindoos and Chinese have derisively asked which form of Christianity they are to embrace. And **I might** go on **to** speak of the waste of energy, the overlapping, the underhand proselytism, the petty persecution, the puerile rivalries and the like, as further proofs of the injury that is done. Aye, we need to " lay to **heart,"** as the **Prayer** Book **puts it,** " the *great danger* we are in by our unhappy divisions "— danger to CHRIST's religion and to our own souls. But I must now turn **to a** third **point. We** must clearly understand

3. **That it is** the will of GOD that *these divisions, whatever they may be and whatever occasioned them, should be healed.* I say this because many good people despair of ever seeing an end to them ; they believe them to be inevitable and insuperable. And I grant you the difficulties in the way **are** formidable ; so formidable that **it** is hardly to be wondered at that men should think the **task** hopeless. But our answer to this is—CHRIST prayed **for** oneness ;

He prays for it still—for HE never changes—He wills it; He works for it; therefore it must and shall be accomplished. We only despair when we think of the prejudice and bigotry and obstinacy of men, and forget the power of Almighty GOD. "Is anything too hard for the LORD?" Can He not turn the hearts of men whithersoever He will?[1] He has inspired this passionate longing for reunion; will He not find means to accomplish it? We must never, therefore, say or think that reunion is impossible; it only needs that *we* should desire it as GOD does, and it will be realized. Another point as to which we must be clear is this—that

4. *The divisions of Christendom are not to be healed by any sacrifice of principle, by any suppression of conviction.* It is of no avail that we " make a solitude and " then " call it a peace." Not by watering down our beliefs until nothing is left that can offend anybody ; not by giving up any part of the deposit, " the faith once for all delivered " ; not by keeping back aught that we believe to be profitable, not thus are Christians to be made one. " The world," said Baldwin Brown, " has nothing to expect from a religion which reduces to a clammy colourless pulp the great facts and truths of the Catholic faith." So spake a Congregationalist. Now hear what a Unitarian Journal says : " The attempt to make peace in the Church by the elimination of theology from religion is a kind of pacification by guillotine. It quiets discord by cutting off the disputants' heads. Theology is the *rationale* of religion. It can only be escaped by

[1] Prov. xxi. 1.

losing our heads." [1] We may be quite sure, therefore, that no good can come of giving place, even for an hour, to what we believe to be doctrinal error. We must face our differences ; must discuss them ; must ask for the old paths ; must go back to first principles. The only agreement that can be lasting is agreement *in the truth.* A last lesson, and perhaps the most difficult of all to learn, is

5. *That we ourselves are not infallible ; that* **we may** *possibly be mistaken ; that, after all, others may be right,* **and we ourselves wrong.** Unless we approach the question of Reunion, involving, as it does, the consideration of a hundred points of doctrine and practice, with an honest and open mind, any real progress is impossible. It is very difficult to care more for truth than for victory, but it must be done. Reunion cannot come until Christians are willing to be set right when shown to be wrong ; willing to follow the truth whithersoever it leads them. Now I proceed to speak of what we have to *do.* But first, of what we must be careful *not* to do. I observe that

1. *Nothing can be more inimical to reunion than the spirit of exclusiveness and sectarianism.* And by sectarianism I mean here, not merely the joining of a sect or split from the parent stock, but I also use the word to include that narrow and uncatholic view of Christendom, which leads men to restrict their gaze, to confine their sympathy and charity to their own Church or denomination. And I think that this is a danger to which English Churchmen, perhaps, by virtue of their position, are especially exposed. We must never forget that the Church of CHRIST in

[1] *The Southern Unitarian* (U.S.A.), March, 1894.

England is now much wider than the " Church of England"; that it embraces in its membership all the baptized, no matter to what "denominations" they may have wandered.   Nor must we forget that some who have *not* been baptized—I refer especially to the Quakers—though they do not belong to the *body* of the Church (for "by one SPIRIT are men baptized into " that body [1]) nevertheless belong to its *soul ;* they are *of* the Church, if they are not *in* it, for they exhibit the graces, the tempers, the fruits of the Christian life, the very things among others for which the Church exists.   And, as such, they are not, they cannot be, indifferent to us.   Not only are they in many ways an example to us, but they are in some sense *related* to us, by virtue of their spiritual relations to CHRIST.   How, then, can we deny them a place in our hearts ?   We want, in fact, to obey the Apostolic precept, " Look not every man on his own things "—his own society, his own services, his own successes—" but every man also on the things of others."   I do not hold with the Baptists or Bible Christians—I do not believe that our LORD intended that there should either be the one or the other—but all the same Baptists and baptized Bible Christians are our brethren in CHRIST.   This, then, must be our *first* and imperative care—*not* to be narrow and sectarian in our sympathies, in our goodwill and affection.   There was one who said that he " counted nothing that was human indifferent to him "—how much less anything that is Christian.

2. And we must be equally careful, in the second

---

[1] 1 Cor. xii. 13.

place, *never to taunt, decry or disparage those who differ from us.* At present, as you know, there are those in our parishes who resent it bitterly that others should presume to have different views from theirs. The days of persecution are not quite over, though happily the persecution is of a milder type ; though

> "The war and waste of clashing creeds
> Now end in words and not in deeds,
> And no man suffers loss or bleeds
> For thoughts which men call heresies,"

yet men who think out their religious position for themselves, and then say what they think, still have to suffer for it. What a reproach to our religion it is that it should be so. The lesson of bare tolerance has yet to be learned by many Christians. And those who are tolerant are not always fair ; they speak of opponents in a contemptuous way ; they impute motives to them ; they insinuate doubts ; they disparage their good works ; they damn with faint praise. This is still done, and done by professed Christians. I put it to you, whether it is not a rare thing to find a Protestant, for example, who is strictly just towards Roman Catholics, or a Churchman who can speak with perfect calmness and charity of Dissenters, or a Dissenter who can resist having a fling at the Church. And these are the things which hinder reunion, because they provoke tempers which are averse to reconciliation. This, then, we must *not* do—we must *never* permit ourselves to be unjust or unkind to any of our separated brethren. Any speech or action calculated to wound or to irritate makes for *disunion*; it helps to prolong our shameful separation.

3. But we must go a step farther. We *must not take advantage of the misunderstandings or dissensions which arise amongst Dissenters*, as indeed amongst ourselves. We may be tempted to think that a split in this body or that affords a fine opportunity of winning some of them over to the Church, but we must spurn the temptation. It can do us no real good to yield to it; those who join us because of a quarrel elsewhere may presently quarrel with us; or, if not, what good can it do us that our ranks should be recruited in this way, by men who are not Churchmen by conviction? It may easily do this *harm*—it may engender a feeling of injury and consequent bitterness. If men come to us of their own accord it is another thing, but we must not stoop to entice them away. It is constantly done—there are those who lie in wait for the disaffected—but it is altogether unworthy of a Christian.

4. And there is another thing against which we must guard even more sedulously, and that is *rejoicing in iniquity;* parading the faults, or exulting over the fall of any who belong to another community. Alas, it seems, as things are, almost the natural thing to do. If a clergyman is overtaken by a fault, or a Jabez Balfour is convicted of a fraud, there are never lacking those who point the finger of scorn at the religious body to which he belongs, who seek to make capital out of this misery, who glory in this shame. But *we* must never do it; for the sake of Christianity we must not. I often wonder how those

persons who blaze abroad the frailties of the Church parson or the Dissenting deacon never seem to reflect that, if this is any gain to their denomination, it is a real injury to our LORD CHRIST. They do it, no doubt, to discredit one particular form of religion, but they forget that others will eagerly fasten on it as an argument against all religion. They overlook the fact that in gibbetting this Church delinquent or this Chapel hypocrite they are sawing at the branch on which they themselves are sitting ; they are teaching men to blaspheme ; they are crucifying the SON of GOD afresh and putting Him to an open shame. And this not only by the particular scandal which they publish, but also by their own conspicuous lack of charity in blazing it abroad.

I now approach the last part of my subject—what can we *do*, what steps can we take to promote reunion?

1. Well, in the first place, we can *take care that we understand the position, the views and arguments of those who differ from us.* We owe it to ourselves, to them, and to CHRIST, so to do. Yet, so far as my experience goes, it is seldom indeed that this is done. I am greatly afraid that there are those among us who much prefer to *mis*-understand; whose only anxiety is that the other side should not be able to clear themselves. Their one concern would seem to be confirmed in the opinions which they have embraced, or, as often as not, those which they have *inherited*, to win a triumph for them. To them "orthodoxy is my doxy, and heterodoxy is other people's doxy." Hence they read no books, no religious newspapers even, but those of their own

way of thinking. They never by any chance give their opponents a hearing. In fact, I am constantly reminded, in this long controversy between Church and Dissent, of that episode in Jewish history of which we read in 1 Kings xv. Baasha built a fortress, Ramah, on his border, that "no one might *go out or come in*" to Judah. Presently Asa captured it, but he did not retain it; he simply carted away the stones and the timber; he removed them bodily, and used them to build elsewhere. So now there are those who laboriously build their ramparts between Church and Chapel, and there are those who remove them—remove the obstacles to intercommunion out of the way. And one great rampart is ignorance; hence the anxiety which some betray to remain in ignorance; hence their unwillingness to listen to explanations. The first essential towards reunion, however, is that we should understand one another, and not be the victims of delusions; as it is, we go on hugging our mistakes from one generation to another. I repeat, that we owe it to Christianity and to CHRIST to take pains to get at each other's real reasons and beliefs; we may possibly find that, after all, they do not differ so very widely from our own. We may find that we have made mountains out of molehills, or, per-chance, have been charging at windmills.

2. But we can do more than this. It is all very well to study; perhaps it is the first thing to be done, for if agreement ever comes it will be on a dogmatic basis. " If there is ever to be a communion amongst the various denominations of Christians "—I quote Bishop Boyd

Carpenter—"it can only come by the honest, patient . . . and unself-willed study of the book of GOD."[1] But the next thing is to learn from living contact with those who differ from us. We must, therefore, sedulously cultivate kindly and brotherly relations with them, must welcome opportunities of knowing them and of hearing from their own lips what it is that separates them from us. I do not know that such intercourse will minister *directly* to dogmatic agreement, but it will do much to break down prejudices and to inspire kindlier feelings. And it is for this reason—I might almost add, for this reason only— that I value so highly the gatherings which have been held at Grindelwald and Lucerne. They are of little or no value from a theological point of view—they are not likely, I mean, to lead directly to theological agreement— for many who take part in them are in no sense theo- logians, and are hardly competent to discuss theological questions. But I believe that these meetings have nevertheless done real service in making Churchmen and Nonconformists better acquainted with each other. They have met under pleasant conditions, have rubbed shoulders, have had their private intercourse, and have learned to know and respect one another as they never did before. I could wish, therefore, that such meetings might be multiplied. But why must we go to Switzerland for them? Is nothing of the kind possible in England? Yes, something of the kind, something much more likely to lead to agreement *has* been held in England—I refer to the Langham Street Conference, where a few repre-

---

[1] *Guardian*, May 17th, 1893.

x

sentative Churchmen met an equal number of eminent Nonconformists for quiet conference and prayer. This is the " more excellent way "—the leaders are always nearer to each other and more amenable to reason than the rank and file ; besides, the latter constantly misconceive the real points at issue. A little knowledge is a dangerous thing—in theology as elsewhere—and " fools rush in where angels fear to tread." There are learned and capable men on both sides and in all denominations ; let them meet quietly and discuss these disputed points calmly. The Grindelwald Conference has suffered greatly from the temptation to "play to the gallery," from efforts to win a cheer from partisans, from the desire to score a temporary triumph. In a private meeting this fatal snare is absent.

" But what is there," you will perhaps ask, " *for us* to do ? You have suggested nothing, apart from prayer, for men who are not experts to attempt." Then I will suggest it now. You can promote reunion in a very simple and effectual way. The holier our lives, the more candid and truthful we are, the more we conquer envy and jealousy and meanness, the more hope for a reunited Church. Reunion is very largely a question of character. Disunion is the result of deterioration. " It is only," as John Wesley observed, " only when our love grows cold that we can bear to be separated from our brethren." Division has been caused by giving way to nature—S. Paul pronounces the Corinthians " carnal " because of the divisions amongst them : reunion can only be attained by yielding ourselves to the grace, the charity, and gentleness of GOD. So that reunion is mainly a question of character. If we Christians were but Christlike, our difficulties would disappear at once. Every selfish or sordid or lukewarm Christian is a difficulty; so is every uninstructed Churchman. This, then, is the "conclusion of the whole matter." Let us yield ourselves to GOD, Who is kind to the evil and the good, and sendeth rain upon the just and the unjust; let us follow CHRIST, Who " had compassion on the ignorant and on them that are out of the way "; let us open our hearts to the teachings of His good SPIRIT, and so the prayer of our LORD shall be accomplished. " The gift of unity "—I think it was Dr. von Döllinger said this—" will not be grasped by any rash human hands; it will come down from above in the indwelling of the HOLY ONE, and will come, as all other blessings, when the Church is ready to receive it."

THE END.

www.ingramcontent.com/pod-product-compliance
Lightning Source LLC
Chambersburg PA
CBHW021756110726
47902CB00006B/1534